The Shanghai Diary

To Jacki;

Peace —

The Shanghai Diary

Ursula Bacon

Milestone Books

The names of some of the people have been changed to protect
their privacy

Milestone Books
E-mail: bacon@bestseller.com

Hara Publishing
P.O. Box19732
Seattle, Washington

Dedication

To Thorn always
and
To my wonderful children, Ron and Marly
and
In memory of those who perished.

Acknowlegements

*To all of you who have touched my life and
brought me your gifts of love and
to a special friend whose support of my endeavors
is boundless, my deepest gratitude.*

Table of Contents

Foreword

*T*here must be a reason why it took me so long to write this story. Perhaps I thought no one would want to read it, but I changed my mind.

I have lived in America since 1947, and only at the persistent urging, constant nagging and final threatening of family and friends have I stepped back into the past to chronicle the "Shanghai Years." Few people have ever heard of the 18,000 or so middle European refugees who found shelter in Shanghai from Hitler's Nazi Germany — the country that eventually would permit the extinction of six million Jews and millions of other "undesirables" of the Third Reich. The rest of the world had closed its myopic eyes to the horrors of Nazi Germany, closed its ears to the pitiful cries for help, and consequently barred its doors to those trying to escape from the nightmare of genocide. America, Mexico, Canada, South America, Central America, Australia, New Zealand, South Africa, not to mention the European nations and their colonies, all were unwilling to accept refugees into their countries.

Shanghai, restless metropolis of footloose adventurers, fortune hunters, home to the black sheep of Europe's upper crust, and breeding ground of sinners and pleasure seekers, kept its gates wide open and at the drop of a chopstick, offered shelter to Europe's desperate Jews.

Several books have been written about the "Shanghai Jews," all of which report on daily events, furnish dates and data, describe conditions and politics of these Shanghai refugees. One of these is not only probably the most accurate account of the Shanghai Years, but also touches me because I know Ernest G. Heppner, the author of *Shanghai Refuge,* Nebraska University Press. He and his wife, Illo, have been life-long friends. I have relied heavily on his unerringly thorough and fastidiously correct research of major events and dates. His work has refreshed my memory. I am grateful for his important contribution to a little-known segment of Jewish history in the Nazi years.

I am not writing a book, I'm telling a story. I'm glad you're listening. Once I started the process, I couldn't stop. My subconscious mind, the storehouse of my being, prodded me with pictures and events of the past. It's all here. I remember.

In order to make this story richer, but nonetheless true, I have interwoven the narrative with the lives of those who so deeply touched mine, and whose indelible selves are forever present in the heart of my yesterdays.

The Shanghai years — from our arrival in May 1939 to our departure in August 1947 — were an unforgettable experience — not just for me but for all other refugees. More than 18,000 middle European refugees had found a strange, uneasy and fragile, but comparatively safe place to wait out a terrible war, and to grimly celebrate the end, when it came, of the incredibly mad and senselessly cruel Hitler regime. Relatively few people know the story about the Jews who fled to Shanghai, China and the challenges they faced at the other end of the world. I hope I have successfully described the Shanghai of those years — the customs, the traditions, the heartbeat of another culture — the sights and sounds of the Orient. And, oh yes, the smells of a metropolis once called "the armpit of the world, the slum-scum of the Orient and the boil on the hide of China." Just ask any sailor!

Shanghai was all those things and more, but it was also teaming with humanity — exotic, eccentric and exciting. The city danced with bright colors, beckoned with exquisite art and teased with strange, new sounds. More than anything, Shanghai gave us shelter from a gone-mad homeland. One day, the war was over, and we heard the heartbreaking news of the fate of six million Jews. And after that, names like Theresienstadt, Treblinka, Maidanek, Chelmo, Auschwitz, Bergen-Belsen, Dachau, Buchenwald, Sachsenhausen, Sobibar among them, were forever burned into our souls. Suddenly, our misery of the Shanghai ghetto paled in comparison to the horrors of the death camps. Shanghai turned out to have been the paradise for survivors.

I am eternally grateful. I survived, and lived to tell about it.
To you, Shanghai — *"chien-chien! chien-chien!"*
Thank You! Thank You!

Ursula Bacon

Prologue

March 1939

*T*he sound of a car squealing to a halt, boots crunching on gravel, followed by the thunderous pounding of fists on the front door, brought our household up and wide awake in the early morning hours of a rainy, blustery day in March. Harsh, loud voices accompanied the stomping of heavy feet up the stairway in the direction of my parents' quarters.

Had they come for my father? Terror struck my heart.

My father had been forced to sign his business over to the Gestapo the day before, and according to Lothar, our faithful factotum, he had fumed and cursed the God-damned Nazis out loud at the barbershop — for all the world to hear. And someone had heard and had turned him in. It could have even been the old barber himself who had cut my father's hair for more than twenty years. Loyalties switched sides easily in those days. Old friends turned foe, others just turned away.

Fraulein Amanda, tying the belt of her robe hastily around her middle, came flying into my room in the dark and unceremoniously yanked me out of my bed. Dragging me by my arm, she made a mad dash for the big, old armoire, pulled me in and shut the door softly behind us. She groped her way through my clothes, slid the secret panel aside, carefully rearranged what she had disturbed and closed it. There was barely enough room for the two of us to fit into that tiny space where I used to play hide-and-seek as a little girl.

Pulling me tightly against her, she urged, "Sh! Sh! Keep still."

Fraulein Amanda had been my governess for more than seven years and her role as teacher and companion had grown into a strong bond between us. I could feel her slender body shaking as she shared the fear that boiled up in me and clutched at my throat. Her warning was unnecessary: I couldn't have uttered a sound anyway. Everything that the grownups had whispered about with fear in their eyes, everything that had taken the color out of our lives for months, was coming true.

The Gestapo had come for my father.

We heard more shouting, clattering footsteps retreating down the stairs hastily; then came the slamming of the front door which echoed throughout the house like a death knoll. An engine raced, and we listened to the sounds of a car moving away on the gravel path that led to the tall iron gates and then into the narrow village road.

In a way, the silence that followed was worse than the brutal intrusion. Dead silence. It felt as though the house had died.

We clambered out of our hiding place and raced up the wide hall to my parent's wing at the other end of the second floor. We didn't bother to knock. Mutti sat at her dressing table, her hands folded into her lap, her eyes far away and lost, her voice toneless.

"They have taken your father away ... to some Gestapo head-quarters. That's all I know. I called your Uncle Erich," she said haltingly. "He is wonderful. Nothing seems to shake him. He assured me he knew what to do. Fortunately, he has a lot of friends everywhere. We've got to move fast to get your father out."

She straightened her shoulders, firmed up her voice and said, "I'll pull myself together, and start thinking. But first, I'll get dressed." She gave me a forced but reassuring half-smile, held on to me for a moment, and sent us back to our part of the house.

"Go about your day. I'll be in to see you as soon as I have something to tell you. Go on," she urged, "I'll be all right."

The hours crawled by at snail's pace. Our fears and worries lay heavily on the air and like a dark threatening cloud followed us everywhere. Maria, Lothar, old Burdach, his wife Trude and the rest of the household tiptoed aimlessly around, their faces worried, their voices low. Fraulein Amanda stuck to her tutoring schedule, but I caught her staring out the window and losing her place in my lessons. We both picked at our lunch, pushed the food around on our plates, and waited for something to happen. I was scared, and my insides jiggled and quivered in a most unpleasant way.

Finally, by late afternoon, we heard a car pulling up at the house, rushed to the window and saw my Uncle Erich emerge. Of all my uncles, he was my favorite. Tall and slender, a militaristic look about him, the Baron von Wartenburg was an imposing figure, and had a reputation to match. Mutti greeted him at the front terrace, and the two of them disappeared into the house.

In just a short while, my mother walked into our classroom with Uncle Erich at her side. I ran into his outstretched arms. I didn't know what to say, so I cried. Gently, he untangled himself from me and walked over to the big table where Fraulein Amanda quickly cleared away the schoolbooks and writing tablets.

"First things first," he held on to my hands. "In order to get your father out of the clutches of the Gestapo, we have to show proof that all of you are leaving the country. That's the only thing that will work. But there's no time to chose a country. That's a long process these days. I couldn't even buy a small country," he winked at me in an attempt at humor.

"All over the world" he continued, "nations have closed their borders to refugees. There is only one place that takes in refugees now — no questions asked, no visas necessary. You're going to Shanghai, China. I was lucky! I managed to book passages for the three of you. Your mother has the tickets for your ocean voyage. Fortunately, your passports are in order. That alone is worth a million less worries.

"Your ship is the *Gneisenau*. She is sailing from Hamburg tonight and will make port in Genoa in seven days. And, that's where you'll board her. It gives your parents time to make all the necessary arrangements to leave. And you, young lady," he looked at me, "have quite an adventure waiting for you."

His voice sounded funny, his dark eyes looked moist and he squeezed my hands until they hurt. In a rare show of affection, Fraulein Amanda stood behind me, her hands resting on my shoulders. My mother's face was still, and her empty eyes looked out of the window into nothingness.

The big room fell silent. Outside the wind whipped the bare tree branches and drove raindrops against the tall French doors. Thick clouds, heavy with more rain, hung over Marienhall, our home, matching our dark mood.

"Now comes the difficult part," Uncle Erich's voice broke the momentary silence. He sighed deeply. "I'm afraid your childhood is about to come to an abrupt end, dear child," he paused, looking at me strangely and said, "I have located the Gestapo station where your father is being held, and I've decided that you'll have to get him out. Yes, you! Not one of us grown-ups should go. It could put us in danger of being arrested by the SS. But I believe they will leave a young girl alone. They won't know what to do, and, therefore, will do nothing." My uncle's eyes, boring into mine, were like harsh words I would never forget. With his voice still low and raspy, he continued.

"Lothar will drive you in my old hunt car to the Gestapo building. He will drop you off, drive on, park further down the road and wait for you. You will go inside, ask for the officer in charge, tell him your name, and explain that you have come to ask for the release of your father, Martin Blomberg. Show them your tickets to Shanghai. Be polite, smile and act sure of yourself, but humble. If they ask why your mother didn't come, just say that she has the Grippe."

Uncle Erich softened his gaze and smiled at me. "Fortunately, you are quite tall and look a lot older than your age. With your blond hair and green eyes you're the picture of a German Aryan. Besides," he added with a sigh, "you have been around adults all your life and behave like one most of the time. I am confident that you can handle this situation. Don't be scared. Let me assure you, it will work. I have already set the wheels in motion, passed on a good deal of money here and there to ease the way. Those SS men may have black Nazi souls and their festering hate-all-Jews mottos, but they also like money — probably like it a lot more than the hate they peddle.

"You have to get going now. I'll be here when you get back," he promised and pulled me to my feet. "Come on, Katrinke! Do not be afraid. You can do it." He always made me laugh when he used my little-girl nickname.

"I'll go along, Herr Baron," Fraulein Amanda announced in her best iron-clad, no-nonsense teacher's voice. "Nothing you say will stop me. The child needs more help than Lothar. I'll stay in the car when she goes in to get her father, but on the way there and back … I'll be.…" her voice trailed off and she got busy with her handkerchief.

Without waiting for a reply, she brought our coats, barely let Mutti hug me, rushed us down the stairs into the rain and into the car. Lothar had the motor running and drove off. During the hour-long ride Fraulein made no attempt at light conversation, but instead, took on the role of a vicious, nasty Nazi official. She prepared me for what lay in store for me. She pelted me mercilessly with cutting questions, corrected my answers, taunted me with insulting remarks and directed my mannerisms. Even though I was frightened and unsure, I listened carefully. I had always been an eager pupil and a fairly obedient child. I was given little room to be naughty or stubborn, Fraulein Amanda saw to that. But on that night, she was different.

Just before we arrived at our destination, she opened her arms, pulled me close, and for the first time I heard her pray.

❧   ❧   ❧

The man inside the grim, grey stone building with its barred windows and narrow hallways that smelled of fear, was tall, sandy-haired, with a cold face and colder eyes. He looked sinister. His black SS uniform was something Death would wear, if Death dressed for a funeral. His thick, dark eyebrows rose high on his narrow forehead; surprise registered on his face as he looked me over. Not a word was spoken. He scrutinized our three tickets to China I handed him. Finally he nodded and barked a sharp order to the older SS underling who had delivered me into his presence, and who had remained at rigid attention next to me.

"Get that Blomberg Jew, give him to his Jew-girl here, then get them both out of this place."

With a vicious motion of his hand, the SS officer sailed our papers across his desk and on to the floor where they landed at my feet. He gestured impatiently for me to pick them up, and sharply turned his back to face the window.

The older SS man, a short but husky fellow, grabbed me roughly by my shoulder, steered me out of his superior's luxuriously furnished office and brought me to the entry way of the Gestapo building. Our footsteps echoed in the empty hall. He looked around him furtively and when he had assured himself that there was no one there to see us, he released his hard grip on me, and spoke in a quiet, almost kind voice.

"I know your family. My son is a printer's apprentice and works at your father's place. Your father is a good man. I do what I do because I have to," he stopped suddenly and looked at me as though seeking approval. His gaze dropped to the floor for an awkward moment of silence. I had nothing to say.

"Now, listen," he finally continued, "You wait outside; I'll get your father. Then you're on your own, and you better move fast." With that he pushed me gently out into the rain, and shut the door behind me. I hovered close to the building, trying to find shelter from the spring storm. The cobblestones in the courtyard that went all the way to the gate where two SA men were on duty in a guardhouse were wet and slick. I closed my eyes for a moment, picturing myself walking beside my father out of the gate and going home. Going home.

I waited. Time lost its meaning. I felt part of the seeping, dreary wetness, frightened and cold to the bone. Every once in a while I heard doors slam. I heard the clinking of iron against iron, the hissing noise of rattling chains. Loud voices shouted orders and obscenities. And cutting through the air like a sharp knife came high shrieks of pain, hoarse, animal-like noises of protest and deep, gut-wrenching sobs.

I tucked our precious tickets to China inside my coat to keep them dry and pushed my hands deeper into the pockets of my coat, when the older SS man appeared from a side door and motioned me to come over. He was holding on to a large burlap sack that was streaked with dark stains. I could tell it was heavy by the way he strained to hold it upright.

"I'm, sorry," he whispered, to me, then raised his voice for all others to hear. "Here's your filthy father, you Jew-swine. Get that heap of shit out of here before I change my mind."

He thrust the ends of the sack into my hands, and with his eyes urged me on. "Go on, young lady," he hissed, "don't freeze up on me. Your father is all right. He looks worse than he is."

Blindly, I grabbed the rough burlap with both of my hands, and could feel my father's feet pushing against the coarse fabric. I started to pull the heavy sack over the cobblestones, when I heard a low moan. Oh, my God. His head must have hit a stone. With each pull and stop, the end of the sack connected with the hard, bumpy ground. That must hurt. Tears mingled with fat raindrops on my face. With my back towards the gate, I put all my strength to work.

Hurry! I told myself. Hurry! Hurry! I pulled some more, afraid as I dragged the damp, lumpy sack forward inch by inch, that if I hurried too much I would hurt my father. After what seemed an eternity, and when I was about halfway to the gate, the old SS man suddenly appeared at my side and without a word, grabbed the sack, lifted it into his arms and ignoring the few uniformed men who had gathered to watch and sneer at my ordeal in silence, carried the load to the gate.

"Open up," he ordered the men in the guardhouse, "I've got to get rid of this stinking Jew swine and his Jew-girl."

The gates swung open; he took three big steps into the dark street, dumped his load, and under his breath said, "Good luck, my child. Go with God."

Behind me, the heavy wooden doors creaked shut, and I was alone in the night. I tried breathing deeply to stop the wild beating of my heart. But another anguished moan from inside the sack brought me back.

I looked down the street, and saw the big car backing towards me. There was no one in sight, not a human being, not another automobile; just a starless night sky, and me with my father in a bloody potato sack. Lothar jumped out of the car, and without a word, grabbed the sack and gently hoisted it on to the floor of the car behind the driver's seat. He pushed me in, the doors slammed, the motor roared to life, and we were moving away from the pit of hell.

When I saw Fraulein Amanda's face ghostly white in the dim dome light of the car my fright returned.

"Don't look," she ordered. I couldn't obey her and watched her with my insides quivering, as she took one of the hunting knives lodged against the back of the front seat by a leather restraining strap and boldly ripped the sack open all the way. And there my father was with his knees tucked up under his chin, naked, bruised, blood-streaked and bleeding. I had never seen my father without clothes before.

"Don't panic on me me now," she snapped. "Scoot back on the seat, tuck in your legs, so that he can stretch out. From what I can see, I think all that bleeding is from surface cuts. I think he's coming to."

She poured some cologne on a clean handkerchief, and when she gently rubbed away at a dried-on blood streak on his bare shoulder, a nasty scratch appeared. Satisfied, she dropped the handkerchief and piled some blankets on top of him and turned to me.

"They must have hit him with a sharp, pointed ... something ... may be a nail." She stopped quickly when she heard me gasp in horror and I started to sob.

"I'm sorry, my dear, I shouldn't have said anything," she looked crushed, "but...."

"Do you want me to pull over and stop the car?" Lothar asked from the front.

"No! No! Keep going. The sooner we get him to bed the better."

Suddenly Vati's eyes opened. He looked guardedly around, cleared his throat several times, moved his head back and forth and whispered, "Are they gone? Are we going home? What is the child doing here?"

Fraulein let out a deep sigh and ignored his last question, "Thank God! Yes we're going home. Try to stretch your legs, and drink this." She pressed one of Uncle Erich's slim silver brandy flasks against his mouth. Vati took a couple of sips, shuddered, coughed and pushed her hands away in protest. He moved his legs slowly as he stretched under the blankets, moaning softly and rolling his shoulders back and forth, as though testing ... testing....

"What did they do to you?"

"They beat me. I don't think they broke any bones. I don't want to talk about it, I'll never talk about it, Fraulein Amanda. Please. I want to rest." He closed his eyes again.

The car sped through the night, splashing through the heavy rain that made fat rivulets on the windshield. I sat petrified, listening to my father's shallow breathing. Fraulein put her arm around me again and held me close.

"You've been so brave and courageous. I am proud of you. Try to forget this day, this night. There are still a lot of good people out there. Please believe that. I don't understand the others. I don't understand them at all...."

Tears rolled down her cheeks. She made no effort to wipe them away. Of all the sights that night that made pictures in my head, Fraulein Amanda's crying touched me the deepest.

Lothar honked the horn several times as he drove through the gates of Marienhall and brought the big car to a stop. Lights came on; people appeared, anxious faces peered at us. Strong arms reached in and carried my father up the wide stone steps and through the open door into the house.

Before Mutti could say a word, Vati's blood-streaked arm came out from beneath his blanket and took her hand in his.

"I'm all right," he said. "I could have walked, but I have no clothes on. They kept them. I'm all right," he said again. "Just sore."

Fraulein Amanda led the way to our wing. "Let them take care of him now, and let us get some rest. You've done a fine job, and your father is going to be all right. Believe me."

All right, I wondered? Would any of us ever be all right again? And what about the people who did this to him? People who did these unspeakable things every day — all over Germany. What would happen to them?

It was ten o'clock when Fraulein tucked me in bed and slipped in beside me on top of the silky-soft eiderdown quilt. She rested her head besides mine and held on to my hand.

"I'll stay until you've gone to sleep. Good night, my child. Dream a lovely dream. Dream about fairies and flowers, rainbows and kittens and a walk at the seashore. Good night."

I made myself into a ball under the soft, silken quilt in the comforting darkness of my familiar surroundings and stared into the quiet night for a long time. Why did people want to hurt people? My father was good. He didn't do anything bad. Why did they hurt him? Why?

Fraulein Amanda was breathing deeply; she had fallen asleep. I snuggled up against her, closed my eyes, and told myself a story. A happy story.

Chapter One

March 1939
The Year of the Hare

*W*e made it! We escaped! Father, Mother and I made it out of Germany in the middle of a cold, fog-shrouded March night. Stealing out of town like thieves, leaving the scene of the crime of being Jewish. I shall never, ever forget those last few days we spent at home. Horror, fear and panic closed in on us like an evil fog, sinister and unforgiving. Like the whirlpools of a grey and churning river it threatened to pull us down, swallow us, and leave no sign of us behind. I don't want to remember getting my father out of the Gestapo's prison. I'm petrified that just thinking about it could bring it all back. But we made it; we did!

At last, we were on board our ship. There I was — tucked away in my little pocket of a cabin adjacent to the bigger one of my parents, about to sail on the steamship, *Gneisenau*, on our way to China. Still docked in the harbor, we were not scheduled to depart for another three hours. My parents had locked themselves and me into our suite, afraid some Nazi could find us and order us off the ship. "After all," Mother remarked, "we are on a German ship and that is as good as being on German soil — Nazis everywhere." How we made it to Genoa is another story.

We were still shaken from the ugly scene that played out at the Breslau train station, as we waited among the other silent clusters of travelers on the platform to board our train to Genoa. A quietly dressed, middle-age couple with two girls about twelve and fourteen years of age were standing amidst their four pieces of luggage at the edge of the crowd just outside the terminal. A couple of Hitler's brown-shirted SA men swaggered by, stopped at the little family which was most probably fleeing the country just as we were. The four people seemed to be shrinking into each other in a futile attempt to become invisible. One of the SA men made some remark that caused them both to break out in coarse, boisterous laughter. The other Nazi began twirling an iron crowbar expertly in the air, and with calculated accuracy suddenly brought it down hard on one of the family's bulging suitcases. The sharp points of the iron tool ripped a deep gash into the leather. In order to retrieve his weapon from the suitcase, the man yanked sharply, the rip widened, and with a death-knoll-tinkling, several gold coins escaped from their hiding place between the leather and the lining. The gold pieces twinkled and danced on the marble floor for a brief moment, then came to rest at the shiny, black boot-clad feet of the two Nazis.

My father, whom I called Vati, stood as still as a rock, his eyes averted, glued to the floor. He was gritting his teeth so hard that I could hear a crunching sound. A strong muscle jumped on his right cheek, ready to burst through and attack the world. Mother's hand flew to her mouth as she stifled a soundless scream. Within seconds, shouting an endless barrage of Jew-swine-filthy-Jew curses and insults, the two burly Brownshirts herded the family on a fast trot out into the street and out of our sight, pulling the treacherous luggage behind them on a small cart. The mother, the father and the two, lovely young girls would most probably not live to leave Germany. I looked at mother who silently mouthed the words, "May God be with them," while fat tears sprang from her dark eyes.

Fortunately, we made it onto the train without an incident. However, when hours later the train stopped on the scenic Brenner Pass — the border between Germany and Italy — the famous words, "Juden raus!" (Jews out!) echoed through the train's compartments. What had gone wrong?

Vati woke with a start from his restless nap. His eyes flew wide open reflecting the raw panic the three of us felt. "What in the name of God could they want now?" he hissed through clenched teeth. "We've been checked and checked and stamped and approved. We are leaving the country. We'll no longer be soiling their precious Aryan souls with our presence. So, what more do they want?" Exasperated, he dropped back against his seat.

Not knowing what to expect, our hearts filled to the brim with fearful anticipation, we quickly clambered out of our first-class compartment onto the platform where a row of black-clad SS — Hitler's "Elite Corps" — had assembled. Yelling and shouting curses, they ordered us to form a line. Father was drowsy from the sedatives Mutti had been feeding him on the long train ride, and we both held on to him to keep him from slumping over. Luckily the cold, fresh Alpine air helped to clear his head and braced him enough to allow him to stand still. When all the jewish passengers were assembled, an SS officer appeared, and flanked by his men, walked down the line as though reviewing the troops. Arrogance painted his face with disdain and disgust glinted in his eyes, as though he was about to be contaminated by the act of merely looking at Germany's human refuse.

Ever so often he jabbed his swagger stick sharply at an unlucky person, who then stepped forward, and obeying the harsh command to wait. When the officer came to where we stood, the swagger stick pointed in quick succession at Mutti first and then at me. What could that mean? Cold fear clutched at my throat, but I didn't dare look at my mother. Reluctantly, I let go of my father's arm, and stepped forward, head down. What are they going to do to us? Why did they choose us?

The twenty passengers, both men and women who had stepped away from the line, were hastily ushered into the terminal. Men were separated from the women, while some one shouted a rude order: "Mund halten!" (Shut your mouth!) Along with several other women, Mutti and I huddled against a wall in some hallway facing a row of doors. The door directly in front of us opened and a coarse-looking woman with a round, flat peasant face, dressed in a dark, non-descript uniform appeared, quickly pointed at one of the well-clad women in our group and ordered her to follow. The door shut behind them with a groan of warning.

What were "they" doing behind the closed door? I had overheard whispered scraps describing what the Nazis did at Gestapo Headquarters, and knew enough to be frightened of what may lay ahead. We were still in Germany! Pictures of gothic torture chambers appeared behind my eyes and in my mind I heard horrible screaming no one else could hear. The door opened with a creak, the Jewish lady appeared seemingly undisturbed by her experience and walked away in the direction from which we had come. Mutti was next. She too returned after a short while. She had a faint smile of encouragement on her face for me and the rest of the terror-stricken group. No words were spoken.

When the Nazi woman came for me, I followed her into a room that was furnished with a few glass-front cabinets like those found in a doctor's office, and attached at one end of a long, black oil cloth-covered table were two strange metal contraptions sticking up into the air from each corner. The woman looked me over briefly with cold, stone-gray eyes. Nervously, I tucked at my clothes. I was wearing my old school uniform which consisted of a pleated gray flannel skirt, a matching short jacket over a white cotton blouse and sturdy knee socks.

"Pull down your underpants, lift up your skirt, lean against the table and bend over," she commanded without further explanation. How humiliating. I felt my blood heat and rise to my face, burning my cheeks while I did as ordered. I had never undressed in front of strangers. Was she a doctor? Would she examine me? For what?

"Do you carry any jewels on your body?" she asked harshly pushing against my exposed back side.

"No, Madame," I managed to gasp as her cold, rough hands roamed in quick jerky motions over my body. Finally her thick, stubby fingers painfully probed the inside of my anus, and soon found the even more private opening in my body. Making strange, choking noises and gasping for air at the same time, the woman thrust her unforgiving fingers deeper inside me and pushed and pinched and rubbed, hurting me. I held my breath in pain, afraid to utter a sound. An eternity later, she exhaled loudly and withdrew her punishing hands. I felt a trickle of warm moisture make its way down the inside of my thighs, but I paid no attention to it. All I wanted was to get away from this evil woman and find my parents.

"Pull up your under pants, you dirty Jew-swine, and get out of here," she said in a steel-edged voice. Her face was flushed, a row of fine perspiration stood out on her upper lip. Her hands were tucked out of sight behind her back. Shaking with fright, sore from the agonizing examination and feeling soiled and dirtied — a dirty Jew — I hastily arranged my clothing, and with my eyes glued to the floor, I stumbled blindly out into the hall. I hoped my face did not show my shame. I wondered if she had performed her disgusting act on my mother, and the other women. What would Mutti say? As soon as I was at her side, she looked strangely at me, took my hand in silence, and we walked back out to the platform, where a Nazi soldier with the thrust of his head, chin-high, motioned us to board the train.

When we reached our compartment, Vati was asleep. With his tall, slim frame slouched and bent slightly forward, his suit seemed too big for him, and the collar of his white shirt stood a good two fingers away from his neck. His face looked haggard, etched with deep lines along his mouth. A new worry frown had settled permanently on his forehead. Every few seconds restless face muscles jumped under his clean-shaven skin, and his eyelids fluttered wildly as though protesting a bad dream. His body jerked and jumped every so often, making his sleep a far cry from rest and forgetfulness.

We knew that he had been through hell after being arrested by the Nazis that gray and early morning eight days ago. I remember how horrible he had looked after we picked him up at Gestapo headquarters just twenty hours later. So far Vati had not uttered a word about what "they" had done to him; and knowing him, Mutti predicted, he most probably never would. But we had heard enough to know that beatings were common, as were a variety of fiendish methods of physical punishment and unspeakable acts of torture for Germany's Jews. It was also widely known that SS and SA found great amusement and delight in the suffering they inflicted on their captives. Such heroes!

Mutti didn't look her usual lovely self either. Her dark eyes were surrounded by deep shadows and filled with worry and fear.

Her fine ivory skin had lost its lustrous glow and her shiny black hair had turned a muddy grey almost over night. Like the sun disappearing behind a dark cloud, her warm and inviting smile had vanished from her face. She moved without that natural ease and poise that used to make people look at her twice.

Settling into her seat, she collapsed against the velvety upholstery, closed her eyes and after a moment of stony silence she whispered, "What did that awful, smelly woman do to you?"

"Nothing," I lied. "She was looking for diamonds and jewels, she said. She let me go when she didn't find anything. Really, Mutti, she just looked me over and asked me if I had anything hidden on my body. Then she called me a Judenschwein and let me go."

Mother reached out for me and cupped my face in her ringless hands. "I don't want anything ugly to happen to you," she said in her soft voice. "All this is hard enough as it is. I am so sorry we didn't plan better. I'm so sorry," she sighed deeply. Exhausted, she closed her eyes against the world, pulling me close.

I really didn't understand what that nasty woman had done with me, but I knew it was ugly. There was no need to tell my mother. It was over, done with. We were not detained from leaving Germany, and that was all that mattered. The painful memory of rough, insulting hands on my body would fade with time. I was going to wish it away. I wasn't going to tell nor would I dwell on it. My parents carried enough of a load. I was getting older by the minute.

Vati woke up one hour before we reached Genoa. He appeared bewildered and puzzled for a moment as though trying to figure out where he was. He straightened himself and with a familiar gesture of his hands, adjusted his tie. Relief flooded his face when he saw Mutti and me sitting across from him.

"What happened?" he wanted know. "I must have dozed off while I was waiting for you to come back. What did they want? We had been cleared by customs before we left home. What did … those … those monsters want?"

"Nothing. Nothing at all," Mutti's voice soothed and assured. "It was no more than a nuisance, really, more Nazi brute power play. A routine check, one more calculated act to bully us. They know how scared we are and they play it to the hilt," she sighed. "Some woman did a spot check looking for people smuggling jewels out of the country," she continued. "When she found nothing on us, she let us go. Relax, dear, here we are, in Italy — bella Italia." Unsuccessfully, she tried to sound gay, but we all knew we weren't going on holiday to Italy.

"I won't rest," Vati replied wearily, "until we are in China. We are still in enemy territory," he said under his breath.

Then with both my parents shuttered in their hearts against the harm of the world we were leaving, the rushing of the wind, the clicking of the rails and the occasional lonely wail of the train whistle were the only sounds that pierced the apprehensive silence in our compartment. .

Arriving at Genoa to friendly Italian faces and a generous display of jovial Mediterranean temperament under sunny skies, brought us momentary relief from the doom and gloom we had lived for so long and had packed along.

Boarding the *Gneisenau* was uneventful, and at the same time nerve wracking. The ship was German, the crew was German, the captain was German; the people of our homeland had become our most feared enemies. Now we would be among them in close quarters for almost four weeks.

☯   ☯   ☯

The first things that fell out of my one and only suitcase when I unpacked it, were my three empty diaries — each a present from a different friend. Maria gave me the thick one, bound in dark red leather with a shiny brass clasp. With tears running down her apple cheeks, she said she had picked a diary with only three hundred pages — that's more than I would need.

"You'll be back soon," she had tried to assure herself and me, forcing a smile as she dabbed at her face with one of her lavender-scented, lace-edged hankies. She made me promise to write everything down everyday, so she could read all about our life in China. As the oldest of the Burdach family, Maria was head housekeeper and watched over her three brothers, her two sisters and their mates, to see that Marienhall, the home we had fled, ran smoothly. The whole family, including Grandmother and Grandfather Burdach had been managing the estate long before my grandfather, the Old Baron, had given it to his son. My father always said the Burdach family had belonged to the land a heck of a lot longer than the Old Baron and had a lot more class. The young Burdach children were my playmates on the few occasions I escaped Fraulein Amanda, and between the eight of us, there wasn't a corner of the fields, or the gardens of our fairy-tale forest we didn't know. We swore in unison, that we all had seen the "White Lady" — the sad ghost of Marienhall — float through the hallways and the attic, trailing yards and yards of a filmy silk gown — moaning and weeping. Her dark hair streamed behind her like silk ribbons as she moved lightly from room to room searching for her lost child. Never mind what Fraulein Amanda said. We knew a ghost when we saw one.

Governess and teacher of mine for seven years, Amanda von Goettlingen presented me with a diary covered in rough, stone-colored linen she had artfully painted with colorful wildflowers. There was also the pale blue leather one — Mutti's gift from my last birthday. I had a lot of empty pages to fill. Perhaps that was a sign that we weren't going to be back very soon, and I would have a lot of days and weeks, a lot of months and even years to write about. Lothar, our faithful factotum, had given me not one but two fountain pens, assuring me that wherever I would be, someone would have a bottle of ink.

It was time to depart. Through the open portholes we could hear the strains of an old German folk song being played by the ship's band. We all knew the words of this friendly song well. Now the words were bitter: "Muss I' denn, muss I' denn zum Staedtele hinaus, Staedtele hinaus, und du mein Schatz bleibst hier...."

("Must I leave, must I leave this friendly, little town, friendly little town, and you, my love stays here....")

We had not chosen to leave our homeland. We had not chosen to leave our loved ones behind. We were fleeing all that we knew, all that we treasured. We left it all, including our hearts. The band kept playing the song over and over again as we felt the first gentle motion of the big ship making her way out of the Genoa harbor.

Our next stop would be Cairo.

❧   ❧   ❧

Actually, I was excited now that we were on our way to China! Just think, I was traveling to China. Nobody I knew had ever been to China — India, yes, but China, no. I kept thinking of what I had learned about that country ... Marco Polo ... big-bellied, golden Buddhas ... lotus blossoms ... cool green jade ... ivory trinkets ... pagodas ... rickshaws ... dancing paper dragons ... rice paddies and water wheels....

When I read about that far-away land, I saw lovely pictures of dainty Chinese ladies in long silken gowns with velvet slippers on their tiny feet, strolling in beautiful gardens. Their shiny black hair was twisted and sculpted into tall hairdos that almost touched the gaily painted umbrellas that shielded them from the bright sun. Seven-story pagodas stood out against deep blue skies, butterflies fluttered about the snowy-white heads of huge chrysanthemums and whimsical birds hovered over the branches of blossoming trees. Pristine water lilies floated on clear ponds, and colorful ceramic house gods squatted and scowled from the corners of slanted tile roofs guarding the house against evil spirits.

It was all so cheerful, so inviting and so intriguing. It was a strange and different world from mine, but it certainly looked pretty on paper. What an adventure it would be. But before I'd get there, I planned to enjoy the sea voyage. I made believe we were on holiday. Fraulein Amanda always told me to seize the day, make the best of it and never live in the dark. She also said to dance and sing while the music played, and cry later!

I promised myself that in my first letter to her I would write, I would follow her advice.

Mother had left the connecting door between our cabins slightly ajar, and I could hear spurts of my parents' conversation. They were still disturbed that we were on a German ship. They talked constantly about the events of the last few years and berated themselves over and over for not having seen "it" coming. They panicked over the lack of funds. Taking money and valuables out of Germany had been verboten, and when caught in the act of smuggling (their own things), people had paid with their lives. We had witnessed that only a day earlier at the train station. My parents had the allowed sum of about fifteen American dollars with them. Uncle Erich, who had helped us secure our passage to China, had purchased several thousand dollars worth of "board money," which was no more than currency-mocking coupons with which to tip the crew, pay for extras, or purchase items from the on-board gift boutique. Only the crew and regular passengers could convert "board money" coupons into real currency at the purser's office at the end of the voyage. Jews did not have that privilege.

By the time we decided to check out the gift shop, all worthwhile and resalable merchandise was gone. Things like cameras, binoculars, travel clocks, Mont Blanc pens and other fine gift items that could easily be turned into cash in Shanghai had been snapped up. The gift store shelves were bare except for a few pieces of typical tourist junk, swastika pins and other Nazi memorabilia.

Except for "how-do-you-do-hello-goodbye-please-and-thank-you," my parents spoke no English. How would they make a living, they worried. How long would we have to stay in China, and would we make it to America soon? How-why-when-where-and-who questions were tossed into the air and left hanging with no answers.

Our cabin stewart was an older man who was very kind to us. Apparently, he had not been consumed by the Nazi doctrine, and secretly made no bones about it. He told us that there were four-hundred and fifty-six jewish refugees on the ship, all headed for a new life in Shanghai. His name was Guenther, and he didn't have too many kind words to say about the city that was about to become our new home. For more than twenty years, he had sailed to the Orient on freighters and passenger ships and considered himself an "old China hand." I loved to listen to him; he knew a lot about that part of the world. He called Shanghai the armpit of the world, the slum-scum of the Orient and the boil on the hide of China. He was quite eloquent in his description of the big city on the banks of the muddy Whangpoo river.

"It's a filthy, boiling-over-with-evil kind of a city," he said. "God must have looked the other way when the Devil moved in," he added, his hands folded as though praying. "All sorts of hooligans roam night and day and will snatch the teeth right out of your mouth before you know it. So watch out! When you walk down the street, when you are in a restaurant or a hotel lobby, when you shop in the stores, you will hear every language in the world spoken. You will see people from every nation on the globe, and you must guard against having your pockets picked by an expert."

Always the practical one, Mutti's logic rose to the occasion. "We have no choice," she told Guenther. "We can't turn around and go back There's no other place to go. I'm certain that even Shanghai is better than Gestapo Headquarters," she said.

Just the same, for the rest of the voyage, Guenther appointed himself tour guide to our destination and made it his job to tell us everything he knew, or had heard about Shanghai — city of sin, city of evil and bad smells. I listened spellbound to every word he had to say. When I didn't understand something, he wouldn't explain, just commented that I was too young to know. "But," he added reassuringly, "you'll learn quickly."

In a weak moment, he admitted that Shanghai was exciting, a teaming metropolis full of interesting, adventurous people, hidden treasures and beautiful arts. He also added that Shanghai was a city of trade. "You can buy anything, trade anything and make a living," he assured my father. One had to learn the way things were done.

"The Chinese are crafty traders, and bargaining is a matter of honor, of 'saving face,'" he explained, and gave Vati a quick lesson on trading a handful of nails, worn-out batteries and a basket of tin cans. He certainly took us under his wings.

For the first three days, we stayed sealed in our cabin and took our meals there, expertly served by Guenther. I had been frightened and disturbed when I discovered bloodstains in my underpants when I undressed for bed the first night aboard ship. I wondered what that monster-woman had done to cause me to bleed. Next morning I no longer hurt, and again decided not to tell my mother. I didn't know why, but I felt some things were better left alone. Maybe the less attention paid, the less fuss made, the easier it would be to forget unpleasant things.

Stretched out on my bed, I stared out the portholes at the ocean rushing up against the side of our ship, and hoped Mutti would let me go on deck some time soon. On the fourth day, Guenther brought us a note on creamy linen stationary from the ship's captain, who introduced himself in a sprawling, heavy handwriting. He mentioned that he was a good friend of my uncle, Paul von Warteburg. Apparently the two men had attended the same military academy, and kept in touch throughout the years. Captain Hans-Klaus von Oberon requested our presence at tea in his quarters at five o'clock this very day.

The visit went well and left my parents assured that it was all right to enjoy the voyage. Captain von Oberon's manner was formal and a bit stiff, yet Mutti insisted that she sensed that he was sympathetic to our plight, especially in view of his friendship with Uncle Paul. The captain said something to the effect of "not inventing more phantoms than already existed," and slipped in a casual remark that his ship was just that, a ship.

The conversation skirted dangerous territories and stayed with lighthearted talk about people, places and the comfort of common ground. When we finished our tea with all its delicious trimmings, Captain von Oberon invited us to join him for dinner at his table the following Saturday evening. He then went to his gleaming teak desk, and retrieved a small package from one of its deep drawers. With a conspiratory smile, he bowed from the waist as he handed it to my mother.

"Compliments and best wishes from the Chadwicks — your London friends," he said,

My father's eyes popped open, he looked questioningly at his wife. But before he could say a word, Mutti rose from her chair, quickly tucked the package into her purse, clasped the handsome captain's hand, thanked him profusely for a lovely, lovely afternoon, for the surprise from London and ushered Vati and me out the door.

"We'd love to join you for dinner Saturday night," she cooed a bit too sweetly in parting. Captain von Oberon kissed her hand, and insisted we tour the ship's impressive public rooms in the company of his first officer. There was nothing else to do but to accept.

"This is quite a hotel," Mutti commented. There was a graciously appointed library/writing room where the walls were lined with bookshelves clear to the ceiling, bursting with leather-bound books and others clad in colorful linen-like coverings. There was a large general salon, an enormous dining hall, a brass-leather-and-mahogany card room where a long, mirrored bar stretched itself across one wall. There was a handsome "Gentlemen's Room" and a "Ladies' Salon." Everywhere huge chandeliers sparkled from lofty heights, enormous gild-clad mirrors reflected the grandeur of fine paintings and graceful furnishings — all of which added to the general feeling of total luxury.

Back in our cabin, Mutti quickly explained that several months ago, she had paid for my old baby nurse, Hedwig's holiday in England, and had given her a sealed package with instructions to deliver it to family friends in London. And as soon as our way out of Germany had been established, Uncle Erich made the final arrangement to get the contraband aboard ship and into the safe-keeping of his brother's old friend, Captain von Oberon.

"I wrapped up the several pieces of my jewelry which weren't insured for Hedwig to drop off at the Chadwicks, in London. They had offered to help. And, now," she added triumphantly, "here they are. We're no longer poor!"

With that she broke the red seal that bore her initials, hastily removed the string, tore off the wrappings, dumped the contents on a small table and let out a painful cry

Instead of gleaming rubies, sapphires and sparkling diamonds in their gold and platinum settings, a pitiful assortment of glass beads, broken bits of mirror, stones and few short nails tumbled dully from their hiding place.

"Oh, no!" Mutti wailed — a heart-breaking sound — "Hedwig stole my jewelry. She stole our future. She stole our safety. Why? We've always been kind and generous to her. We kept her on after her work was done because she was getting old and had no place to go. Why would she repay us in such a treacherous fashion?"

Vati put on arm around her shoulders and I curled myself around her on the other side. But no matter what we said, my mother was inconsolable and wept bitter tears for the longest time.

I was lost, too. Our old Hedwig, who "blew" on my scraped knees to help heal the deep scratches from a nasty fall; who held me when I woke up scared from a bad dream; who taught me how to read long before Fraulein Amanda appeared on the scene, who loved me and scolded me, who brushed my tangled hair ever so gently. My Hedwig, who had been my world from the day I was born, had treated us so shabbily. She stole from us. She had hurt all of us. Finally, I went to sleep with the gentle motion of the dark sea cradling our big ship. I dreamt of home, of Marienhall. When I woke up the next morning, my face was wet. I wondered if I had cried all night long.

And Mutti? Well, she never spoke of Hedwig again.

The next night we dressed for dinner for the first time, left our cabin and found our table in the elegant and imposing dining room. An older couple from Berlin were our dinner partners. At first the conversation was halting and sparse, but the irresistible charm of Mr. and Mrs. Herrnstadt their worldly manner, their openness, soon paved the way for lighthearted chatting. I was so glad to see my parents' faces come to life again. Peter and Marina, as I was allowed to call them, immediately included me in the conversation, and treated me just like a grownup. I really liked them. They became my best friends.

I would enjoy myself on this trip, I confided to Mutti later that night. With her deep brown eyes smiling at me, she replied with big sigh, "Oh to be a child again … innocent and free of worry."

She was wrong. I was not free of worry, because whatever waited for my parents in Shanghai waited for me too. I looked around me at the passengers and I could tell a refugee from a "normal" traveler at a glance. The Jewish passengers moved about in an air of subdued participation — awkward and hesitant. Their troubled eyes radiated their uncertainties, their voices were toneless, afraid to be heard. We were truly "all in the same boat."

It wasn't until we passed through the Suez Canal, that my parents started to talk to other passengers, joined them for high tea, or met them on deck. They all talked in hushed voices about "home," the place of comfort and tradition, what their lives had been like, and what loved ones they left behind. I met a few children my age, but soon discovered my preference for being with older people — after all, that was all I'd ever known.

As one golden-blue day merged with the next, and the weather got warmer, I spent most of my time on deck reading one of the books from the ship's library. After dinner, we returned to our cabin, where another book waited for me. I began to feel at home. All I needed to make life complete, was Fraulein Amanda's presence and her daily lessons. She had handed me a list of books to read — some in English and some in French — in hopes I would find a few of them on board ship. "They are classics," she commented, "and every decent library will carry these titles." She was right. I was head first into reading Rudyard Kipling, and Mark Twain was waiting his turn. I missed my teacher. Each day I studied the big map that was displayed on deck where colorful pins showed the progress we made, as the *Gneisenau* plowed through the blue waters. China was coming closer and closer.

We had entered the Indian Ocean, when one of the ship's screws broke. The *Gneisenau* continued on to Singapore with reduced speed, where repairs would be made. No complaints from us. None of the refugees was in a hurry! Once in dry dock, we spent seven hot and humid days while the crew replaced the damaged blades. "Normal" passengers were invited to stay in comfortable local hotels, but Singapore was British territory, therefore Jewish refugees were not permitted entry into the city. Mutti said the English were afraid that the refugees might stay, and the British Empire was not going to have that.

Back on the high seas and full steam ahead, The *Gneisenau's* graceful white bow plowed through the blue sea under dazzling, blue skies, and life on board felt so normal at times that I was beginning to believe I was indeed on a world cruise — a holiday. Even my parents lost some of their apprehensions and were more at ease. Mutti's eyes were bright again; Vati picked up a good tan and his features had lost their haunted look. He stopped his fretting about not having money, and Mutti referred less and less to the condition she termed as "the loss of identity." I wasn't quite sure what she meant.

I liked to hang on to the smooth, sun-warmed wooden rail of the ship as we sailed under deep blue tropical skies. I watched the dolphins, those friendly, flying fish of the Seven Seas, as they played along side the *Gneisenau*. Rising from the sea, the big fish arched against the sky, shedding sparkling rainbow droplets of salt water. At night, I was held spellbound by the endless parade of schools of phosphorous fish whose passing lit the dark waters with glowing streaks of light. Overhead, billions of stars winked against velvet eternity, close enough to be reached with a tall stretch. The air was fresh and balmy, the wind gentle and the soft strains of a waltz from the Salon spilled into the night and mingled with the steady hum of the ships mighty engines. I loved everything about the sea. I could have sailed forever.

We made port in Manila and Hong Kong, where Jewish passengers again had to remain on board, looking out at the land not unlike prisoners behind bars. Between Hong Kong and Shanghai we ran into a powerful typhoon that howled and roared and tossed our 23,000-ton ship around as though it were a walnut. Most passengers had a greenish cast to their faces, stumbled along the hallways hanging on to ropes, and avoided the dining room with their eyes closed. Eating a meal during the raging of the typhoon wasn't easy. Unless I held on to my plate it would race to the other side of the table at top speed and crash to the floor as the ship rose high on a monster wave and crashed back into a deep trough of the rough seas. I had a good time. I wasn't seasick; I ate with a few other seaworthy passengers in the dining room, and loved going to sleep to the rocking and rolling and yawing motion of the turbulent ocean. My parents didn't do as well, especially my father who confessed sheepishly that anything bigger than a storm in a teacup made him seasick.

Overnight, the storm flew out to sea, the ship's movements were steady and reassuring, and the sky was as innocent as the new day itself. And then, our voyage was over.

Our "holiday" had come to an end; much too soon, I thought. I had silently wished for another breakdown of one of the ship's screws which not only would slow us down, but would have to be repaired. No such luck! We packed our meager suitcases, Guenther took them on deck, still grinning in gratitude from the large bundle of "board money" Vati had stuffed into his hands. We waited and watched as we left the deep blue China Sea, entered the Yangtse River and eventually chugged along in the sluggish, yellow waters of its tributary, the Whangpoo. The landscape was dismal, flat and far from inviting. Small, colorless villages, alarming mounds of rubble, bombed-out, crumbled buildings hovered in mute protest along the shoreline. I leaned against the ship's railing, no longer feeling like a tourist. I was looking at my new home. Mutti wondered out loud if that ugly, muddy water was any sign of what was to come. Shanghai — the armpit of the world, the slum-scum of the Orient, and the boil on the hide of China? What a recommendation for a city!

The *Gneisenau* had reduced speed so much that we barely seemed to move. A motor djunk came along side, halted at an open loading door in the belly of the ship, and the harbor pilot came on board. He would navigate the big vessel through the heavily trafficked river into her docking slip. Our "hotel on the waves" gave one last mournful blast, the anchor dropped, the engines stopped, the gangplank came down and connected us to our new world. And what a world it was.

Chapter Two

May 1939 — The Year of the Hare

Shanghai's waterfront offered an imposing view of a wide street lined with massive stone buildings that ranged from square and squat to tall and towering. Colorful flags whipped gaily in the wind from several rooftops. Mutti gasped, and pointed to a large, gray stone building. From its balcony flew the offensive red-white-and-black flag of Hitler's German Reich — the huge, hateful swastika fluttered mockingly in the breeze under a clear China-blue sky.

My father took one look at the arrogant display of Nazi presence on foreign soil, and turned to Mutti. "We shouldn't be surprised, after all. Don't you remember the Fuehrer's threatening promise? He said that his 'arm was long and would reach around the world.' We have come more than halfway across the globe," he sighed, "only to see that the madman kept his word."

"This must be the consulate, Martin." Mutti had recovered her voice and she sounded calm and soothing. "And judging from all these flags, this must be consulate row. Let's just hope Herr Hitler will have to eat his words. Let's not cross bridges that haven't been built yet; let's not create phantoms."

My mother! Always finding words that smoothed over the ugliest moments and lessened the sting of the insult. With a combination of Jewish resignation and boundless courage she held together the fragile threads of our souls.

No more time to ponder or to worry. We each grabbed our suitcase, and without a look back, walked down the gangplank. We had no idea what was to happen next. We had been informed on board ship that a representative of the new Jewish community would meet us, and take us to a shelter. We had no idea what that meant.

Beginning to perspire profusely in the moist heat, we put our suitcases down, and as though looking for strength and encouragement from each other, held hands, and began to take in the scenery around us. It was quite a sight!

Why, it was nothing like the pretty pictures of fragrant gardens, petite silk-clad ladies, butterflies and flowers. The air was thick and moist filled with the strangest, pungent odors. Not at all pleasant. Mother insisted it was heavy with the smell of human excrement and urine. It turned out she was right.

Coolies in dark cotton pants and sweat-stained tunics, each with a wide, peaked straw hat tied under their chin, with flimsy straw sandals on bare feet, carried heavy loads suspended from a bamboo pole on their shoulders. The muscles on the calves of their legs bulged like knotted ropes. Their loud sing-song that sounded something like "Yeho-Heho," mingled with the cries of street vendors offering their goods. Thick throngs of pedestrians snaked their way through the streets. Hordes of people on bicycles, their bells clanging shrilly, competed with carts and automobiles for the slightest hint of a break in the traffic. An armada of rickshaws pulled by sweat-dripping coolies darted in dangerous maneuvers in and out of the teaming mass of urgent humans. A few wildly honking and swerving automobiles added to the confusion of the city's traffic.

In this symphony of sounds and smells, filthy beggars — men, women and children — their bodies barely covered by pitiful rags, exposing nasty sores, littered the dockside and packed every available nook and doorway of the handsome, broad river front street. In high sing-song voices, they cried out for alms. Food peddlers cooked and fried their offerings over portable charcoal fires; peddlers offered their wares from baskets suspended from a bamboo pole. Turban-clad, bearded Sikhs in dirty khaki uniforms, complete with swagger sticks, directed traffic and appeared ornamental rather than effective in the midst of the surging crowd.

And above all this clamoring hubbub, there hovered over the city a mass of dirty, cloying air as thick and as moist as a hot-water-soaked sponge that threatened to drown us. Breathing was like sucking on warm, wet cotton balls. How could we get used to that, I wondered.

Like many of our fellow refugees, Mutti pressed a snowy handkerchief against her nose to ward off the offensive smells. Dressed in our thick European travel clothes, we soon were hot and sticky. Finally several men appeared on the scene and made their way to where we were waiting. They introduced themselves as representatives of the new Jewish community. One man stepped on a wooden box and over the din of the city tried to make himself heard.

His name was Werner Silberman, formerly of Berlin. He informed us that we would be transported to a place called Hongkew, an area adjacent to the International Settlement. Hongkew had been "won" from the Chinese in 1937 by the Japanese war machine, and was still occupied by the victors who invited Jews to settle there.

He went on to explain that Shanghai was divided into several areas: the International Settlement, leased by the British for ninety-nine years, was the heart of the city, beginning at the river front. Then there was the Concession Française, a pleasant residential area, tucked in where the International Settlement ended. The huge Chinese Quarter was off-limits to foreigners, he warned, unless of course a person wanted to vanish from the face of the earth.

"One step inside those gates," he warned, pointing vaguely to his right, "and you're gone, disappeared, never to be found again." I wondered what the Chinese do to foreigners there, and why. I had a lot to learn.

I listened carefully as he continued his description. I learned, Hongkew, our destination, sat on the other side of Soochow Creek, just a few blocks away from where the *Gneisenau* had docked. That part of the city was occupied by the Japanese since the Chinese-Japanese war of 1938, and bore the scars of destruction from air raids and shellings. It certainly wasn't the high-rent district, Mr. Silberman said, shaking his head in a funny way, but it was a beginning. Five buildings in that area had been set aside for Heime (temporary shelters) for arriving refugees, providing a free-of-charge roof over their heads until they were able to make their own arrangements for living quarters. The sooner people moved on, the quicker room and aid became available for new arrivals. Shanghai's Jewish community of old-timers was a bit overwhelmed by the thousands of refugees seeking shelter. Few had any money to speak of and depended on the Heime for a place to sleep and some food in their stomach — at least it was a beginning.

Two large trucks rumbled toward our hot and weary group of travelers which had thinned out a bit. Some of the refugees had been picked up by family members or friends who had preceded them to the Orient. How nice it must have been for them to be met by familiar faces — relatives who already knew their way around.

We crowded into the open truck bed, sat on our luggage and held on to each other as the driver slowly weaved his way through the heavy traffic. When a big bridge came into view, we were told it was the Garden Bridge that crossed Soochow Creek and that it had two owners. The first half of the bridge belonged to the International Settlement, and the second half was claimed by the Japanese. Soochow Creek divided the city into two territories: the English "occupied" International Settlement and the Japanese occupied Hongkew. The first half of the bridge was patrolled by British and the second half by Japanese soldiers. But just the same, people were free to come and go as they pleased. Sometimes the Japanese soldiers played the role of the big conqueror and pestered the Chinese citizens crossing the bridge by searching their meager bundles. More often than not, they confiscated a few handfuls of rice, food items, a trinket or whatever caught their eye. These two nations had hated each other for centuries. Chinese people called their enemy "apes."

After we crossed Soochow Creek the neighborhood changed drastically. Grubby row houses with open storefronts lined one side of the waterfront street. The sidewalks were littered. Chinese women sat on low stools in front of houses, smoking cigarettes and shrieking at toddlers and noisy children. Some women were nursing their babies, swatted at flies which rose in hordes from the spills of dirt-clogged gutters only to land on the nearest heap of foul trash. Here and there a brazen rat scurried around in broad daylight between the shabby row houses that sat next to the gaping holes of bombed-out buildings. On the river side of the street, the docks hosted rusty and tired merchant ships of all sizes that screamed of neglect and old age. Perhaps this was the graveyard for rust buckets no longer seaworthy, someone on our truck suggested.

From their resting places in the stinking gutters, mangy dogs with whip-like tails, and eyes inflamed and dripping puss, chased unwelcome flies. Children played on the street oblivious to the small rivers of urine that trickled into the gutters, and they skipped nonchalantly around the small heaps of human feces. Here and there, men and boys, with their backs turned to the street, faced the wall of a row house and urinated. Kids squatted in the middle of the sidewalk right where they played, doing their business.

"Spitfire." Mr. Silberman explained that little Chinese children wore pants that were split open on the bottom for convenience. He held his nose in a mock gesture of shutting out bad odors.

I hadn't seen a garden with petite ladies yet. However, the whole scene of load-toting coolies, sing-song vendors, food purveyors, penny-seeking beggars covered with sores and grotesquely swollen legs, rickety rickshaws and bicycles and throngs of people on the move, had not changed. Mutti looked from Mr. Silberman to me and said, "Well, this is Shanghai, after all. It's not Paris, London, Rome or home."

Right there, young and as green as I was, I made up my mind that I would have as little as possible to do with China. I would keep it at arm's length. Shanghai would serve as a waiting place. A place to go from to a place of "home." I would think of myself as a girl Robinson Crusoe — shipwrecked on an island, waiting for a ship to rescue me and bring me back home.

The kaleidoscope of new impressions was too much for one day. Mutti closed her eyes, shutting out the chatter and clatter that never ceased. Vati looked around with a closed face, constantly wiping thick beads of perspiration from his face with his soggy handkerchief. If it was this hot in the month of May, I said to myself, what would August be like? I was dripping too, and, like my father, had taken off my jacket, but it was not much help.

Barely avoiding a collision with a wildly weaving, rattly old automobile, our driver suddenly turned away from the harbor side and entered the web of crowded, narrow intersecting streets of inner Hongkew. Finally, we came to stop at a large, run-down building that squatted in an equally run-down courtyard where a handful of refugees had gathered to greet the new arrivals.

A dark-haired lady in a simple cotton dress stepped forward when the truck squealed to a stop, and with a friendly smile welcomed us in a heavy, unmistakable Viennese dialect. We climbed down from the truck, grabbed our suitcases and on unsteady sea legs, followed her into the building. A blending of fried onions, stewed cabbage and a hint of 4711 Cologne greeted us when we entered a large hall-like room. Several rows of wooden tables and benches for eating and meeting occupied the center of the hall. The rest of the area was divided into cubicles equipped with two to four cots that were separated from each other by flimsy sheets or thin blankets hung on clotheslines in an attempt to provide a semblance of privacy.

The Austrian lady, who introduced herself as Frau Wilna, directed us to chose an unoccupied cubicle and lock our luggage when we left it. She warned haltingly, clearly embarrassed to suggest thievery among "our" people.

She recovered her poise and explained that Wayside Home was one of several refugee shelters where people stayed until they were able to be on their own. "Some refugees have lived at the homes for over a year, and they may never leave," she said. She told us that a "soup kitchen" served simple "Eintopf" (one-pot) meals, and warned us about buying food at the open markets — especially fresh fruit.

We were instructed to wash all our fresh fruits and vegetables in potassium permanganate … to kill bacteria on the skins. Watermelons, were off limits because Chinese farmers cultivate their crops with human fertilizer, and to make the fruit heavier injected them with dirty, unboiled water. Typhoid and cholera still existed in Shanghai and diarrhea was as common as a cold in the nose.

Never, she cautioned us, "eat or use anything that has touched the floor. If you drop your handkerchief, wash it." Her litany of dangers lurking to pounce included beggars, gangsters, pickpockets, thieves, purse snatchers, treacherous rickshaw coolies and crooked shop keepers.

Her final stern advice was not to change U.S. dollars into Chinese yen with street money changers who would cheat us and rob and kill us. Use the American Express office for currency exchange. Don't buy anything from a vendor without haggling.

"Always ask the rickshaw coolie the amount of the fare to a destination in advance, then offer him half as much and stand fast. And, for God's sake," she added emphatically, "do not ever rescue a Chinese human being. Not a baby, a child, man or woman. If you do you will be responsible for the life you saved. You will have interfered with Buddha's will and have to pay for it."

Next, preceded by a gush of apology, Mrs. Wilna finally drew us a picture of the bathroom facilities. "Hygiene," she called it, "is bad here. It's very bad. We have only two cement bathtubs, and no hot water. Someone rigged a cold water shower. It, too, is primitive. Worst of all are the toilets." She took a deep breath before continuing. "We do not have water closets, just honey pots," she confessed, and described the shameful wooden barrel-like receptacles for human waste.

"Please," she urged, "help us keep that area as clean as possible. What with hordes of flies and other insects, it's a cesspool of disease just waiting to get you. A coolie comes every morning to empty the pots and cleans them after a fashion, but there are so many of us, that we often, uh, overflow...." She looked embarrassed and flustered having had to mentioned the subject at all. Some people, she said, unable to cope with the honey pots, actually walked all the way to town every day to one of the hotels on the bund, where they have bribed servants with a few "coppers" (pennies) to use a bathroom. I thought of Guenther, our steward and his description of slum city. He knew what he was talking about, I just hadn't really believed him.

Stunned by the process of living in a festering slum with dangers at every turn, we dragged our luggage to the next empty space that held three cots, and ate our first meal in Shanghai, a spicy Hungarian stew. Later, Vati standing helplessly in the "doorway" of our quarters vowed, "We won't stay here but one night. I promise. This is unbearable," he shuddered.

Again Mutti's calm took over. "Let's take one thing at a time," she said. "We have found a cheap hotel, and that's better than no place. Tomorrow," she quipped, "we'll move into the Ritz."

Vati just looked at her, shaking his head.

Exhausted and depressed from trying to absorb and digest all the strange and new impressions of the day, Mutti pulled the sheet that served as our "door" closed and dropped onto her cot. Vati and I followed suit. Nobody said a word for a long while; listening instead to the conversational hum from around us. There was a sudden movement in the cubicle next to my cot when a hand dented the sheet, and a man's voice shouted a friendly "willkommen." The owner of the voice announced that he was Joseph Podowski, and that he came from Stettin, Germany.

"We're from Breslau," Vati replied, "my name is Martin Blomberg. Forgive me for not getting up to meet you, but we're pretty tired. It has been a long day and we need some time to ourselves. Like everybody else, I guess we are overwhelmed, and haven't had time to sort out the reality of it all."

Mr. Podowski cheerfully wished us good night, adding his promise to meet the following day. How could we not meet? We're were living in each other's pocket.

Mutti retrieved our nightwear from one of the suitcases, and before turning in we had to find the well-described bathroom. We followed the posted cardboard sign and ended up on the roof of the building. The location of the honey pots was easily identified by the overpowering odor of human excrement and urine that assaulted us.

Mutti took one look at the obscene row of "honey pots," that squatted on the open roof top, partly sheltered by a makeshift tin shed-like roof, pinched her nose shut and closed the ineffective, flimsy curtain behind her. Within minutes she reappeared, motioned me to do what I had to do, her thumb and forefinger never leaving her nostrils.

I don't want to talk about that place — except that going to the bathroom on a roof of a building under a tin umbrella in plain view of any one on the neighboring roof tops, was a bit unnerving. Both Mutti and I were close to tears, but I was too tired to let go. Crying was just one more effort I didn't want to make.

I joined my mother in the so-called "bathroom" with its two cement tubs and several chipped and stained sinks with rusted faucets. A thin stream of cold, yellowish water trickled stingily from clogged openings. I reached for the soap; there wasn't any. A young woman with thick, wavy long hair, who was doing her toilette at the sink next to me, handed me a bar of fragrant lavender soap.

"Guten Abend," she smiled. "You must be new here, otherwise you would know to bring your own soap and towel. Ask Frau Wilna to give you some towels; soap you have to buy yourself."

I shared the soap and one end of our benefactor's towel with Mutti who thanked the young woman profusely, embarrassed that she had not given a thought to the possible absence of some of the mundane objects of daily grooming.

Back in our cubicle, Mother pulled the sheet across the opening to our space and warned me to keep my underwear on. "There are so many people around us, we don't don't know what to expect," she muttered in a low voice. A few minutes later, when Vati returned from his trip to the men's quarters, his face was even grimmer than before, his eyes flat, his breath shallow.

"Good God in Heaven," he whispered hoarsely, "what kind of a hell hole is this place? This is horrible! This country invented gun powder and porcelain before anyone else on the globe. The Chinese weave the most intricate patterns of fine silks, they carve ivory and jade pieces that defy European craftsmanship and artistry, but they can't build a damn water closet, a bathtub ... have clean water? This is the twentieth century. What have I done to us? What?"

He sat on his cot and buried his face in his hands. His body shook, and harsh sounds of sobbing emerged from behind his slender fingers. I was stunned. My father, that strong, tall, erect man was crying. I had never seen him like that. My whole insides quivered.

Mother stepped over to the huddled figure of despair, wrapped her arms around his shoulders, brought him close to her, and shushed him, speaking softly. I couldn't hear what she was saying, but Vati soon recovered from his outburst and said good night in a quiet, controlled voice.

I stretched out on my cot and looked around me. Mutti had hung our traveling clothes from one of the the rods that held the sheets dividing the cubicles. The main bare-bulbs ceiling lights that illuminated the big hall were still on, and the place two hundred people or more called "home" for the night, was buzzing with conversation. There was laugher, chattering and visiting without a thought for those bone-weary, worn-out souls who yearned for silence and sleep.

Adding another layer of discomfort was the oppressive, humid and fetid air. It was so hot and stuffy in our tight quarters that I doubted I'd ever go to sleep. Then I realized with a jolt, that I had never ever slept in the same room with my parents. I had never seen them undress. I became even more uncomfortable at this forced intimacy which I had never experienced before. I closed my eyes against the light. I tried to shut out the busy noises around me, and forced my mind to create the same dream world I had had been able to conjure up ever since I was a little girl, lonely for someone to tell me a story.

I returned to my big room at Marienhall, with its lovely furnishings, silken down covers and rich side drapes. I always loved the tall French windows that stood open and looked out to the gardens, with the sheer white curtains that billowed in the jasmine-and-rose-scented air. The mysterious rustling of the wind in the trees outside talked to me and a full moon made dancing shadows on the lofty ceiling.

I must have been asleep for a while when I woke up to the heartbreaking sounds of Mutti's soft sobbing. As I shook myself awake, I heard harsh panting noises and rhythmic motions coming from one of our neighbors quarters. I heard people talking in foreign languages, their voices hushed. Outside of our circle, people were coming and going in the night. Occasionally a child cried, a baby complained; and all around me were the unpleasant, clinging odors of crowded humanity.

Some of the lights had been turned off, but the big room was far from dark. I wanted to go to my mother's side and say something nice to her, but I didn't know the words. I was sad, forlorn, empty and hollow. Purposefully, I forced my mind to reach back and create again the soul-soothing images of the same dream spun from yesterday's beauty and safety.

Chapter Three

August 1939

*W*e have been in Shanghai for three months now and a lot has happened since our arrival. After spending that first awful night at Wayside Heim, Vati could not hide his deep depression as well as his frustration. We were sick to death of waiting for our turn to visit the smelly bathroom areas, we lapsed into a worried silence at one of the tables in the common room drinking cups of dark Russian tea a kind lady had brought us. I kept forever looking for signs of decisions I expected from my parents. Actually, I didn't know them well at all. Growing up with my Nanny and Fraulein Amanda, spending long weekends and holidays with Uncle Erich and Aunt Antonia on their country estate in Rothenburg, or at Uncle Carl and Aunt Helene's Villa Hochstein in the mountains, I never saw much of my parents. None of my father's sisters had children, and at an early age, I had been designated to be the ersatz child whenever their need for having a youngster around the house rose to the surface. I was used to being around adults, and Fraulein Amanda told me often that I was the oldest child she had ever known. Maybe that upbringing would come in handy now. I had a feeling I would have to do a lot of taking care of my parents. They seemed more lost than I was. But then, I wondered just what it was that I could do. I was just a kid! I had butterflies in my stomach and deep worry clutched at me with icy fingers. If only Fraulein Amanda were here; she would know what to do.

I was brought out of my troublesome thoughts when a man and woman, perhaps in their middle thirties, stopped at our table, wished us a good morning and sat down next to us. The man introduced himself as Joseph Schiller; his wife's name was Lucy. Mr. Schiller had a slim narrow face, serious brown eyes behind thick glasses, and head shock full of wavy, light brown hair. He was of stocky, muscular build, but his hands were slender with long fingers and well-shaped nails. In spite of the serious set of his face, a warm, kind of a chuckle sparkled in his eyes. He explained that he was an accountant from Frankfurt who had left a thriving practice behind that had given him a comfortable living (We heard that story a hundred times a day). A deep sadness clouded his features when he announced in a shaky voice that they had sent their two girls on a children's transport to England for safety. Just a few weeks later, he and his wife had fled Nazi Germany almost overnight. In a stroke of pure luck they had made passage on the Italian ocean liner, the *Conte Bianco Mano*. The Schillers arrived in Shanghai just a few days ahead of us and had been staying in the shelter ever since.

Lucy Schiller was a frail-looking woman with a surprisingly strong face, curious grey eyes, and a whimsical, almost challenging smile about her full mouth. Her reddish-brown hair was rich and wavy, cut fairly short and moved freely with her every gesture. Like us, they were dressed in their "good" European clothes, too hot and too confining for Shanghai weather.

The Schillers deplored the conditions of the shelter in gentle terms as though not to insult their well-meaning host. Like the rest of the refugees, they were strangers in a strange land, were trying to learn their way about as fast as they could, and were hoping to leave the shelter as soon as possible to a place of their own.

Mrs. Schiller, reached over, touched my hand and confided that her oldest daughter was just about my age, then her voice turned to tears. Her husband put his arm around her and lovingly reassured her that the children were sure to be all right.

"The girls are fine. I know it. Not only that, but those dear little brats most probably have a lovely room with a view of an English garden and a real bathroom of their own. A honey pot to them, means nothing more than a bowl full of liquid gold to put on their breakfast scones."

Mrs. Schiller straightened herself, and said something to the effect that every once in a while she claimed a moment of self-pity, and the conversation turned to other matters. The Schillers purpose to stop at our table became clear when they mentioned they had found a large room that rented with a real water closet. The room was not far from the shelter, but the rent would cut deeply into their meager funds. It was true that rents had soared when the native population in Hongkew caught on quickly to the opportunity to charge hefty prices for the most primitive living quarters.

"The place is furnished with a double bed, and two old-fashioned sofas, two easy chairs a table and six chairs, as well as two large chests," Lucy Schiller took charge of the womanly concerns. "There is even a corner shelf big enough too hold a few pots, dishes and a hot plate," she concluded.

I was surprised how quickly my parents responded to the strangers. The couples seemed to like each other instantly. When Mutti suggested looking at the room, and perhaps sharing it for a while, Lucy Schiller's face lit up as she reached over to take my mother's hand in a firm grip and shaking it several times. We looked at each other, laughed out loud for whatever reason, and took off to examine the room.

We walked down one of the busy, cluttered and noisy streets of Hongkew for the first time and learned that they all looked alike. Narrow two-story houses clung to each other in a row stretching the length of a city block, broken up only by a gate-like entrance in mid-street that led to the inside lanes. The whole width of each house was a store front that had no door, stood wide open all day long, and was boarded up at night. We saw a man making peanut butter, someone selling boiling hot water from a cement cauldron that was heated from below by a bright fire. There was a candied fruit vendor, a dried herb business, a rice kitchen, a fabric merchant, a primitive tea house and a Chinese pharmacy. There was a sort of lending library where the books were attached to a thin chain and customers of all ages read their selection squatting on their haunches or sitting on tiny stools on the street. There were people in the business of making cotton stuffing for quilts and robes, others were selling smoked and dried duck, fish and other undistinguishable items.

On the street itself, without the formality of a store front, were people in the ear-cleaning and barbering business. The barbers were digging around in their customers' ears with a thin bamboo stick, ends wrapped in cotton. Others were being shaved from cheek to cheek. Business was brisk, people were waiting their turn patiently, squatting on their haunches in the dirt-littered streets. We walked and gawked, dodged in and out between street vendors selling everything from a bowl of rice, to sewing threads, to brooms and brushes. And for those who could neither read nor write, studious-looking scribes in long, black robes, a round silk cap on their heads, were busily taking their dictation for letters behind a tiny folding table in the middle of the crowds.

"The Chinese people are serious about business," Vati remarked. "Every enterprise is a one-man-band. We have a lot to learn how things are done here." I could see fear and worry climb right back into his eyes. I wondered what a kid could do?

When we entered the lane on Chusan Road where the house was located, Mutti almost fainted. I held on to her, as her hand flew to her face to pinch her nostrils shut to keep out the stench from the garbage that almost overwhelmed us. Shanghai life in the low-rent district was the real world; and it wasn't a pretty one.

The house we sought was just an ordinary narrow link in the chain of dwellings sitting in a filthy, stinking, equally narrow lane of rows of houses — ten to a row — often as deep as a city block. An eight-foot stone wall separated one area of row houses from the next. Cement garbage bins with heavy iron lids hulked against the wall every sixth row to accommodate the tenants' refuse. Boiling under the hot sun and steamed by the humidity in the air, the combination of rotting fruit peelings, spoiled leftovers, raw bones, dead cats, drowned puppies, carcasses of rats, fermented with human feces, sprinkled with urine from chamber pots, and the lifeless body of a newborn baby, plus clots of blood and lumps. Long before the garbage bins were emptied, they reached a state of overflowing ripeness, spilled their foul contents into the alleys, and hosted swarms of fat green-and-purple-bodied flies that promised to spread diseases faster than the wind.

Mutti averted her face, held her hand over nose and mouth, until we entered 2745 Chusan Road.

We viewed the modest "apartment" which was simply the one and only large room in one of the ordinary row houses owned by a Chinese family. The room was on the ground floor — about twenty-five feet long, twelve feet wide. It was fairly clean, the simple furnishings were on the shabby side, but clean as well. The bathroom was primitive, and smelled musty and reeked of mildew. The walls and floor were rough and raw, unpainted cement, as were the short, square bath tub and the small sink. There was no hot water of course, but the shining glory was the water closet, a real toilet with a pull chain.

We had been told that the reason for the lack of modern conveniences was due to the city's inadequate — and in some areas non-existing sewer system. During the rainy season with its long-lasting storms and heavy downpours, the sewers overflowed and spilled their foul, stinking contents into the streets. The toilets we so cherished were illegal, as was book pirating. What a joke! Much later as our China-savvy expanded, we discovered that there was little in Shanghai that wasn't illegal.

"Anything seems better than spending another night at the shelter," Vati urged. Mother nodded and with hand signals translating numbers to the Chinese landlord and signing his piece of paper someone must have provided to him that stated the rental terms in English, we took the room. By late afternoon, the Schillers and the Blombergs were hauling their suitcases out of Wayside Home, heading for the "apartment." Mutti whispered in my ear that it was better to share a room with two strangers than with two hundred. "And," she smiled encouragingly, "nothing lasts forever. All things come to pass!" More of my mother's logic!

The rest of the house was occupied by the landlord's family consisting of at least four women and three men of various ages. I counted six or seven children of all sizes who were dressed clean and neat, their glossy, dark hair cut short or braided with bright red ribbons that bounced with every move they made. We never discovered who was who, but that was all right, it didn't matter. As was often the case between Chinese and foreigners, we remained invisible to one another.

Mutti and I put our few belongings in one of the tall chests, stored our suitcases under the sofa in our part of the room, while the men visited. I had offered to help Mrs. Schiller unpack, and was surprised when she pulled out a desk lamp whose green elongated glass shade sat on a brass neck and base. Wrapped in a thick woolen shawl, the lamp had made the journey undamaged.

"Why would you bring a lamp of all things?" I asked. "How do you know the electric current is the same here as at home? Why bring a lamp?"

She laughed softly and said, "Just you wait and see. This is a magic lamp. It is a true treasure." With the tip of a metal nail file, she deftly unscrewed the plate that served as the base of the lamp. Carefully, she removed a few white cotton balls that came into view. Her slender fingers reached inside the neck of the desk lamp, and slowly pulled out several tissue-wrapped items. When she peeled the filmy paper away, there emerged: two heavy gold chain bracelets, a dozen gold coins, a string of pearls, two diamond lapel pins, a diamond necklace and several beautiful gem-studded rings, all individually wrapped in thin tissue paper. A treasure, a shower of jewels.

"Oh," Mutti gasped who had suddenly appeared behind me, "weren't you scared to death your jewelry would be discovered?"

Lucy shook her head "No … but," she mused, "I did have some bad moments. When we packed our suitcases under the watchful eye of a Nazi inspector, Joseph argued with me not take the lamp. He had no idea I had stuffed my jewelry in its hollow neck. I really wanted these pieces to go to our girls; but obviously I knew we could sell them if times got really bad," she took a deep breath. "I told my husband that I gave my things to a good friend for safekeeping. So our argument about packing the lamp was as natural as it could be. Finally the Nazi inspector had heard enough. He rudely snatched the lamp out of Joseph's hands, said something like, 'Let her have her way. It's only a worthless piece of glass, and it will probably break anyway.' He sounded disgusted. I quickly wrapped the lamp in that shawl and dropped it in my suitcase.

When we finished packing, he sealed the luggage with the official Nazi seal. I was home free!"

Mother admitted she had never thought of smuggling things out. Her big jewelry pieces had been confiscated three months before we left Germany, and she would not hide the remaining things and risk discovery.

Mutti explained that the two Nazis inspectors who supervised our packing looked for hidden jewels everywhere. "They squeezed our tubes of tooth paste and shaving cream. With a wooden stick, one of them stirred through my jar of face cream. He even poked into the two tins of shoe polish and broke every piece of chocolate into bits."

Mutti's face reflected the memory of the cruel insults she had endured from the two young Nazis while she packed the few things we were permitted to take out of Germany.

"I guess I didn't plan very well. My mind was set on just getting out alive," she said. She didn't mention the horrible body search experience on the Brenner Pass by the crude Nazi woman who enjoyed violating and hurting the women she examined, and neither did I. I was still working hard at forgetting that nightmare.

Mrs. Schiller quickly packed her jewelry away in a small silk pouch. She seemed embarrassed to have shown off her treasures which immediately established her as a woman of means in the general atmosphere of resigned poverty. Sensitive to the mood of loss around her, she quickly changed the subject and offered to make a cup of tea for everyone. I liked her.

Lucy, as I was permitted to call her, turned out to be a wonderful friend. Resourceful, curious and adventurous, she spoke to everyone who gave her the time of day, asked a thousand questions and quickly learned her way about. Missing her own daughters, I became her ersatz child tagging along excitedly, as she explored our strange new territory. Like two sponges soaking up water, Lucy and I were determined to become "Old China Hands" in record time. We discovered what the open market places had to offer — how to check fruits and vegetables for freshness, give a pinch here and a poke there, and haggle for the best prices to the bitter end. I quickly learned how to count in Chinese and picked up several colorful local expressions that gave my bargaining over goods real China savvy.

On some of our excursions into the Chinese world, Vati accompanied us, leaving his depressing lethargy behind. I realized how quickly he absorbed new information when it came to "street smarts." All of us quickly picked up a smattering of Pidgin English — the Chinese/English jargon of vendors and coolies. Soon my father's dubious fluency with the English language became a hodge-podge of words, a smattering of this and that, all pronounced with a heavy German accent. Languages may not have been his strength, but he certainly made himself understood in the streets of Shanghai. But finding a source of income was another subject.

Still under the stranglehold of British colonialism in 1939, foreigners could only be traders and business owners, not employees. Some international companies did hire foreign secretaries and on rare occasions employed a European accountant. Filipinos and people of Portuguese ancestry had a better chance of getting jobs in foreign establishments than anyone. The work force labor, was strictly Chinese, and for a good reason: they learned to survive on three bowls of rice a day and live ten to a room. The poverty level defied imagination; these workers existed in squalor and unspeakable sanitary conditions; they died like flies.

During all this time Mutti stayed in the room. Her usual vigor and courage seemed to have left her the moment we settled in our new surroundings — primitive as they were. "I can't stand the rickshaws," she mused. "people pulling people; how awful. And all that horrible hawking and spitting, blowing their noses between their fingers and flinging that … that … that … stuff into the wind, then wiping their hands on their clothes. I want to throw up. Dead babies in garbage cans … the filth … the poverty … the beggars … the children … the stink … the noise.…" She looked exhausted, tears filling her eyes.

"But we're safe, aren't we?" Vati interrupted her litany of objections. "We don't have to worry about the Gestapo, the SS the SA. This is not paradise, I know. Just think of it as a 'waiting place,' a temporary resting place, before going to America or returning home. Time will pass, and we'll make a go of it, you'll see," he encouraged her.

"I'm sorry. Of course I'm grateful. I'll just need a little time. I'll adjust," she promised, "I'll gather myself. But I'm not just sitting around," she said, pointed to Mr. Schiller. "I'm learning English. Joseph has loaned me his dictionary and he speaks only English to me; he speaks quite well."

Mr. Schiller bowed with a comical gesture, "Thank you madame," he joked, "I aim to please." He confessed that languages had always fascinated him and he made learning them his hobby. For myself, I was only too glad that Fraulein Amanda had been such a dragon of a teacher. Monday we used to speak French, Tuesday German, Wednesday English, and then started the whole thing all over again. She had begun her strict regime when I was only three years old and she'd never let up. Now, when the Schillers and the Blombergs sat around the table at meal time, they spoke English only. All but my father, he was knee-deep into pidgin English. His face broke into a grin when we corrected him, but his heavy German tongue wouldn't let him pick up the subtleties of pronouncing English words properly. I didn't think he cared. He was beginning to get along with the Chinese people, and that pleased him.

      ☯   ☯   ☯

I watched my parents worry over pennies. Each evening Mutti brought out her diary which she used to keep track of the few dollars she was guarding. But things were looking up, I thought. Vati, whose instinct for trading reached new heights, had managed to sell several items we really didn't need. Mutti and I each owned a fine manicure set, a leather sewing kit and several beautifully bound diaries.

"No need to have two of the same," Vati announced, grabbed one of the sewing kits, left the house and returned one hour later with a big grin on his face and enough money for four weeks rent. Next to go was one of the elaborate leather manicure sets, which fetched enough money to live on for a whole month. Selling these items made us look at our few things, including our clothes, in an all together different light.

"Vati, I have three leather-bound diaries. I'll keep one, you can sell the other two," I offered. He smiled and thanked me.

"Let's wait until we run low on funds. It's a good thing to have to fall back on," he assured me. "We don't have that many things to sell; I have to find a way to earn a living."

Then came a stroke of luck. On one of our exploratory trips Lucy and I ended up at Cafe Vienna, where she treated me to an iced lemonade. The small tables sat close together and we could easily overhear several conversations at the same time. That was when we learned from a Russian furrier that "...those refugees had better sell their furs before the rainy season sets in." The pelts in Europe were tanned differently than those in Shanghai and fur coats would rot away from the damp and mildew in two season. The leather would turn to mush and all the fur would fall out.

Lucy wasted no time. "Just a minute, my dear," she breathed my way. "I'll be right back." She got up and went over to where the men we had overheard had been discussing the fur business.

"Good afternoon, gentlemen, I am Mrs. Schiller. I understand that you are in the fur business, and I have two fur coats I would like to sell. Can you help me?"

The upshot of Lucy's inquiry was the sale of her furs and my mother's to one of the furriers who bought European furs. Leave it to Lucy, she was always on top of it all.

She paid for our drinks and we hurried home. The moment she burst into the room, she cornered Mother with her news. Mutti pulled out her beautiful black broadtail coat from under the sofa and asked, "Can I sell my coat for twelve months, ten months or eight months worth of living? Or is that not enough? What do you think?"

"I have no idea," Lucy replied thoughtfully, "all I know is that they buy fur coats."

With her uncanny and admirable nose for opportunity, and her tireless efforts to get to the bottom of things, Lucy managed to make the fur dealers come to us. After more than two hours of strenuous haggling, all parties were satisfied, and my mother had enough dollars in her kitty to last us at least another six months.

We celebrated our windfall with a trip to the Cafe Vienna for a piece of their delicious nut torte, topped by a thick dollop of whipped cream. (We didn't even worry if the cream was pasteurized!) The grownups drank several cups of strong hot coffee, and I was given black tea with lots of sugar in it.

"We met with our friends, the Herrnstadts, from the *Gneisenau* the other day," Vati said. "they too have applied for their visa to the United States. It is difficult and takes so much time. The German quota is full, what with people trying to get out of Germany by the thousands."

"I don't believe the Americans, and that includes President Roosevelt, have any idea of what is going on in Germany," Joseph Schiller said, his face set in worry lines. "I met a man at the Swiss Consulate the other day, who claims to have seen a communique via the Red Cross, that describes how Jews are disappearing in large numbers — men, women and children — and that the so-called work camps are really concentration camps. The Nazis are killing Jews like flies, and the Jews have no place to go."

Dead silence fell over our little group. Finally my father broke the mood. "It isn't just America who closed her doors to Jewish refugees. It's all the other countries as well — it's Canada, England, France, Switzerland, Australia, New Zealand, Mexico and South America to name a few. They are all afraid that they are letting in welfare cases who would drain off funds dedicated to their own citizens. Don't they know how industrious Jews are? They'd work their hands raw if they could come to America. What are the Americans afraid of? It's the land of milk and honey, where the streets are paved with gold, where opportunity never stops knocking on your door — isn't it? Under those conditions, newcomers willing to work, will do well," Vati ended his unusually long speech with a sigh.

"I don't believe it is quite that way," Joseph interjected, his hand keeping time with his words. "America is barely emerging from a deep nationwide depression, and they want to take care of their own first. If there isn't any work for their citizens, you can't blame them for not taking in people competing for the few jobs available."

"I'm not talking just about now," Vati explained, leading with his chin. "I'm talking about 1937 and 1938 when Jews were still able to leave Germany with all their holdings intact, which would have meant a tremendous boost to American economy. We would have been wealthy refugees, not the beggars we are now," he concluded somewhat on a bitter note. Perhaps he was remembering the many times he had turned down the opportunity to take his wealth out of Germany and had refused to do so for one reason or another. All of them good ones, he thought.

Throughout our residence in Shanghai, the United States of America was the beacon of hope that everyone of us dreamt of. And for me, there seemed to be an inevitable certainty that we would get there.

I often thought that we marked our days in Shanghai by counting the ways we invented to overcome the irritations — which were miserable, but endurable. Food preparation, for example was vexing for five people living with one hot plate between them. Cooked, fried or steamed food had to be measured by just enough to go around for five, no more, no less. There was no way for leftovers to survive in the heat. We shared everything with the Schillers, who were the most ideal roommates under any conditions. But still our life together soon came to an end.

August proved to be the hottest month of the year. The locals referred to the hundred-plus temperatures as "Tiger Heat." Everybody wore minimum clothing, practiced sitting still and avoided movements. Our clothes stuck to our perspiring bodies during the day, and at night the thin sheet to cover us soon stuck to our moist skin like glue. Swarms of mosquitoes found exposed body parts with unerring accuracy and left us scratching the huge bumps their stings left behind. Some mornings I woke up and did not recognize my own arms and legs. Once I counted more than three hundred bites. The discomfort of the itching was bad enough, but we knew that mosquitoes carried malaria. The disease was no stranger to the Orient.

But that wasn't all that happened at night. When all the lights were out, soon one could hear soft rustling sounds like running a piece of crinkly tissue paper over a hard surface. At first I thought I was back at home and the leaves were calling to me on wings of the wind. Nothing so romantic. I turned on my little flashlight and saw a battalion of fat, black cockroaches marching from out of nowhere. They were scurrying all over the room. Mutti turned on a light, and we caught the ugly visitors scuttling away into cracks and crannies we didn't know existed. I remembered Mrs. Wilna's warning to keep everything spotless, never to leave a crumb of food around. But the nasty, little black menaces were persistent. As soon as the light was turned out, again they came back and with them the high-pitched whine of mosquitoes announcing their impending attack. Great summer nights!

Lucy was the one who brought some relief to the itchy situation that plagued my father and me, but left my mother unaffected. She discovered that the incense-burning offerings by the Chinese were not made to their gods. A certain type of incense was actually a mosquito repellent. For a few coppers she bought several coiled pieces of incense and placed one in each end of the room. As they burned away, a frail column of smoke rose from the coil and filled the air with a strange, but not unpleasant scent. It worked! Even though mosquitoes managed to get to me often, we became less attractive to our nightly visitors.

Every once in a while our living conditions overwhelmed me, and when the temperature rose above the hundred mark and the humidity rose as high as it could go without raining, I succumbed, like others, to a strange and debilitating lassitude. For the first time in my life, I had an inkling of what the grownups called "depression." I was just very sad. I mourned our lost lives. I yearned for home — the stately rooms, the presence of familiar faces, the soft sounds of summer days floating through the tall French doors of the house; the breeze that moved the sheer curtains, the smell of grass and flowers and trees … the feel of it all. It was all gone. In its place were the strange and unpleasant cooking odors of our Chinese landlord's charcoal stove that lingered heavily in the hot air, and the screeching, ear-splitting sound of their tinny radio music. Shanghai old-timers fully believed that the Chinese played their awful music loud enough to irritate foreigners to get them to leave the area.

Trying to escape the heat, people played out their lives in the lanes and on the streets. From open windows came the rushing, clinking sounds of the shuffling of the tiles of our neighbors' around-the-clock mah jong games. But it was the first hour after dawn that disturbed us the most.

At the crack of morning, the residents of the lane placed their honey pots in a neat row outside their front doors. Soon, one could hear the unbelievably strange, guttural grunting-groaning sound made by the coolie announcing the arrival of his two-wheel push cart for the collection of human feces. He stopped at every door, opened the lid to his wooden cart and dumped the contents of the filled-to-overflowing wooden barrel-shaped pots. As soon as he departed from a row of houses and disappeared into the next, women charged on the scene carrying a bundle of arm-long sticks in one hand and a bucket of water in the other. Soon came the rhythmic noise from swishing the bundle of sticks around inside the "family toilet" … chett-chett-chett-chett-chett-chett. The noise heralded the activities of a nasty, but necessary chore. The dirty water was dumped into the lane, and not even the song of a nightingale or the descent of millions of rose petals from above could have washed away the odor that stubbornly lingered all day long.

     ❧   ❧   ❧

Though we hadn't admitted it yet, sharing the room with the Schillers was getting on everyone's nerves by the end of the second month. We tried valiantly to disregard the annoyances that came from the lack of privacy, and struggled valiantly to keep our irritations to ourselves. Mutti had sewn several sheets together by hand and the makeshift curtain divided the room into half. It didn't help. There was only one entrance to the room. No matter what time of day, no matter how consistent our no-see-no-hear policy was, we had to pass through the Schillers portion of the room — three people coming and going countless times, night and day. We had to do something! And our friends were just as desperate as we.

The Schillers were visiting with new friends at the little Vienna Cafe for which Joseph had started to keep books. He provided the same services for a man making soap and for a Berliner who was going to export Chinese silks. Soon, the Schillers would find a place of their own, Mutti predicted.

Vati has been searching for a business opportunity and vowed that as soon as our funds from America arrived, he would start something.

The money coming to us was several hundred dollars which my Aunt Helene had arranged to be sent through the American connections of her late husband's bank. Helene, trusting her personal safety to her semi-Aryan background and reclusive lifestyle, had remained in Wiesbaden.

"What do you think you can do?" Mother asked.

Without another word, Vati got up, pulled out his suitcase from under the bed, and retrieved an aluminum container about the size of a child's shoe box with a handle on its broad side. Next he produced several rubber rollers with flowery patterns carved all over their surface. He attached one roller to the aluminum container and explained how this apparatus filled with paint left patterns on the walls that a person couldn't distinguish from expensive wall paper. He added that when the paint was changed to another color and applied over the first layer of the pattern, interesting designs emerged.

"I'll go in the painting business," he announced triumphantly.

It turned out that Vati had helped finance a young man's idea for manufacturing this innovative decorating device to take the place of wallpaper several years earlier. When Vati's protege had become successful and returned with gratitude to repay the loan, he gave my father a set of his equipment. Vati must have had an inkling that it could be useful in our China exile.

"But you can't be a house painter here in China, and not only that," Mutti replied, "you know nothing about painting."

"I don't intend to paint myself, I'll be the boss. I've asked around, and I'm learning how foreigners do business in China. They find a Chinese partner, or a comprador — a sort-of local front man who can wheel and deal in his language with his people according to local customs and business manners. He gets cumshaw (Pidgin English for commission) on each job. The more jobs he brings in, the more money he'll make," Vati ended, pleased with himself.

Mutti continued with objections and obstacles to my father's idea, but in spite of the black little cloud she kept sailing over his future plans, she didn't dampen his spirit. On our daily walk to the city to check with American Express to see if "the money" had arrived, he talked incessantly about his objective. He had met a

Chinese gentleman, a Mr. Yung, who was eager to associate himself with my father and his idea for a business. How Vati conversed with Mr. Yung, how he made himself understood, was a mystery to Mother and me.

"We even have a name for the business," Vati announced. "We're going to all it 'China Art Painting and Decorating Company,' translated into Chinese it is: Tsun-gei Nisei Fenshi Gungtse." I laughed when I saw his happy face. Apparently the two men had surmounted the language barrier with full credit to Mr. Yung who spoke an excellent English. My father, well, he spoke "pidgin."

It was also decided that as soon our funds were in, we would look for some modest living quarters in the French Concession. Vati had heard about a small school run by French nuns in that part of town and intended for me to attend classes.

French, I would be speaking French again. Fraulein Amanda's promise that had sounded more like a threat when I balked at some lessons, surfaced in my memory. I could still hear the high pitch in her voice, "One day you will be grateful for the languages you speak and for all the lessons you have had. You'll think of me, and you'll thank me."

"Thank you, Fraulein Amanda," I said.

August was also the month the Schafers — Aunt Clara, Uncle Arthur and Cousin Margot — my mother's sister, her husband and their daughter — arrived in China. The stories they told about the ever growing Nazi terror and their relentless policy to banish the Jews from their teutonic world shook us up — all over again.

Mutti was thrilled to have her only sister safe and sound, and Vati was only too glad to take over their introduction to China living and helped them get settled. The Schafers rented a place in Hongkew. My uncle, an accountant, saw an opportunity to work in the Jewish community and Joseph Schiller happily took him under his wing and introduced him around to some of small business owners.

My other uncle and his family were still in Breslau, still waiting for daughter Suzie's hope chest linens to be embroidered. Every time his name came up, Vati became angry all over again, and between the sisters, tears flowed freely. But no amount of tears could wash away the reality of the danger their brother lived in every day.

❦   ❦   ❦

On the thirty-first of August, Vati and I walked over the Garden Bridge onto the Bund, stopped in at the American Express office, and left with more than five hundred American dollars in his newly acquired money belt. Our "funds" had arrived. Now Mutti would have several years of living expenses in her possession, providing of course everything remained the same. Well, it didn't stay the same.

Just one day later, on September 1, 1939, Hitler marched into Poland with his goose-stepping armies, his mighty tanks preceded by his Luftwaffe which cleared the path ahead. Great Britain declared war on Germany, France followed suite, and the fires of World War II that would eventually engulf all of Europe started to roar across the Continent.

What did the war in Europe mean for us in China? We didn't know. It was one more uncertainty with which we had to deal and more heart-wrenching thoughts about those we left behind: friends, family ... Marienhall ... my beloved uncles and aunts whose background may have been mostly aryan, whatever that meant, but whose hearts did not beat for the Third Reich. Outspoken as they were, with Nazi ears listening everywhere, it was almost predictable that Nazi revenge would catch up with them. Foremost in our minds as we heard the news was the question: Would Hitler's personal war against the Jews exacerbate? Would he dare to eliminate them as he had threatened?

"May God be with them," Mutti's lips moved silently.

I remembered a Chinese proverb and thought how unconsoling it was: "Only tomorrow can give us the answers for today; and tomorrow never comes."

Chapter Four

September 1939 to January 1940
The Year of the Dragon

*G*ood news: My parents rented the first floor of a modest, fairly new house in the Concession Française that sat behind a six-foot wall in a pleasant lane of five rows of houses — only four lanes deep. A small patch of lawn edged by narrow flower beds and a few blossoming bushes may not have been a replacement for the park-like grounds and the fairy tale woods we left behind, but it was the Garden of Eden compared to the lane on Chusan Road. It was even clean.

Our timing was good because the Schillers had gently hinted here and there that they had come upon a small apartment in a newly rebuilt lane. Joseph's bookkeeping clientele was growing, and he could support a place by themselves. Time had come for everyone to move on. We couldn't have asked for better partners for sharing three hundred odd square feet of living space for four months, twenty-four hours a day, and remain fond of one another. Lucy and Joseph were just about our best friends, forever.

Peter and Manon Herrnstadt had moved to the French Concession in late June and told my parents about the pleasant and reasonably priced Place de Fleurs as the little housing complex was called. Vati and I finally managed to get Mutti out of the house the first week in September, and we took a rickshaw into the city — my mother protesting our mode of transportation all the way — and then some.

We stopped for tall glasses of iced lemonade at the lovely, venerable Cathey Hotel on Nanking Road — a special treat for our circumstances — then took another rickshaw to Rue de Kaufman and Place de Fleurs. Surprised and pleased with the contrast of pleasant streets in the residential area of the French Concession, set apart from the noisy, bustling, traffic-choked main thoroughfares of the city, Mutti relaxed and quickly became interested in the little apartment. The front room was slightly larger than the one we shared with the Schillers, but it was cheerful and bright, with freshly painted walls in a soft, warm shade of pale apricot.

"We can really stretch our legs here," Vati sounded excited.

A few steps down a narrow hall was a small kitchen with a few tiny cupboards, a snow-white porcelain sink, a double hot plate and an adequate wooden icebox. A friendly window peeked out at the rear to the next row of houses — all neat and orderly looking. What a difference these surroundings would make in our lives.

Adjoining the kitchen was a bathroom, but contrary to the grey and rough cement finish of our Hongkew dwelling, this one was done in pale blue ceramic tiles, all shiny and clean, with a real bathtub and a hot water tank on a gas meter. A few coppers would buy us a hot bath.

The pleasant Russian lady who was showing us around, turned out to be the owner of the little lane complex. She told us that she had rented the upstairs to a refugee couple from Leipzig who were moving in a few days.

"There are also two gentlemen from Berlin — good friends — who are interested in renting that back room if you wish to sublet," Mrs. Vorchenkoff mentioned, and gave us their Hongkew address should we want to meet them. That bit of information decided the deal, I guess. No matter how much I wanted that room for myself, I knew that we would probably take in a renter.

"We'll take it," my parents announced in unison. Mutti's face was alive. She looked around the big room, and I could see that in her mind she was placing furniture, hanging curtains and tossing pillows.

We would move in the following week. My father already knew where we could buy some inexpensive rattan furniture and a wardrobe. It was amazing how he was getting to know his way around Shanghai — a city that had grown and stretched all over like a bad haircut. It was quite astonishing considering how little English he spoke. But he was friendly, curious, inquisitive and people, even the Chinese, liked him. I wondered if he ever had an enemy in his whole life. To overcome the language barrier, he expressed his love for children by making funny faces and silly "Chinese-sounding" noises at the kids on the street who giggled and laughed at him. He always had a copper or two and a few pieces of candy in his pocket and was usually followed by a pigtailed, spit-fire-pants-clad band of admirers. Tall and gangly, skipping gaily ahead of the wiggly horde, he no doubt was the Pied Piper of Shanghai. In those moments he created the best times under the worst circumstances. I wanted to be that way, too.

          ◐   ◐   ◐

The two bachelors from Berlin turned out to be quiet, pleasant gentlemen, who had become traders in whatever commodity the Shanghai market had to offer. Max Selig and Kurt Vogel had a lot in common with my father — they were "doers" in a gentle and unassuming way. Oh, yes, they wanted to rent that back room.

"We're gone all day," Mr. Vogel explained. "We don't cook, we keep things tidy, and make little noise." Perfect!

The arrangement worked out quite well. Everyone had learned to live in tight quarters — literally in each others pockets. Mr. Selig said that we were friendly strangers caught in the same predicament.

The day we moved in, an old rattly truck held together by magic only, delivered our new wardrobe to hold our few clothes; two armless, backless couches, a fairly large round table and chairs, and a cot for me. Mutti borrowed Lucy's sewing machine and accompanied by her friend, dared the streets, purchased a few pieces of fabric of pleasing colors and made curtains, pillows, bolsters, and padded cushions for the simple wooden chairs. Mutti added two little tables, a small writing desk and some lamps with silk shades that delivered a soft, cozy glow to our modest quarters in the evening.

She insisted we keep to ourselves, explaining that she had heard enough tragic stories and she wasn't collecting material for a book. However, she reminded me every day to write in my Tagesbuch, my diary. Father cheered us on with his little sayings — things like "Since we don't have anything better, then this has got to be the best!" or "Never worry about the future, it will happen anyway." Or, "Don't complain, unless you can do something about it."

He also declared with great pathos, "When the Jews spit in the river, all the fish die" When I asked him what that meant, he just chuckled and said that life would have the answer for me, when I asked at the right time.

Grownups! I don't always understand them.

When Gerda and Albert Cohn from Leipzig moved into the upstairs attic room, it only took a short time for my mother and the younger woman to become good friends. The Cohns were in their late thirties, he was Jewish, she was not. Gerda chose to stay with the man she married and, as some others like her, left her comfortable home and family behind.

Every once in a while there were five (and sometimes seven) of us around the table for tea in the afternoon, a game of cards in the evening, and company to shop for food at a nearby Chinese market. Together, we walked all the way to Avenue Joffre, one of the main streets of the Concession Française, where Russian immigrants who had fled the 1919 Bolshevik Revolution ended up in Shanghai. They had opened restaurants, stores, boutiques, beauty salons and with the presence of the next generation, built an excellent classic dance company, the Ballet Russe.

We met some of the other refugees who had flocked to the lane called Place de Fleurs. But true to Mutti's wishes, we stayed much to ourselves. Living in a part of the city that was mostly occupied by foreigners and Chinese middle class was far removed from our Hongkew experience. Even though still strange, unknown and difficult, life in Shanghai took on a sort of pseudo-normalcy. We no longer slept under a blanket of fear; a knock on the door did not send us into a frozen shock, and seeing a policeman or a Chinese soldier in uniform evoked only a second or two of hot panic. Hitler's shadow had grown smaller, and was hiding out in the back room of our terror-ridden yesterdays. After all, we lived on the other end of the world, and according to my father, we also lived on the other side of a war.

When we spoke of "home" Mutti's eyes clouded over, and a subtle hue of pain settled over her face. Her father, Hermann Burger had died just eight weeks before we left Germany, and she was worried to shreds about the safety of her seventy-eight-year old mother, whom she left in the loving care of Ana-Marieke, grandmama's faithful housekeeper of more than forty years. We had not heard from them in months.

Only two uncensored letters had reached us from Germany, and from what we could tell the hunt-chase-and-kill pursuit of the Jews had steadily intensified, and was being compared to the most devastating pogroms of Poland and Russia. The *Shanghai News* reported Hitler's army sweeping over Europe like an iron broom clearing away people and countries like so much debris, and claiming them as new territories. What if he couldn't be stopped? What if…? These frightening thoughts were uppermost in our minds, in our conversation and dressed up as nightmares, invaded our sleep.

"It won't happen," my father said wishfully. "I believe these early victories are a surprise-kind-of-a result of unpreparedness on the part of France and all the other countries. They'll recover, they'll fight back. There are too many against one."

Mother prayed her husband's words into "God's ear," and from the stubborn set of her mouth, I could tell she had indeed reached the Almighty's attention.

Mail from Germany arrived in Shanghai by freighter at snail's pace. The careful wording in the letters — news playing hide and seek between the lines — often took a long time to interpret. Not everyone of our correspondents had the gift of conveying happenings in such way as not to attract the interest of German mail inspectors, and at the same time make themselves understood. Hard to decipher or not, the news was not good. It became quite clear that we were lucky to have left Germany when we did. It didn't matter how difficult our circumstances, Shanghai was a lot more attractive than Hitler's Germany.

٭   ٭   ٭

I started classes at the Sisters of Sacre Coeur. After one hour of being tested on a variety of subjects by Sister Angeline, that included speaking in French, English and German, she placed me in a class with all the older girls. I had passed her machine-gun like questions with flying colors in three languages.

Except for geometry and algebra, learning came easy for me. I loved being around books again, (there's no room in a refugee's suitcase for more than one book) and enjoyed being with girls whose birth place was either a European country, North Africa, the near East or the Orient. The Sisters were just as strict as my teachers back home; their intent was to pound knowledge and the Holy Trinity into our heads — no nonsense! Sister Monique had a long willowy whip-like branch on her desk and was known to flip it on an unsuspecting chatterbox with unerring accuracy. She quickly got the attention of the offender without interrupting the flow of her lectures. No nonsense! Sister Magdalene taught catechism, conducted the rather minute choir of a few good voices, and smelled of mothballs and cinnamon. She came from Lyons in France, and had made the convent her life. The other Sisters were cut much from the same cloth — hard lessons, lots of prayers and Hail Marys, and only an occasional spurt of laughter.

It was all right with me. I thought school was great. I spoke French again daily, improved my English vocabulary, attended mass and catechism class, was given a beautiful ivory rosary, and to my mother's horror, crossed myself at the dinner table.

I had become a Jewish girl, with Lutheran ancestors and Catholic manners. Mutti voiced her concern about my checkered spiritual upbringing, but my father insisted that it couldn't hurt to cover God's major bases.

"Next, she'll take up Buddhism," Mutti predicted with a sigh. She looked at me with a slight frown in the shape of a question mark on her forehead. She did that most of the time. She had an active negative streak in her which she exercised regularly.

"That's all right too," Vati laughed, "she'll either be confused, which I doubt, or she will learn that more than one road leads to Rome, and more than one ideology leads to God. If she does no more than live by the Ten Commandments, she'll turn out all right."

Why do grownups have this rather impolite habit of talking about you in the third person, when you're right next to them? Grownups; they can be most irritating at times.

At any rate, I was glad to be able to go to a school, of any kind, and especially liked the small convent atmosphere, nuns, chapel, rosary and all.

This particular convent of the order of Sacre Coeur had been established by missionaries years ago, was well endowed and was able to provide free tuition to about fifteen Jewish refugee girls. I was lucky to have been accepted. The nuns even furnished us with our school books and school uniforms. The latter were dark blue cotton jumpers, long-sleeved white shirts in the fall and winter, which were exchanged for light blue cotton jumpers and short-sleeved blouses in spring and summer. Being used to my wearing gray and plaid uniforms, Mutti poked gentle fun at our outfits, and jokingly said we resembled a bunch of overgrown penguins.

         ☯   ☯   ☯

Vati had followed through with his plan for the China Art Painting and Decorating Company, spearheaded by Mr. Yung who brought his business expertise and the unwritten laws of Chinese trading manners and methods into the partnership. Vati's new partner had quickly found a source to manufacture rubber rollers, and hired a man to carve new designs onto their surface.

"If they can do it on ivory, wood and stone," Vati remarked, "they can do it on rubber." He was right; some of the designs this man produced were intricate floral patterns, fire-breathing dragons, butterflies and birds on the wing, flowers, mountains, clouds and raindrops. The China Art Painting and Decorating Company was on its way.

And so was life in general.

Some of the stories Vati brought home each day from his house-painting career were hilarious, and at the same time pointed out the pitiful knowledge the two men possessed when it came to painting walls. Most of their problems arose from not knowing how to mix paint which did not come pre-mixed in tin cans, but was only available in powder form to be blended with all sorts of other stuff. If the mix was done incorrectly, the "paint" didn't stay on the wall, but sort of evaporated in a day or two. When the humidity was extraordinarily high on certain days, the paint just ran down the walls in thin trickles of tears. Then there were the problems with the day laborers — the coolies — who had their own strange rhythm of coming and going on jobs. My father with his Germanic upbringing of the-on-time-work-hard ethics discovered he had a lot to learn. (Mostly patience.)

"These coolies are something. We hire one person to stand on a ladder and one to hold it. We hire one person to paint the walls, and one to watch. For every one-man job we have to have two people — if not three." Vati reported with something between a sigh and a chuckle in his voice.

One thing they all had in common: their excuses for absence from work. "Grandmother" in Nantao, or Wotsin, or Tanpu died. "Honorable grandmother die, must go funeral, bamby. No go honor grandmother, bad joss (luck)."

"I've never known a people who had four or five grand-mothers," Vati laughed, as he reported on the events of his day. He was pleased that he had found a way to earn a living for whatever time it would last. In spite of all the problems, business was thriving.

Mr. Yung called on "better" Chinese hotels, gambling estab-lishments and opium dens, and there were plenty of them. According to his appraisal of Shanghai business prospects, these were the places that not only needed constant repairs and redeco-rating but also had the money to pay the costs. To the great embar-rassment of my mother and to the even greater amusement of our friends, Mr. Yung also called on houses of prostitution that were often attached to any one of the other dens of iniquity.

The closest I had come to seeing those petite, pretty ladies in long silk gowns, with tall hairdos parading about on the pages of my childhood books, took place in the houses of ill repute — romantically referred to as House of Flowers. I wasn't too sure what that meant anyway. I just had a good time. Those young ladies were quite pretty, and some were awfully young. They wore lovely, long silken gowns in glorious colors with deep slits on each side revealing their slim, shapely legs as they moved. Black velvet ballerina-like slippers or expensive high-heeled French shoes hugged their tiny feet. Their faces were heavily powdered, their lips a brilliant red, kohl outlined their beautiful eyes and a thick layer of mascara enhanced their eyelashes. Mr. Yung explained to me that these beauties were well educated ladies who entertained the gentlemen who patronized the establishment with songs, dance, poetry and important conversation.

"Are they sing-song girls," I inquired. I had heard that there were popular establishments in China called Sing-Song Houses, where men congregated to relax from their business world, chatted, sipped tea and listened to the Sing-Song girls recite poetry, dance with fans and sing their songs. Something like a European cabaret, I guessed.

Mr. Yung, cleared his throat, looked around as though searching for enlightenment, thought about it, and finally said something to the effect of, "Well … yes … ah … yes … they are something like … like … sing-song girls in tea houses, but they are more … ah … well … let's say, they are … ah … more … advanced."

Not at all satisfied with his answer, I asked Amah when I got home.

Amah was a jolly, slightly round Chinese woman with a dimpled face, thinning hair pulled straight back into a bun, snappy dark eyes that missed absolutely nothing, who arrived daily at Place des Fleurs and took over the housekeeping chores for all the tenants. She did the laundry and ironing, scrubbed and cleaned, went to market, and on the side, she expanded my limited knowledge of the "birds and the bees" to a thorough understanding of the "boys and girls" — including a colorful introduction to what went on in the "Flower Houses." Accompanied by hysterical giggles, and jumping up and down from one foot to the other, Amah had the best time telling "Young missy" what men and women were all about.

"Massa and Missy makee jig-jig, bamby (stands for by-and-by) makee baby, bamby happy. No good catchee girl-child, bamby wantchee boy-child. Too many girl-child no good. Young missy, no makee jig-jig; no wantchee catchee baby," Amah concluded, shaking her finger at me.

Once she got started on a subject, it was almost impossible to make her stop. On and on she boiled over in a mixture of Shanghai dialect and her choppy Pidgin English, getting more and more explicit about what Massa and Missy do at House of Flowers and everywhere else, giggling herself breathless and using wildly descriptive hand and body language to get her point across. Fraulein Amanda would have fainted dead away, a long time ago — not to mention my poor mother's reaction to this unsolicited, free-for-all information about the facts of life.

Well, I had been educated all right; no wonder Mutti wouldn't talk about that subject. Most probably she didn't know as much as Amah about it anyway. So much for that.

So, we painted and decorated houses of ill repute. These "honorable" establishments, too, needed refurbishing, and I went along with Mr. Yung, to present our estimates. The "ladies" of the houses loved the effect our rubber-roller wonder created on their walls. After all, as Mr. Yung declared, "They like their place to look pretty, they do spend a great deal of their time in their bedrooms."

These "advanced" Sing-Song girls treated me like an honored visitor and "little sister" at the same time. They were the first to call me ta pee-tse which means "big nose" in their language. Well, they were right! Compared to their button noses, mine was certainly big. I laughed at the childish pranks they played on each other and on their servants. I marvelled at their empty-prattle-gossipy ways, their high-pitched voices, their expressive moods, and their uncensored shameless sense of humor when they discussed their occupation and their clients. I learned some more.

Giggling behind their dainty little hands, they showed me their favorite jewelry made of jade, pearls and gemstones and brought out some of their hand painted silk fans. With great dexterity, they flipped and flopped their fans open and shut, hid their powdered faces behind them and played all sorts of eye-to-eye flirting games with non-existing visitors. Every gesture had a secret meaning, every flip of the fan sent an inviting message — all of them suggesting forbidden things.

They also practiced their English vocabulary on me, which was somewhat limited to expressions related to their business. Did I ever learn some more! And, it didn't stop there. We sipped tea from delicate China bowls that had matching lids, and some rather explicit jig-jig scenes painted in the bottom of the bowl by an artist's clever hand with a very busy mind. Mutti would have shrieked, dropped the bowl and passed out. I suppose, it was the ladies' way of advertising. I wasn't too interested. That was a grown-up matter, and I had so many other things to think about.

Next morning at class, I was back at the rosary, catechism lessons, English composition and a lot of Shakespeare. At early afternoon chapel, I fervently prayed to a variety of saints that none of the Sisters, and especially Mother Superior, would ever discover where I spent some of my afternoons. I would surely be kicked out of school and sent to roast in hell.

My worldly education was further expanded by occasional visits to gambling houses and opium dens, as they required a paint job here and there. Mr. Yung was dead set against letting me tag along to those places. Apparently houses of ill repute were more acceptable and decent to him, than establishments that catered to opium and games of chance. However, like a good hotel, these places dedicated to vice were rated Number One places among the locals — a rating comparable perhaps to a certain seal of approval in other countries.

Shanghai's gambling establishments were traditionally simple, unadorned buildings with tin roofs. A scattering of round tables filled the smoke-filled halls where people played mah-jong, poker, roulette, dominos, dice and card games as well as tossing sticks from bamboo containers. Noisy groups of Chinese men and women engaged in mysterious betting — shouting numbers, gesturing with finger signals to make their bets. Neat bundles, piles of yen and stacks of American dollar bills changed hands at a rate faster than the tick of a clock. To ease the summer heat, ceiling fans circled night and day, but did no more than move the same old sticky air around. Large floor fans directed their stream of air against huge blocks of ice that sat on burlap-covered wooden tables bringing some measure of cooling. The ever-present rushing sound of shuffling ivory mah-jong tiles on wooden tables, the slamming down of domino pieces, the unrestrained shouts accompanying either a win or a loss, blended with the enthusiastic conversations of kibbitzers, waiters and servants, was deafening.

Mr. Yung told us that Chinese — from coolie to merchant king, man and women alike — loved gambling and made and lost fortunes, only to return to the tables and their finger games to try their luck again.

"We bet on anything," he grinned, "the frequency of a cricket's chirp, the length of a frog's leap, the speed of a cockroach, and how many twigs in a bundle of twelve. Losing at gambling is merely bad joss, loosing face is a disgrace."

The opium dens were another story. Mr Yung violently opposed my setting foot in these places.

"Opium is bad, very bad. It runs your days and ruins your life. People smoke opium to dream big dreams, and to get lost in the world of the poppy. You don't want to go there; you don't even want to see," he urged. When he saw the determination in my face as I shook my head in disagreement, he continued to discourage me.

"You don't want to see the people who have turned into walking skeletons. They are so thin and brittle you can see their bones sticking out through their shabby clothes. The skin is stretched so tight across their faces, they no longer resemble a living person. They might as well have been buried for years, life no longer holds meaning, and the only reality they know resides in the bowl of their pipe. When these poor wretches run out of money, they are turned out into the gutter where they die along with the rest of China's refuse. You don't want to see that," he pleaded.

But I did go, and I did see, and Mr. Yung was right. It wasn't a pretty sight. The air had a cloying odor of sweet smoke and was as thick as a morning fog. In the less expensive parts of the opium houses, people crowded like sardines on rough, wooden bunks stacked two high and four deep, either asleep, smoking or cooking the opium in the bowl of their pipes. In the "first class" part of the Wu Chen Li's House of the Happy Poppy comfortable lounges separated by handsome teak tables were arranged in circles, low light muted the murals of flowered garden scenes that graced the domed ceiling giving the room a dreamy, far-away quality. Rich Oriental carpets hushed the footsteps of attendants, and a hazy softness dulled the senses. Patrons indulging in one pipe or more were well dressed and seemed to represent the wealthy segment of Shanghai's population.

Mr. Yung was not impressed with my observation. "Poor or rich, it doesn't matter," he huffed, "they're chained to the pipe, they live by the smoke and they'll die by it too. Don't get any ideas that this is glamorous. Smoking opium brings bad joss."

Laying a firm hand on my elbow, and motioning to my father that it was time to leave, he steered me out into the sunlight. The oppressive air was getting to me by then, I felt a bit woozy, and without further protest, I followed Mr. Yung only too gladly into the courtyard, where the gatekeeper bowed from the waist and closed the huge iron gate behind us. Even the hot, humid mid-summer Shanghai air with all its street odors was a relief from the smoke-filled room of Wu Chen Li's House of the Happy Poppy.

☯   ☯   ☯

It had been relatively easy to secure painting contracts for the China Art Painting and Decorating Company. After the first introductory call at a prospective customer, things fell into place rather quickly. Mr. Yung and his assistant, a young man who tagged along just to give his boss the necessary statue and "face," measured the areas that required painting, did his multiplication magic on his abacus and arrived at a cost at about double as much as it should be. And then the fun began. At least one hour of haggling, bargaining, threatening and gentle insulting went on before the bottom price was reached. Both sides had won. And, that was important. Losing face was worse than death by the fiery breath of a dragon.

Then, one day a most astonishing thing happened. Mr. Yung was ill and could not present the painting estimate for a three-floor paint job at the Park Hotel. Vati insisted I go with him after classes to help interpret. By then I had picked up a fair smattering of Chinese street talk — enough to find my way around, bargain for a good price, as well as threaten my way through, using interesting long-winded, wildly colorful curses of which Fraulein Amanda would not have approved.

Mr. Chien-Su, the manager of the Park Hotel, ushered us into his office, and appeared nervous and ill at ease when I handed him the estimate. He took a long look at the numbers, bowed politely, thanked us for coming, and to our great surprise, affixed his chop to the dotted line. Next, as customary, he counted out the money for half the amount to start the job. Here I had been all prepared to drink tea and haggle and chisel for a while but nothing happened. The man did not bargain and my father made an unheard of high profit on that job.

When Mr. Yung heard about it, he laughed his head off, then he became serious and explained that business men just did not haggle over prices with a foreign "business woman." How strange. Mr. Yung and Vati decided that from then on, I would occasionally present the inflated estimates, and see how it worked. It worked! The only time we had to resort to haggling was on the rare occasion when the owner of an establishment turned out to be woman. She didn't care that I was a female and a foreigner. These women bargained, pleaded, cajoled, whined, cried, yelled, threatened and haggled as though their life was at stake. I learned to play right along with them; it was too funny for words. But it was a game to be played, or else lose out.

Time was running fast; days rushed into weeks and we experienced our first typhoon season with its slashing rains, high winds and cooler temperatures. Sewers backed up and flooded some areas with foul-smelling waters from the big city's belly, full of human waste and God-knows-what. Rickshaw coolies in bare feet sloshed through the rain-filled streets seemingly unconcerned with the threats of typhoid and cholera that clung to every drop of the sewage-tainted waters that swirled around their ankles. Children played in the death-breathing "lakes," sailing little bamboo and paper boats on the crest of waves that boiled up from disease-breeding gutters. And if that wasn't enough, hordes of fat, lice-infested rats scurried to high ground, not afraid of anyone, carrying the death sentence of thousands of humans on their horrible bodies. Drowned rats sailed by silently in gutters and bobbed about in low-lying areas wherever poisonous sewage waters had accumulated in deep puddles and fetid ponds.

We shook our heads, got booster shots for typhoid and cholera, and avoided leaving our safe little house during the typhoon season as much as possible. Mutti returned to her gray mood and refused to go out at all. Instead, she spent her days at her recently acquired sewing machine. She had gone into competition with the local tailors, and was doing alterations and some dress-making for the ladies at Place de Fleurs, who soon recommended her to their friends. Vati had protested violently at first, muttering that no wife of his was going to work, especially not doing alter-ations. Mutti just put on her best Mona Lisa smile, did what she wanted to do, and proudly added her earnings to the kitty. My father had opened an account with the British Hong Kong-Shanghai Bank, but my mother preferred to keep her earnings close at hand — in a worn-out blue knee sock of mine tucked away in a far corner of the wardrobe.

"You know, Martin, work has never dirtied anybody," she parried. "Remember how I grew up? My father's distillery and the little tavern were the work place for the whole family. We worked it, it fed us. And that's what were are doing now. Who we were is no longer of social interest. Who we are inside is what counts; it is more important than ever. Work's never hurt anybody. It isn't hurting you."

Vati's objections were silenced. Surely, he must have known by then that my mother got her way, most always. She kept on with her sewing, and that old blue sock of mine grew fat with dollar bills.

Winter was not really cold, but it was damp and had the disposition of a dour, disappointed old maid — so my father observed. A persistent fine mist hung in the air almost daily. That fine veil of moisture — not enough to produce raindrops — was enough to cling to our garments and skin with clammy persistency. It was an uncomfortable, bone-chilling cold, not measurable by degrees of celsius, only by the misery it brought. Leather mildewed and grew beards; white spots and blotches of mildew settled on our garments, and everything smelled dank and musty. In spite of some electric heat in the house, we were never really warm and dreamed of a roaring fire in a big fireplace. A warm fire ... that got my memory going, until I made myself miserable dwelling on the past — home.

Just thinking of crackling fires breathing pine-scented warmth and comfort connected my mind instantly to holiday celebrations at Marienhall, but especially at Aunt Antonia and Uncle Eric's lovely old Schloss Rothenburg. In the quiet of the night, when I thought no one could hear me, I cried for the lost yesterdays, and my heart was not noble enough to be grateful for the present. I wished myself back — back to the excitement, the joy, the family, the sleigh rides under starry winter skies … presents … secrets and surprises … the magic … music … festivities … the fragrance of Christmas baking … Maria … Liesel … Lothar … the tall, sparkling Christmas tree, fresh greens and shiny red-cheeked apples in huge copper bowls … a roaring fire in every room … pine cones … and late at night, the whisperings of glowing embers … the echo of music and singing, lively chatter and gay laughter. Everything was gone, lost forever. Despite some of the Christmas celebrations that took place at school, it just wasn't the same; it was all so strange, so foreign, so unreal, and so … nothing. Mutti made an effort to celebrate Chanukkah, but it too, did not hold the magic of the past.

Our first holiday season in Shanghai was difficult for me. It wasn't the best for my parents either. I was really homesick and lonely. I was moping around, withdrawing into an unhappy world of my own making, and hovered constantly at the edge of tears. None of which escaped my mother, who cornered me one day, and insisted I tell her what troubled me so.

At first I tried to act as though nothing was wrong, but I couldn't fool her anymore than I could believe she hadn't heard me crying at night. Finally, between big sobs and equally big tears splashing down my face faster than I could wipe them away, I told her about my sadness and longing at the approaching holidays. I yammered and stammered, I whined and complained, until I embarrassed myself.

But Mother, with her usual patient and logical approach to everything, let me sob and blow my nose and sob some more. When I was finally finished with my soggy tirade of raging against my fate, she took my hands into hers, looked at me with a wisp of a smile and gave me a good dose of her logic

"Memories are wonderful and we all have them. They are part of us. But we need to treat them like a favorite picture book that we enjoy looking at, and when we close the book, the pictures stay on the pages. If you let the past live your life, my child," she guided softly, "then the present has no value, and the future is doomed to failure. Look at what we once all had — those fine and generous gifts, be grateful for them, but recognize the new gifts coming your way. Live in the present, take what life has to offer, adjust, and if nothing else, make a memory of everything. And," she added with a big sigh, "in the depth of my heart I know that everything we are given now, we will be able to put to good use at another time. You know what your father always says, 'After this time, there comes another!' But for now, that gift is our life! What is more precious than that?"

Oh, I knew she was right, and she was wise, so wise. Everything she said made sense, but it didn't bring back yesterday. And, at that moment, that's what I wanted. I wanted to retrieve my world that was lost forever.

Chapter Five

1940 to January 1942
The Year of the Snake

*T*ime really did pass swiftly. Life in the French Concession in Shanghai, China, had settled into a colorless routine and had taken on a form of resigned orderliness. Still uneasy about the strangeness of a strange land, we kept much to ourselves. My father's share of the painting business was making us a modest living, and to Mutti's great delight, she was stuffing the earnings from her sewing into a second knee sock of mine. Vati made noises about renting a house, or larger apartment, but every time he brought up the subject Mutti voiced the same objections.

"Martin, you know that we're not staying in China much longer," she piped up. "We have our affidavits for America, we are registered at the American Consulate, and we have applied for our visas. With the war going on in Europe, nobody is leaving Germany, and the German quota must be opening up. Even Mr. Armbrewster at the consulate said so," she paused for a moment, looking at Father for signs of agreement.

"It's not worth our time and money to move to a more expensive place, buy more furniture we won't take with us to America anyway," she emphasized. "Let's just stay here, save our money, so when we go to the United States, we will have to depend on no one. Not only that, but we might be on our way to some modest wealth," she looked at him questioningly.

"Oh, my dear," he chuckled, "we will have some money, and we won't be the paupers we were when we arrived here, but we'll be far from wealthy. And that's all right. Surely our holdings in Germany will one day be returned to us. This war can't last forever, and furthermore, you know how I feel: Hitler won't win," he predicted.

Vati took Mutti's suggestion to heart and we stayed put in our little place. We had become good friends with our two bachelors in the back room, who had turned out to be star renters. But I'll never forget the first time Mutti invited the two friends for dinner. When we sat down at the table, Mr. Selig handed mother his dinner fork and asked for a soup spoon with which he proceeded to eat the roast, the potatoes and the vegetables after he had cut everything into small bits with his knife. My parents chatted about this that and the other, ignoring our guest's odd eating behavior.

Much later my mother told me his story. Mr. Selig had been picked up by the SS and brought to a Gestapo holding station. She said he had tears streaking down his face, as he recalled to her how he and about twenty other Jews had been given pitchforks and ordered to line up against a building in close rank — three steps away from the wall. No sooner had the prisoners taken their position, legs spread apart for balance, their pitchforks pointing upward, when men came tumbling down from upper floor windows and landed on the pitchforks. The horrible screams of the victims, the loud and cruel laughter of the Nazis, and the blaring trumpets of a band playing the German national anthem were a distorted symphony of obscenity to human suffering and even worse, to human indifference to inhuman treatment.

Max Selig concluded his horror story by saying that the Jewish prisoners had been warned not to let go of their pitchforks, or they would end up on the upper floor and be pushed out of the windows by their vicious captors. We never set his place with a fork again.

I was glad I wasn't present when he talked with my mother; I didn't want to know. I was terrified. One could only guess what was happening in Europe after almost two years of war. Every once in a while we heard some news via Hong Kong. At other times a friend of our bachelor renters who worked at the Swiss Consulate managed to bring us some letters through the Red Cross from friends and from our servant family the faithful Burdachs. The writers of these letters put on false return names and addresses, and their messages were carefully garbled. The mantle of fear and terror that the Hitler regime had dropped over the Jews of Europe also covered those sympathetic to Jews — those who reached out a helping hand, those who defied the Third Reich.

The news from war-torn Europe was devastating. Hitler's armies had overrun Poland and had invaded western Europe. France, Holland, Belgium, Denmark and Norway played unwilling hosts to Nazi soldiers, suffered their Third Reich arrogance and their harsh rules of conquest. Jews were rounded up at an alarming rate and were shipped to work camps in the East.

"I can just imagine what a work camp is like," Vati pondered, his eyes remembering the indignities, and the torture he had experienced at the hands of the Gestapo. When he wore a short-sleeved shirt, I could see the scars on his arms from the slashes he had received at the hands of his Nazi interrogators at the Gestapo station. I wondered, what had they done to him? He still would not talk about it, not to anybody.

"I'm so worried about Mother and Ana-Marieke," Mutti said with tears in her eyes. "And, we haven't heard from Arthur in months. Why didn't he have sense enough to leave?"

Arthur was her youngest brother, who had a wife, a teenage son and daughter. My uncle had an opportunity to obtain passage to China in August 1939, but Aunt Rosa must not have felt threatened. She wouldn't leave the country, she announced, until my cousin Susie's hope chest linens had been embroidered with her initials. My parents came apart when they heard the foolishness.

"I was as shortsighted as a blind owl in sunshine about getting out of Germany," my father declared, his voice laced with anger, "but to wait until some damn linens bear her daughter's name is liable to cost them all their lives," he ended bitterly. "Who in the hell cares about that damn hope chest? That stupid woman," he bellowed. "If Rosa wants to stay behind to wait until those damn sheets are embroidered — let her. But get those children out of

Germany," he shouted. Frustrated and furious, he voiced his fear. We never heard from them again.

Ever so often we went to Hongkew to visit with the Schillers, Mutti's sister and some of our other friends and caught up on the news there. The several shelters (Heime) were still full. Conditions had not improved for those who lived in them. But for many there was no other way. Then, there were those who like us, had received financial help from relatives or friends in America. Others had sold some of their treasures and used the money to start a business of one kind or another in Hongkew, as well as in the International Settlement or in the Concession Française.

Joseph had become active in the Jewish "government" in Hongkew and was well informed about refugee affairs. My father thought Joseph to be quite "political." Our friend knew all bout the Jewish Shanghailanders and the role they played in supporting the refugees in the shelters. Shanghailanders were Jews of many different nationalities who had lived in the city for many years and who had done well for themselves. Several of them had acquired enormous wealth, and were generous with their contributions to the less fortunate. Joseph also worked with American committees to solicit funds to help feed the hungry who had not a copper to their name.

"Nothing is ever enough," Joseph sighed, as he continued to describe the pitiful shelter conditions. And of course, more refugees were still trickling in.

Desperate for money, people sold everything they could do without, and kept but the clothes on their backs. Others had become clever traders of goods, and took "things" on consignment. The sidewalks on one Hongkew street were lined with refugees displaying their personal belongings from suitcases. It was amazing that everything — an old handkerchief, a scarf, a pair of under-pants, buttons, a lone lid from a long-gone pot, a broken hand mirror, powder puffs, bent-out-of-shape knitting needles even empty tin cans — could fetch a price.

I saw and I heard, and all of a sudden, I was more grateful than ever for what we had. Silently I thanked Aunt Helene's friend in New York for his generous gift, and my father for his drive to earn a living and better our circumstances. I was lucky!

Christmas 1940 had come and gone without much fanfare. I embroidered some hankies for the Sisters of Sacre Coeur, and Mutti had baked some special pastries for the convent. I admired the Sisters for their unquestioning faith which I respected, but did not share. However, attending chapel held a certain appeal for me. Out of respect for the nuns, I had followed their lead during worship which held no particular meaning for me. I just thought it was a nice break from classes, and I liked the candle-lit stillness of the chapel where I could let my thoughts roam at will. Sister Angeline was certain she had made a convert out of me, and awarded me a high grade for Chapel. It was all right with me, if indeed it made her happy.

Neither the rituals or the traditions of the church called to me, nor did the fear of the Devil and Hell's fires bring me to my knees in prayer. There was something else, something greater, deeper and mysterious — somewhere, somehow — for which I had no words, nor did I understand it. All I knew was that at times, I felt a warm stillness inside of me that made me feel loved and important. I certainly didn't feel like a sinner, I had nothing to confess; I had done nothing wrong or bad. It was a big puzzle. I wished there was someone with whom I could talk, who would listen and who could perhaps tell me just what it meant.

None of my classmates qualified; they were fun girls, and were terribly busy with their social activities that went hand in hand with the colonial settings of the times and their lives at home. My mother was just too … too … too steeped in her beliefs of Judaism, which she hoped I would embrace one day soon. I kept telling her the same thing I had told her when Rabbi Rosenfeld came to our house in Germany to teach me Hebrew and the Old Testament when I was little more than five years old. No sooner was my first lesson in religion over, when I made an unannounced dash for Mutti's sitting room.

"Mutti," I was breathless. "The rabbi was here. I don't like him. He has a very angry God, and I won't listen to the stories he reads from his book. They scare me. And," I added with my kinder-garten-view of things, "he smells bad, his coat is full of spots, his fingernails are dirty, and he has dried noodles in his beard." Mutti paid no attention to me, instead she asked me to "be good, attentive, and honor the rabbi."

"We are very fortunate that Rabbi Rosenfeld has agreed to take you on as a pupil. He is a very busy man and he is very wise. People look up to him and listen to what he has to say. And you will have to do the same." With a pat on my head, she sent me back to Fraulein Amanda and the nursery.

The rabbi came to the house three more times. He read from his book and tried to teach me Hebrew letters. During all this time, I kept looking out the window, shutting out his voice by singing a silent song in my head, or telling myself a story. He finally gave up on me, and to the great disappointment and irritation of my mother, he refused to return.

On the heels of the departed rabbi arrived Pastor Schultz, a representative of the Lutheran faith, who on his first day immediately made himself as unpopular with me as his predecessor. The pastor was round, (Fraulein Amanda called him portly) bald, had red cheeks and several chins that jiggled when he talked.

"You are born in sin," he pronounced in a deep and sorrowful voice, his face set in stern and unforgiving lines, "and you are a sinner."

That's all I needed to hear. I told him that I had done nothing wrong for a long time, except snitching a piece of candy twice. I further argued with him that I couldn't possibly have been bad when I was just a brand-new baby. While he was droning on about my doomed fate, I went back to singing songs in my head, telling myself silent picture-book stories and looking steadily out the window. After just two of such afternoon sessions, Pastor Schultz left in a big, black huff and a purple tizzy, assuring me on his way out the door that I was full of the Devil.

Nothing had changed since the day the two men of God gave up on me. I grew up without growing a religion. However, there was inside of me an uncharted knowing that Something Big and Something Grand was all around me; always. Maybe it had to do with the stars and the moon, the wind in the trees, the shimmer of a rainbow, or the hush of early morning. Perhaps I would never know.

I had been been thinking about a lot of things. About growing up, and feeling strangely lost at times. I wondered about life in general, of which I knew little — so I kept on examining things as the days unfolded like a kaleidoscope with new patterns forming at every turn. Some patterns were of a reassuring familiarity, others were puzzling and confusing. When it got too much and in spite of my mother's advice to close that "picture book," I retreated to the past — for a little while anyway.

I found myself day dreaming about home, about Marienhall. If I concentrated really hard, I could recall the delicate fragrance of the linden blossoms we gathered for tea making. I could bring back the musty wholeness of the big red mushrooms that hid in the loose, warm earth at the base of old tree trunks around their gnarled surface roots. I could taste the plump, wild strawberries and the big juicy gooseberries in late summer. I closed my eyes, stuck out my chin and soon I could feel the wind rush against my face, fanning out my hair behind me, as Principessa, my horse and I galloped freely at the edge of the wheat fields that bordered the ancient woods of Marienhall. In my dreams I walked again the narrow trails among the tall firs of my childhood's dense fairy-tale forest. The trees were so thick and tall, that they almost blocked out the sky. I tip-toed through the deep, mysterious shadows that moved silently around me, telling me delicious secrets about little people, flower fairies and whispered about the magic of the moon and the stars high above. Secrets, I have always loved secrets.

Not a night passed without my calling up the pictures I carried with me in my mind. I saw the faces of my Uncle Erich, Aunt Antonia and Aunt Helene ever so clearly behind my closed eyes. I could hear their laughter, the sound of their voices as they gestured with their slender, bejeweled hands. I missed them, and I was terribly frightened for them. Had they gone to Switzerland, we would have heard from them by now through the Swiss Consulate. But there had not been a word. If they remained at home, they were caught up in the war.

"War is hell," Vati had proclaimed, "it's hell for everybody, soldiers and civilians alike."

Every once in a while I would catch him staring into space, a deep, dark mood shadowing the light of his hazel eyes. And in the middle of the night, I could hear my parents talk about the past, deploring their lack of vision, about their losses. Mutti cried when she spoke of the family we left behind. Bits and pieces of terrible news about the constant roundup of Jews, the brutality of the Nazis and about concentration camps from which no one ever returned, continued to come to our ears. Where was our family? When would this war be over? And who would still be alive? My parents must be thinking and talking about the same things. All those what-ifs, those speculations, wishful prayers and crazy thoughts … I had to shut off my mind. I had to stop thinking.

Our friend, Max read the Shanghai News religiously every day, and discussed the headlines with us over cups of strong coffee or tea on many an afternoon. When he was through with the paper, he gave it to me neatly folded, and I read the news word for word, page by page, the advertising and everything. We were inundated with rumors, gossip, perspectives and tales of night-mares. But just the same, life went on — uneventful and quiet. Or so I thought.

Accompanying Vati occasionally to the sites of a paint job that Mr. Yung had secured was fun. Not only did I feel somewhat important to be able to help my father in his business, but I had the opportunity to see a lot more of Shanghai than my mother would have appreciated, had she known.

Beggar children in the street reached out their painfully, skinny little arms, singing their plea in pidgin English: "Massa, Missy, no mama, no papa, no money, no whiskey-soda, no moto-car…."

At every corner, from every doorway, ragamuffins offered the products of their thievery, "Massa, Missy, rea' gold, rea' silver, plenny good, you look-see…. No good, you bling back tomollow…." (As though one would ever find them again.)

When Mr. Yung enlightened me that these beggar children and their adult counterparts, thousands of them, all belonged to a "Beggars Union" which was run by a Beggar King, I felt a lot less sympathetic to what I had considered to be their misfortune. These people chose their trade the same way another person may decide to become a clerk, a waiter or a carpenter. Mr. Yung went on to explain how enormously wealthy the Beggar King and his lieu-tenants were.

Street urchins, mostly young boys, offered different opportu-nities: "Massa, Missy, want-chee see boy-girl? Want-chee see girl-

girl? Boy-Boy? Wantchee see donkey …?" Pitiful cries from street children advertising things best left untold. More often than not, they were soliciting for their siblings. What I didn't understand, I asked the young ladies at the Flower Houses. Powdered and painted, rustling in silk gowns, strands of jade beads and pearls dropping from their slender necks and with expressive facial contortions, manicured fingers fluttering, they refused to talk about it. All they said repeatedly was, "You no listen. You go your way. Is bad, velly bad. Is ugly. Velly ugly...." Just the same, my carnal knowledge grew at an alarming rate, which at the time only made me promise myself to wait a long, long time, like maybe twenty years, until I even wanted to hold hands with a boy. Ugh!

From the "Sing-Song Girls" I learned how to play mah-jong, how to eat slick noodles and slippery mushrooms with chopsticks, and all about proper tea-drinking manners. I was introduced to the quality of imperial jade, how to test pearls for excellence, and how to count in the Mandarin dialect. Friendly and playful, one of the many "Mei Lings" I met at one of the Flower Houses, taught me her favorite pidgin English rhyme:

"Me no savvy, me no care, Me go mally millionaire.

If he die, me no cly, Me go mally other guy."

Well groomed, polite and charming, perfumed and powdered, doing fine embroidering and painting silken scrolls, they seemed quite the ladies. Their waking hours were filled with gales of laughter, child-like games and generous doses of harmless mischief. They certainly were more fun than my classmates, the dour, serious and quick-to-punish nuns, and even my parents' friends.

      ☯   ☯   ☯

While Max Selig was our historian and international political analyst, his roommate, Kurt Vogel appointed himself our entertainment specialist. He kept us informed on the dates for symphony concerts, he insisted we attended chamber music events, recommended American movies, and secured tickets for the Ballet Russe. I loved the ballet. I was enchanted with the graceful dancers in their traditional customs, the music, the fantasy and the magic. It reminded me of home.

Kurt took us walking to several of the well groomed, quiet, tree-shaded city parks in the International Settlement and in the French Concession. He was the one who discovered that the best piroshkies were served at a pleasant Russian restaurant, Cafe Deedee, on Avenue Joffre. I didn't know what a piroshki, was, but became hopelessly addicted to these little meat-filled potato-pastry dumplings. He introduced us to another Russian restaurant where we listened to balalaikas accompany colorfully dressed singers whose tragic songs bemoaned the loss of their beautiful homeland — dosvedanye, Mother Russia. He also insisted we go to Hongkew to catch a performance staged by our refugees of *The Merry Widow* — my parent's favorite music of all.

At first Vati objected vehemently. "I have seen *The Merry Widow* performed by the best talent in Berlin, in Breslau and in Vienna. I want to keep these images alive and not spoil them with some mediocre performance."

"Martin," Mutti scolded him unceremoniously, "don't be a snob. You probably will have to take back your words. What you don't know, because you haven't bothered to find out, is that Rosl Albach-Gerstel is singing the widow, and you have been one of her biggest fans."

"I didn't know she was in Shanghai," Vati sputtered "She's the greatest. Why didn't you tell me?"

Mutti just laughed. "You didn't ask!"

Everybody was more than pleasantly surprised by the excellence of the performance of Lehar's charming operetta — the fine voices, the professional execution of the production and the quality of the well rehearsed small orchestra. The old Hongkew movie house was filled to bursting. When the final curtain came down, the audience, along with my father, rose to its feet as one. Kurt and Vati were whistling shrilly through their teeth and applauding until their hands were hot and red. We were the last to leave and took along the gift of having witnessed a fine performance — not in Berlin, not in Breslau or Vienna, but in a half-bombed-out, Japanese-occupied, miserable suburb of Shanghai, China.

We rode home in a pedi-cab, humming along with Mutti who knew every word of the popular arias. By the time we had redone act three, we were home.

"The Hitlers of the world can destroy and murder innocent people, they can torture, terrorize and starve them, but they can't kill the soul of a people and they can't kill music and art. They can't kill the love for music. Beautiful music lives forever, and," Mutti's voice cracked a bit, "it's portable. We took it along with us." She had tears in her eyes.

For weeks we talked about that night, and the fact that amidst the filth, the heat, the worries and the endless uncertainties, our refugees had the spirit to "make music — such beautiful music." Mutti smiled her Mona Lisa smile, as she closed the subject.

"Anybody can sing and dance and celebrate in good times. That's easy, and we don't give it much thought. But when we are able to celebrate life in any form in bad times that means to me, that we can rise above our circumstances and express our indestructible spirit, and the gift of life itself." My mother!

In April 1941 the Third Reich Army invaded Yugoslavia. Hitler's march of destruction continued. It seemed that no one could stop him. Two months later, more news.

It was late in June when Vati came home quite agitated, bearing the latest report from the war in Europe. "Guess what happened?" he started. "Hitler broke his non-aggression pact with Stalin; he invaded Russia. I hope to God he gets stopped before his threat comes true — 'today Germany, tomorrow the world.'"

That evening Max, Kurt and the Cohns gathered around our table and discussed the outrageous act of aggression by Germany's mad Fuehrer and his equally mad generals. The discussion was a lively one, everyone contributed ideas and possibilities about Hitler's war, until Max made his final prediction.

"No matter how much he conquers now," he started out thoughtfully, "there is too much land to cover, too many borders to guard, too many people to govern, too many people to feed, and too many enemies all around him. If Hitler hasn't learned from history, his armies will most probably reach the gates of Moscow in the depth of winter — just like another conqueror before him. Napoleon got that far and no further. He lost his war to an empty city and to the ice and the snow, to starvation, lack of clothing and supplies and an angry, rallying Russian people. Napoleon's army was 600,000 strong — the biggest army ever to invade and engage

the enemy. Only 100,000 returned. Mark my words," his hand hit
the table for emphasis, "the timing is right. The German armies
have a long way to go yet before they get to Moscow. Winning a
war is not just having the armies, it's equipment, weapons, fuel,
clothing, food, medicines. I can't imagine how long the supply lines
for a big army across such a vast territory would be. Berlin to
Moscow; that's a long, long way. When those supplies don't catch
up with the men in battle, all is lost. It's not only wishful thinking
on my part when I predict that Hitler is going to lose the war at the
frozen gates of Mother Russia's Moscow. It's a fact.

"You know that history repeats itself," he continued. "Man is
slow to catch on, apparently. We don't learn from the mistakes of
others, we are so smart ... we have to do it ourselves. Hitler's no
different. The conqueror complex — the driving ego — is a
powerful engine that propels man into victory at first, blinds him to
reality and in the end leads him to inevitable disaster. Sooner or
later Hitler will lose his war. What with the Americans in the
picture now, there is no doubt in my mind, that there will be another
front established in the west. Even Herr Hitler doesn't have the
manpower, nor the machines to fight two mighty enemies on two
fronts," he concluded with a vigorous shake of his shiny, bald head
and a smirk of satisfaction on his face.

"Your words in God's ear," Mutti expressed everyone's
sentiment.

I sat through all these conversation with my eyes and ears
open. I loved to listen to grownups — even though they often
puzzled me. But this talk made sense to me and I stayed up until the
last words were spoken and the final predictions repeated like a
chanted mantra...Hitler will lose the war, he will lose ... we will go
home ... he will lose....

When? I wanted to know. No one had the answer.

❧   ❧   ❧

Summer was hot and sticky as usual, but at least we had
disposed of our European over-kill summer garments. Vati took the
heavy clothes to a man in Hongkew who sold them for us. Mutti
had made several dresses for herself and me out of thin, cool cotton
fabrics that were a pleasure to wear. The few things we owned from

sheets to dresses were hand-washed by Amah, who was also a champion at ironing. Everything always looked fresh.

While my mother's sewing activities slowed down a bit, because it was just too hot during the day, Vati's business became hectic. Summer was the time to paint and redecorate in Shanghai, and at times Mr. Yung had more than sixty coolies to supervise. But as Vati said, only thirty percent of them worked a full day. The others stood around, watched, chatted, steadied ladders and drank hot tea, unless, of course, they left town to attend "honorable grandmother funeral." Fortunately, rather than get aggravated, my father had learned to laugh about it. It didn't matter that much, the company was earning him a living.

The summer of 1941, however was most eventful for me. Two things happened. I had my first job and I met a wonderful refugee family from Berlin.

First, Mr. Yung introduced me to an army general (I assumed he was a general because he wore a splendid uniform). He lived in a splendid villa in the French Concession with his three "sisters" who wanted to learn English, and if possible French as well. Mr. Yung took me to General Yi Wai Chen where I met three pretty, giggling young women all of whom were twenty years old. Unless they were triplets, or adopted, they couldn't all be the exact same age, I reasoned. Somehow, they had the same air of lady-like silliness about them as my exotic friends from the Flower Houses.

The general was a stocky, muscular man, with a purposeful manner, and spoke English fairly well. He explained that his business activities were far-reaching, and he wanted his sisters to be able to converse with his foreign associates. It was decided that I would come to his house four afternoons a week for four hours to teach conversational English only. Later perhaps, he suggested, his "sisters" might wish instructions in reading and writing. French was not on the list as yet. One language at a time, he prescribed. He offered a generous fee, and I was in heaven. Before I left, he requested that I confine myself strictly to the east wing of the big villa where the sisters, One, Two and Three (as I called them before they told me their names) resided and to please stay away from any other part of the house. He repeated that he was a busy man, involved in business as well as in politics, and he spent his days in meetings and conferences with important people — men only.

The Sunday before I was to start my new job, our friends from the *Gneisenau*, the Herrnstadts invited us to tea and that's where I met the Levysohns and their two sons, Heinz and Wolfgang. Paul and Olga Levysohn came originally from East Prussia, but had moved to Berlin during World War I, where Paul started a pharmaceutical business. He produced several patent medicines, all of which soon became household words in Germany. Heinz the older of the "boys" was in his early twenties, Wolf, for short, was several years younger.

The conversation turned to the boys and the story of their flight from Hitler's Germany to Italy, where a wonderful family in Perugia took them on as apprentice photographers. Heinz had left Germany earlier to study engineering in Czechoslovakia, but after the Anschluss, fled to Italy rather than return to Berlin. Wolf, who was attending an art academy in Berlin, followed his brother to Italy shortly. The year was 1938, Antisemitism was heating up in Germany, and Italy seemed to be a better place to be. The two young men had a grand time, took to photography like ducks to water and generally fell in love with the charms of this beautiful Mediterranean country. No sooner had they settled in, when Hitler started to play his games with Mussolini. Predictably so, the two dictators formed an alliance, and in March of 1939, Il Duce searched his heart and (surprise) discovered his Antisemitic leanings. Shamelessly, he followed in the evil footsteps of his newly acquired partner in crime, and issued a proclamation demanding the departure of all Jews from bella Italia — pronto!

At first the brothers remained in Milan in secret hiding places. Fluent in Italian and free of any trace of an accent, they easily passed for locales. But when asked for identification papers, they failed the test miserably, and finally were forced to leave the country. But go where? Heinz and Wolf spent the next two months floating in no-man's land between France, Italy and Switzerland, crossing borders at night, not belonging anywhere, not welcomed by anyone. Like pieces of flotsam the sea tossed on the beach on the crest of a wave, and taken back out again by the tides and currents, so bounced the two brothers with a handful of other Jews between countries — back and forth, back and forth. They crossed the borders so often, that some of the guards called them by name as they sent them back from where they had come. Finally, along with five people in the same boat, Wolf and Heinz crossed undetected into France over treacherous mountain territory in the dark of night.They walked into fashionable Nice where a group of people were ready to help them.

The boys parents got lucky and managed to secure passage to China for the four of them. With proof in hand for leaving Europe, the two brothers were permitted to return to Genoa where the family happily was reunited, and together they boarded an Italian ocean liner bound for Shanghai.

Mr. Levysohn found employment with a Swiss pharmaceutical company where he developed several patent medicines, based on the formulas of the products he had manufactured for his business in Germany. He was pleased with his position and comfortable in his new surroundings. After all, working for a Swiss company was like working in Germany.

The young Levysohns were employed in a photo studio in the French Concession, where not far from there, the family rented a small house, part of a large estate, hidden from view in its secluded park-like setting. The property belonged to a lovely Chinese lady, whose wealthy, Oxford-educated merchant husband had been murdered under mysterious circumstances.

Elizabeth Chi who had traveled extensively in Europe and America, effortlessly blended a good measure of western culture with her heritage. She lived in the handsome main house with her grown children, two boys and four girls. The Chi family spoke English, displayed a love for classical music, jazz, art and literature and were quite cosmopolitan in their life style. A deep friendship developed between the Chis and their Jewish refugee tenants. Paul, an accomplished pianist, was in heaven when Elizabeth Chi offered him the use of her grand piano, where he spent "… the best hours of my life."

The Levysohns portrayed a tight, energetic and congenial family. They joked and teased each other, shared inside jokes, and one couldn't help being attracted to their jolly mood and manner. Paul and Olga held hands a lot, inquired about each other's well being frequently, and magically drew those around them into their circle that radiated warmth and sparkled with affection. That included my parents. Addresses and telephone numbers were exchanged that afternoon, and before the week was out, we were invited to have lunch with our new friends in their cozy little house. That was the beginning of a lasting friendship — and more.

Our families visited back an forth, the boys took me under their wing. It was like having a whole new family. Heinz and Wolf dragged me along to the movies and on long walks in the park. Together, we ventured into the the city regularly, discovering new streets and neighborhoods until we knew our way around the International Settlement as well as the more residential French Concession. I felt that I had become a true Shanghailander and almost an old Chinahand. The three of us spent hours just talking about our lives in the past, got to know each other's stories — and all about getting out of Hitler's reach. Then there were the evenings when we sat in Mrs. Chi's elegant drawing room, and listened to Paul playing his favorite music on the piano. We made friends with the Chi boys and girls who ranged in age from fifteen to twenty-four. We never thought much about age differences. Circumstances had made us all grow up in a hurry. We were old and smart beyond our years. But when we got together, we were just a bunch of kids enjoying each other's company. I had the best time.

Wolf and I roamed around in town periodically, and usually ended up on Bubblingwell Road, a broad and bustling street with nice buildings, host to the picturesque English Race Course and all those lovely stores. Whenever we approached the grounds that housed a regiment of America's Fifth Marine Corps, we always walked on that side of the street, so we could see the American flag close up and say hello to the two Marines who stood guard at the entrance to their compound.

When the news reached us that America had entered the war in Europe, we were certain that peace would come quickly to the world. After all, America was the greatest country in the world. What power it represented. We celebrated what my father called "The beginning of the end of the Third Reich." I was glad that America was on our side. Seeing the "Stars and Stripes" fluttering in the wind high above Bubblingwell Road, and exchanging a few words with the Marines gave me a strange feeling of belonging.

My parents made strict rules about my time spent with the Levysohns, where we went and what we did. "Don't make yourself a pest," Mutti warned. "The boys are older, and they may have other interests than spending so much time with you."

Grownups; they're so strange. I knew I was going to marry Wolf.

❧   ❧   ❧

I had become friendly with several American girls at school who had invited me to their homes where I met the rest of their families. We talked about America, and that my parents and I were going to the United States soon, that we were registered at the American Consulate, expected to receive our visas to the United States any day. I asked a million questions about my new homeland-to-be and felt a strange yearning to be just like them — to live in America, to be an American.

That became another dream for me to dream on. Perhaps I could replace the images of the past with those of the future. I had seen post cards and pictures from America, and had been walked through the family albums of my American friend, Janey Langford, depicting all kinds of places — her home, picnics and holidays, vacations and other fun events. I loved it.

Mother and I talked a lot about America. Her oldest brother, my Uncle Joseph with his wife and two daughters, had immigrated to Chicago just weeks before we left for China.

"We will have some family in America. And when my sister also comes to America, the three of us will be together again." she smiled her dreamy smile, and returned to her sewing. The ladies she had met kept her quite busy with their alterations, and continued to recommend her to their friends. Pretty soon, Mutti had a waiting list.

She turned a deaf ear to my father's objections to her sewing activities. "It gives me pleasure to work with my hands, and I'm getting better at it all the time," she announced, pleased with herself. "Besides," she challenged, "what would I be doing with myself all day long?" Vati who rarely ever denied my mother anything, shook his head in resignation with a half-smile on his face.

Each time he went to the Hong Kong-Shanghai Bank to put some money into his account, he always offered to deposit the contents of her knee socks in a "safe place." She refused. "I am more comfortable to have the money right here," she replied. "What if something happened to the bank? After all, this is Shanghai...." her voice trailed off in search of a catastrophe she could conjure up, that could affect the security of the powerful international bank. My father just laughed and humored her.

                    ☯   ☯   ☯

During the year 1941, the China Art Painting and Decorating Company did well. Mr. Yung had turned out to be a fine and trust-worthy partner-comprador, and due to the high humidity and poor quality of the paint, most of the establishments required redeco-rating frequently. Vati's greatest irritation with his painting business remained the way the Chinese coolies worked. "For each job that would normally require one man," he explained, "we have to hire three: one to do the work and two to supervise. One to mix the paint, two to hold the bucket. One to paint a ceiling, two to steady the perfectly steady ladder."

Mutti had to laugh that he expected German efficiency from a people with all together different principles and traditions. Vati didn't think it was funny, but admitted that the coolies' work patterns weren't at all upsetting to Mr. Yung.

"And why not?" Mutti replied still chuckling, "it's his country and his way of doing things."

During this time, I learned more street Chinese from Amah, a few more words in Mandarin dialect, and was pleased when she paid me her highest compliment in her prattling sing-song voice: "Young Missy now ol' Chinahand. She savvy Missy ... bamby she catchee lich man, mally lich man, then she plenty mo' savvy...." She was bound and determined to marry me off.

                    ☯   ☯   ☯

I was excited because Janey Langford had invited me to my first "American" dinner in late November. Mother made me a special dress and I felt real grownup. I was almost as tall as my father, and my feet had stretched at an alarming rate. No Chinese shoe vendor carried my size. Whenever I walked into a store, pointed at a shoe from the window display, pointed at myself, without fail, the clerk would look at the shoes, look at my feet, spread out both his arms wide apart and say, "Solly Missy, this size no got." The spread of his arms suggested that my feet were the size of a canoe and left me praying that they had reached their final growth. A Swiss shoe store on Bubblingwell Road catering to foreign trade came to my rescue and had shelves full of shoes in European sizes — and a lot more expensive.

On the day of the dinner, with Mutti's home-baked pastries nestled in a red-silk gift box in hand, I left the house a bit on the early side. I wanted to take my time, do some window shopping along the way and say hello to the guards at the Fifth Marine Corps Headquarters. Mutti had given me money for a rickshaw, but I wanted to walk.

As I approached the walled-in compound of the American military station, my eyes flew open, and my heart skipped a beat. A large crowd had gathered. Men an women stood in a deafening silence and stared at the long column of Marines carrying backpacks and rifles shouldered, that stretched down Bubbling Well Road. Traffic had come to a halt.

Just then a woeful bugle sounded, calling taps. Slowly, the American flag came down from its tall pole. Strangely afraid, I pushed myself through the crowds, and saw two Marines folding the flag, handing it to an officer with a smart salute, and sharply turn on the spot. They walked towards the entrance, reached for the heavy wooden gates, brought them together, pushed them shut with a final thud, slid a huge padlock in place and joined the column. A command rang out and the Marines started to march in the direction of the Bund, towards the river.

The busy, noisy thoroughfare was suspended in an eerie silence. No honking automobiles, no yelling rickshaw coolies, no bicycle bells clanging, no sounds of shrill bargaining or greetings, no vendors' sing-song, no scolding of boisterous children. Nothing. No sounds, just an ominous silence under a heavy, grey and somber November sky.

Finally, I came to my senses, my feet moved on their own, and I caught up with the last Marine in the column, fell in step with him in my new shoes and a string of questions poured out of me.

"Where are you going? Why did you lock up your headquarters? Why did you take down your flag? Are you coming back? Were you going? Please, tell me," I begged.

I looked up at the tall, broad-shouldered soldier, pleading with him. He kept walking, barely turned his head, and out of the corner of his mouth — hoping not to attract attention, he said in a hoarse voice, "We're going on maneuvers to Manila," he glanced at me sideways, turned his head and kept on marching. Hot tears welled up in my eyes.

"But you are coming back," I insisted between sniffling in my hankie and mopping up my tears, all the while keeping up with his pace, like a yapping puppy dog chasing an elusive paper ball.

He shrugged his shoulders, raised his eyebrows and shook his head. "Don't know, maybe, maybe not. Anyway, young lady, take care, and wish us luck...."

He looked straight ahead, his shoulder set squarely as he marched away. The officer who cradled the folded flag of his country in his arms and who must have heard this brief exchange of words, turned to me, and with a hint of a smile, and a casual half-salute, waved me off.

The Fourth Marine Corps was leaving — shipping out to the Philippines. That was bad news. Our refugee friends had always viewed the presence of United States Armed Forces in Shanghai as a sign of strength, a sign of peace, which gave us a sense of protection and security. Everyone looked up to America — America, the Statue of Liberty, the Golden Gate Bridge, Mark Twain, the Grand Canyon, democracy, opportunities, clean water, fresh air and freedom — precious freedom of just being. Now the keepers of that freedom were leaving.

Hoping I would find out more at the Langfords, I hurried in the direction of their house several blocks away. Even though the people on the street and the traffic had begun to move again, there still hovered a hush over Bubblingwell Road. I felt strangely uncomfortable.

No! The Langfords had not heard anything about the closing of the Fifth Marine Headquarters and the soldiers marching off to be shipped out on maneuvers. The mood quickly changed from festive to worried. Robert Langford, shocked and surprised, to say the least, raced to the telephone and called the American Consulate. The line was busy. No wonder! He then called one of his business partners from American Chemical, a Detroit-based firm. Robert, as I was allowed to call him, had managed the firm's Shanghai branch for more than four years. The Langfords loved living in the Orient as much as they enjoyed their bi-annual visits home. Mrs. Langford, "Tinka" to everyone, did Chinese watercolor painting, studied brush art and was a tireless tennis player. Tall and slender, with a square, stubborn chin, laughing steel-grey eyes, and a mop of wild, red hair, she was a friendly soul who had taken to life overseas with the passion of a kitten for a mouse. Lawn parties and English teas, croquet and polo matches, bridge tournaments, mahjong afternoons and black-tie dinner dances at the country club all fell into her routine with clockwork ease.

Foreigners didn't work themselves to death in the Orient, and Robert was no exception. Golf, tennis, horse races and social activities took precedent over the business — which was well established and practically ran itself. Life was a bowl of sunshine and lotus blossoms not only for the Langfords but for most of the other American and European transplants.

His face was serious, his eyes worried when he returned to the living room. "Richard had just heard about the Marines' pull out and basically knows no more than we do. Shipping out to the Philippines on maneuvers is the rumor. That's all. But he doesn't believe the 'maneuver' part. He has the same concerns as I. something's up with the Japanese. I feel it in my bones," Robert sighed. "I don't like it. I don't like it at all. Tomorrow," he turned to Tinka, "I'll book passage for you and the girls. You're going home."

With her chin sticking far out and up in the air, Tinka announced she would not go home without him and that was it. In a gentle way, they argued back and forth through dinner, until Robert gave in and promised to go home with her and the girls and stay there, at least until he felt good about the political situation.

"I just know the Japanese are up to something. Why would our boys leave in such secrecy? We're famous here in Shanghai for gossiping at a rate that has no rival — but no one had even heard a hint, a whisper…. The marines might as well have snuck out of town in the dark of night."

"Or," Tinka added thoughtfully, "the orders came so fast, there was no time for the news to get out."

"If that's the case," Robert's forehead creased into deep worry lines, "we have serious trouble coming our way."

I couldn't wait to get home to my parents. Tinka promised to send word with Janey at school as soon as she had some reliable news. "I don't want to pass on rumors, get everybody excited or calmed down, which ever the case, and in the end be all wet."

The Langfords insisted their driver take me home. "I just don't feel safe with the marines out of town," Robert attempted a feeble joke. I had a feeling he really meant it.

I thanked my hosts, gave Janey a hug, climbed into Robert's dark blue Ford and was home in ten minutes. Our two bachelors were visiting with my parents, and everyone sat in shocked silence when I told my story.

Max immediately agreed with Robert Langford's appraisal of the situation.

"I'm afraid that it means we are close to war in this part of the world," he announced in a flat voice, void of emotion.

"War? War with whom?" my father interrupted. "The Japanese? They haven't finished their war with China. War with America? Don't tell me they are stupid enough to take on something they can't finish. Why, Japan making war with America would be like a mosquito stinging an elephant," he concluded all stirred up.

"Not quite, unfortunately," Max raised both hands. "I've read a lot about Japan lately, about the Japanese — their history, their ideology, their exaggerated sense of nationalism, and their jaundiced view of Westerners. I could go on and on, but let me just name three things that make them a formidable enemy: One, they have no natural resources; two, they hate foreigners; three, they are every bit as industrious and hardworking as the Germans — if not more so. Blinded by their fanatic and misguided nationalism, they

very well might take on America. As far as I have heard, the union
between Germany, Italy and Japan — the Axis exists, and that can
only mean...." He didn't finish, shrugged his shoulders in a
helpless gesture and fell silent.

Before anyone else said anything, Max raised his hand, let out
deep sigh and said, "One more thing we haven't even mentioned.
What about the Fifth Column?" his eyes looked around the table
questioningly.

Max was referring to the members of the large German
community, mostly Nazis — Hitler's "long arm" — in Shanghai.
The Fifth Column was the Fuehrer's overseas army. After all, they
represented everything we had left behind — a treacherous bunch
of people threatening our very existence.

"We know they're here, and we know they're not just decora-
tion. We'll just have to wait and see. One thing is for sure," Vati
added. "even if it is dangerous, uncertain and perhaps stupid to
consider — but there's a whole lot of country behind Shanghai.
One could just take off. Missionaries and traders have done it.
They've charged off into the unknown, the interior...." my father
looked questioningly at Max.

"You are an adventurer, after all," Max smiled. "Not a bad
idea. Let's keep it in mind. I'm sure we could find people to help
us. There's always Ursula's General Yi and the three sisters."

My father the adventurer. I had never thought of him in that
light. I was impressed with his courage. He always said that
determination paved the roughest road, and single-mindedness
led the way.

"What about Germany's allies, the Italians?" my mother
asked.

Max dismissed the handful of Italians in Shanghai as "...inef-
fective ... typical Italian sidewalk-cafe Fascists ... no more harmful
than a cup of espresso without cream." He did however repeat the
rumor flying around Hongkew that the Nazis have sent a special
envoy to Tokyo to discuss the bothersome presence of the Jews in
Japan. That did not sound good. But, at this point, it was rumor and
we did not dwell on it.

"True, even though we are about as far away from Germany
as we can get," Max went on, "there are a lot of SS uniforms

strutting around on Nanking Road, just as big as life. They're all over town. It's a known fact that besides Madame Mei-Ling's House of Flowers," he winked at me with a quick smile, "the German Consulate is the busiest place on the Bund. People are coming and going all day long, especially Japanese high officers. And," he added, "you can be sure they're not making beer or sake."

I liked Max. At least he always added a little humor, even when the conversation was about serious matters.

The talk continued, lively and agitated, worried and optimistic. Opinions, predictions, ideas, hopes and wishes — opposing here, agreeing there — bounced across the table like ping pong balls at a master's match. It was long after midnight, when everyone finally headed for bed. I had taken it all in, and now had one more worry to add my worry box — impending war in our part of the world.

Two days later, just before class, Janey caught up with me and took me aside. Before she could say anything, I quickly handed her the thank-you note I had written to her parents. Janey tucked the slim envelope in the pocket of her jacket, assuring me she would not forget to deliver it.

"Mom and Dad asked me to say hello. They sure liked you, and they want you to visit more often. They would love to meet your parents and hear more about your family, and how you left Germany and all that. Now the other news, which really is no-news," she screwed up her face in a clown-like grimace: "All my parents heard from the consulate is what we already knew about the Fourth Marine Corps being on their way to the Philippines. Dad and his friends don't believe it; it sounds fishy. The Marines can go on maneuvers right here, just ten miles out of the city, he said. As a matter of fact, that's where they had gone before. Dad believes that if there is to be war in the Pacific, the Philippines is the logical place for our soldiers to be.

"But," she sighed, "we still don't know any more. Except one thing. Dad went to book passage to America for us the next day, and guess what? Everybody is trying to leave Shanghai. The earliest bookings he could get was for some time in March. That's next year — four months from now. It just doesn't sound good," she worried.

"All of a sudden everybody wants to get out of China. Daddy said some of our British friends are trying to get passage to Singapore, Bombay, Sumatra, or even just Hong Kong. But he believes that if there is going to be war with Japan, the whole Pacific is going to blow up. There won't be a safe place, and all those great British colonies are going to be overrun with Japanese soldiers," Janey looked at me with her great, big, blue eyes ... so scared.

I put my arms around her. "I know what it's like to be scared. We got out of Germany by the skin of our teeth. And if there's going to be a war with Japan, we are worried silly about what will happen to us. I guess my father said it best in sort of a humorous way. He said that we are living in great, but rotten times."

We both managed a half-grin and held on to each other. It felt so good to have a friend. Janey dabbed at her eyes, trying to sound cheerful.

"Mom said that worry will get us nowhere, and to go on with our life. Whatever happens, we'll face it then." Janey glanced around nervously and in a little girl voice whispered, "But I'll do extra Chapel, and say a lot more prayers."

Classes that day were as usual, but the Sisters seemed disturbed and restless, and made it a point to talk a lot about Christ's suffering, about courage and about strengthening our faith in the Lord our Father, for He was always at our side. At morning Chapel, for the first time, I truly prayed to that great, mysterious "something-someone" that I knew existed, but to which I couldn't yet give a name.

During recess I slipped into the classroom where the Sister taught geography, and studied the huge wall map of the world. Tiny, handmade paper flags representing a country were placed at various lands and islands of the Pacific. I looked at these flags with different eyes this time than I had during our lesson on Great Britain and her colonies. The little English flag was all over the place and so were the flags of other European nations. Maybe the Japanese intended to change all that. Emperor Hirohito and his court may not be any different then the Germans; they too believed they could own and run the world.

That day the Sisters let school out two hours early and I hurried home.

My parents, the bachelors and the Cohns had become one unit, one household it seemed. On the other hand, the three tenants of Place de Fleurs, Number 475, cherished their privacy, and respected their neighbors' need to be by themselves. Seeing each other was based on invitations, not casual drop-ins. It kept the friendship going.

When I arrived, everyone had gathered around our table, drinking tea and eating delicious, little pastries Max had brought from the Viennese cafe in Hongkew. I mentioned my conversation with Janey, and Max, our politician/historian, took to the news like oil to fire.

"I know that's what the Shanghai News reported. But, believe me, those Marines are going to the Philippines on maneuvers like I'm going dancing on ice," he almost shouted. "America have been well established in the Philippines for decades, and if there's going to be war in the Pacific, and, mark my words, there is, that's the place Japan is going to attack first. You bet, the Marines are headed for war." His words stayed in the air — heavy, oppressive and threatening.

The rest of the afternoon turned into another session of perhaps and maybes, and what ifs and what nots. The one thing everyone agreed on, was that if Japan went to war with America, it would become the war of all wars. "I hate to say it, to think it, but," Max said hoarsely, "there will be more battles fought all over the world than ever before."

I finally curled up with with my homework. I thought the grownups were talking it to death; nothing new was being said.

When we met with the Levysohns the next day, Paul confirmed everyone's concerns. The Swiss community, with access to information from their consulate, had interpreted the situation no differently. War was on the horizon, Mr. Schettli, Paul's boss had warned, and insisted everyone should get out of China. That was great advice for Swiss citizens, they had a place called "home." The Shanghai Jews had no place to go.

But as most people discovered in the days to come, passage out of China was as rare as hearing the roar of the two, life-size bronze lions that guarded the entrance to the Hong Kong-Shanghai Bank. Legend had it, that these magnificent beasts only roared at the sight of a virgin. When I asked Amah what that meant, she went into a bout of high-scale laughter. When she recovered from her attack of merriment, she explained the technicalities to me in minute detail. I learned some more.

❧　　　❧　　　❧

November 1941 turned out to be quite a month to remember. It had been on the fourteenth, that the Fourth Marine Corp packed their gear, locked the gate behind them, and left. Two weeks later, Max came through our door to our house like a bad storm. He was in our room before we heard his knock. Without ceremony, he dropped a copy of the *Shanghai Jewish Chronicle* on the table, I picked it up and read out loud:

German Jews Declared Stateless Citizens

By order of the German Government, a Jew living abroad cannot remain a German citizen. The jew will lose his citizenship if he presently lives abroad, or if he moves abroad after this proclamation...."

The notice went on to say that the assets of a Jew, who, according to the proclamation had lost his citizenship, reverted to the Third Reich.

Nothing new about that. Jewish property had been confiscated at will, with great thoroughness and lightning speed since Hitler had raised his ugly head in 1933. Confirmation of this well known practice didn't stir an eyebrow among our friends.

However the loss of citizenship had a different effect, at least for the moment. We looked at each other in stunned silence. A second later, Mutti managed something between a half-laugh and a slightly hysterical giggle. With her dark eyes glowing, she said to us: "What news! Why in the world would we want to remain citizens of a country that judged us the lowest form of life, killed our people, are probably killing more every day, stole our properties and then kicked us out. Their cruelty and their indifference to human suffering will brand them as monsters in the history books forever. I don't want to be part of them. What's so great about being a German? I don't want to be a German. I don't want my daughter to be a German, and I don't want my grandchildren to be Germans. We're going to America. We're going to be Americans." she took a deep breath; it was quite a speech for her.

"The only thing that is disturbing is that stateless citizens living in a foreign country have no consulate to protect them, no place to turn to if they get into trouble. No one to bail them out. A stateless citizen can disappear like a drop of water in the ocean, and leave no trace behind. Stateless people are nonentities," Max added to the debate.

"We are already nonentities," Vati interrupted. "And just what kind of "help"would a German Jew get from a German consul, who no doubt is a big Nazi, otherwise he wouldn't have been given the post to begin with," Vati rationalized. "I don't believe for a minute that a Jew who got himself in trouble in China would get past the front door of the German Consulate," he continued. "And, the German Consul wouldn't raise a finger to save a Jew. In all the time we've been here now, I have never heard of one single person calling on the consulate for whatever reason. Have you?"

Max looked at Vati a bit sheepishly, "No, I haven't," he admitted. "You're right, of course, Martin." He then looked at my mother and said, "Irene, I'm no longer proud to be a German either. The only thing that saves me from hating myself, is the fact that I am Jewish," he grinned his bad-boy grin, and the mood around the table changed immediately from dark and gloomy, to light and cheery.

The Cohns suggested we hold a "throw-away-our-passport party," but my practical mother insisted our German passports with the huge, offensive, red "J" (for Jew) stamp on one page, and our middle names changed to "Sarah" for women and "Israel" for the men, would be a valuable relic some day. "… If for no one else, then for our grandchildren and their children," she said.

The conversation turned to the fact that no one had ever felt that the Japanese people were Antisemitic. After all, they had welcomed us to settle in Hongkew, the suburb they had wrestled from China in 1937. And, Max, of course, had a much more scholarly and political factor to add. He told us briefly how some Jewish bankers in New York had loaned Japan a great deal of money during their campaign against tsarist Russia in 1904. Jewish people were held in high esteem by the Japanese leaders.

And with that assuring thought in mind, everyone agreed that there was no danger of being persecuted by Emperor Hirohito and his government. I was glad when the afternoon came to an end and we were by ourselves again. After a simple meal of one of Mutti's delicious soups and a loaf of fresh bread from our favorite Russian bakery a few blocks away, we felt no need to talk, and we curled up with a book.

It took me a long time to go to sleep that night. There was so much to worry about, some of which was a great puzzle. War was a puzzle. I thought a lot about it and I remembered the wars in my history books. People killing each other because of differences. The country whose generals killed the most people, usually won. War — nothing to be proud of, including winning, I thought.

❧   ❧   ❧

On December the seventh, 1941 Lucy Schiller celebrated her thirty-seventh birthday, and invited us for high tea. My parents and I piled into a pedi-cab (a bicycle-drawn rickshaw) and headed for Hongkew in the afternoon. Mutti had made Lucy a lovely dressing gown, and I had found a delicately carved pale pink quartz good-luck Buddha on one of my window shopping excursions on Bubblingwell Road. We hadn't seen the Schillers for a while and looked forward to spending some time with them.

Joseph's bookkeeping services were doing well, and Lucy earned some mad money, as she called it, by blocking and finishing hand-knitted sweaters for women who loved to knit but didn't know how to complete a garment. The couple had rented the upper half of a row house in a fairly clean lane. Their quarters consisted of two rooms, and the usual primitive, cold-water, cement-clad bathroom. The latter was shared with their landlord, the Wu Tsien family who had four little ones at last count. The smaller of the two rooms was just big enough to serve as Joseph's work area. The larger room was attractively furnished and presented their living "place," as they called it.

We had a most enjoyable afternoon. The mood was festive, especially since the Schillers had received good news from their daughters. An English sea captain who was a friend of the family with whom the girls lived in London had brought his freighter, the

Sir Henry, full of goods from Southampton to the Shanghai harbor. Snapshots, long letters and pages and pages of diary entries all documented the girls well being. They lived in the country, about forty miles north of London and had escaped the terror of the Luftwaffe's heavy bombing attacks on the city. Even though it was a relief to know that the young Schillers were in fine shape, the news of the destruction of London put a damper on the afternoon. Was it possible Hitler would invade England? The question remained a sinister threat.

It was almost nine o'clock when the three of us finally said our goodbyes, climbed into a pedi-cab and headed for the Concession Française. When we approached the Hongkew side of the Garden Bridge, we noticed that the Japanese guards had been tripled, and a large truck was in the process of unloading a whole bunch of soldiers in full gear. The odd thing was, that the soldiers were quiet — no commands, no talk, no shouting. Their movements seemed furtive and strangely covert. Vati ordered the rickshaw coolie to stop besides the British sentries at duty at the bridge, and proceeded to ask him if he knew what was going on. The young Englishman was polite, but had little to say.

"We've noticed some unusual troop activities on the Hongkew side all day long. It seems that about three hundred or so Japanese soldiers are scattered about — sort of camping out. But, we haven't been told anything, and all's quiet."

"Maybe too quiet," Vati replied.

"Oh, well, sir," the British soldier chuckled, "we can't ever figure out those chaps, they're a queer lot at best. Well, good night, sir." With that he straightened his rifle and stepped back into his guard house.

Our rickshaw moved silently into the night, over the bridge and onto the Bund. Suddenly, I felt funny. There was a strange tingling in my insides and the night grew stiller. All sounds seemed blocked out to me as though an invisible glass bubble had dropped over me. I could see all around me, but I heard only silence. I remembered grownups talking about hearing an "inner" voice that spoke to them. Perhaps that was happening to me. May be there was such a silence before one could hear that special inner voice. But nothing spoke to me; I just felt … funny.

We turned onto Nanking Road where the world came alive again. The street noises returned to full volume. American and British sailors in sparkling white uniforms roared down the street looking for fun and adventure. Shanghai was bubbling over with its usual night activities, bursting at the seams with life. A light veil of moisture made the sidewalks glisten and reflected the bright neon lights. The tingling in my insides stopped. We rode home in silence.

Something woke me up with a jolt early in the morning. It was still dark outside. My little clock on the chair next to my cot glowed green — it was twenty minutes after five o'clock. I sat straight up, and thought I heard some muffled, far-away booming. Maybe a thunderstorm was hovering over the Whangpoo River. A thunderstorm in December? No! Of course not! I sat for a moment in the darkness and listened to the sounds of a new day. All was still. I curled up again, and must have dozed off, when someone shook me awake.

"Young Missy, you wakee up, chop-chop; come on, chop-chop, bad trouble." Amah was standing at my cot yanking at my arm with all her might.

"Amah, what's the matter with you? Why are you here so early? It's only seven o'clock."

Mutti was on her feet, pulling on her robe, and Vati swung his legs out of bed, reaching for his pants.

"What in God's name is going on, Amah," he bellowed.

"Massa, Missy, young Missy bad trouble, no-good Japanese come over bridge, big gun makee boom-boom … is war. English ship on liver go down in water, chop-chop. Is war, bad time come bamby.…" Amah stopped shrieking and started to cry.

We dressed hurriedly, and woke up our bachelor friends. Max and Kurt threw their clothes on and announced that they would go downtown and see what was going on.

"We'll stop at the American or the Swiss Consulate. If there's news, they'll know."

"I'll go with you," Vati offered, but the two men were already out the door.

Amah had pulled herself together a bit, and mumbling an unintelligible stream of words, some Chinese, some pidgin English, all ending in "bad time come, bamby.…" made some strong, hot tea for us. We sat around sipping the fragrant brew and like Amah, prattled nervously on and on, speculating about what might be happening. The Cohns had been awakened by Amah's agitated shouting and had joined us. Vati debated back and forth whether or not to go to town, until we convinced him that Max, of all people, would find out more than anybody.

After a period of inane chatter, we fell silent, and ended up lost in our own private thoughts. I strained to hear that mysterious "inner voice" or experience that strange tingling again, but even inside of me all was quiet. About two hours and countless cups of tea later, a pedi-cab pulled up. Max and Kurt got out slowly, paid the coolie and walked stiffly into the house where five anxious faces looked at the two in worried anticipation.

"It's true," Max sad his voice rough and on edge. "Japanese troops marched into the International Settlement about five o'clock this morning. They sank the British gunboat *Peterel*, seized an American gunboat, the *Wake*, and arrested the ship's captain before he could carry out his orders to scuttle her. All Allied businesses are closed. The American Consulate is closed. At the Swiss Consulate I heard that Japanese airplanes in several deadly waves attacked the American Naval installation at Pearl Harbor in Hawaii. Surprise! The Philippines are under fire, and God knows where else these bastards are striking right now. I'll pick up the *Shanghai News* later"

Max fell silent for a moment, then said, "I'm afraid the war in the Pacific and in the China Sea is on. And I wonder just where we come in, how is it going to affect us?" He sat down wearily and closed his eyes for a moment. "One thing is certain," he mused, "with the war in the Pacific, we are isolated now — cut off from the rest of the world."

"War," Vati whispered, "war has come to find us. Now we're smack in the middle of it."

He turned to me, his eyes serious. "Do you understand now what I meant when I said that when the Jews spit in the water, the fish die? Wherever the Jews go, disaster follows." I nodded my head silently. Poor, unlucky Jews, and I was one of them.

Max disappeared for a moment and returned shortly with his big atlas. Vati took the tablecloth off the table, and Max carefully removed several pages of detailed maps of the Pacific, the Indian Ocean and the China Sea. Mutti must have guessed what Max was trying to do. Without saying a word, she handed him a pair of scissors and piece of white cotton fabric from her horde. She went into the kitchen for a moment, and quickly returned with a cup of cornstarch paste. Max shook his head in wonder when he thanked her.

"How did you know I want to make a wall map for us so we can follow the war in our part of the world?"

Mutti winked at him and smiled. "I'm not telling. If I tell, I lose my power," she teased.

Max pasted the maps on the material and tacked his creation on a wall in the entry way. I was set to the task of making tiny paper flags; red for the British, blue for American, green for the Dutch and, needless to say, yellow for Japan. I glued the bits of colored paper to Mutti's pins, and he placed them on the map, indicating who was where and did what. None of us knew that it would be a long time, and hearts full of worry and misery, before the yellow flags would disappear from our map.

Pearl Harbor Day was fixed in the minds of Americans as December 7th, 1941. for those of us on the other side of the International Dateline — it would always be remembered as December, 8, 1941, a day that promised intolerable suffering and sacrifices to so many nations, and which eventually presented the Shanghai Jews with a whole new set of troubles and undiluted anguish.

Chapter Six

1942
The Year of the Horse

*T*he day after Pearl Harbor, Vati and I returned from our trip to downtown Shanghai to report to Mutti on our fact-finding outing.

Japanese patrols clustered at street corners, on the Bund, on Nanking Road — just about everywhere. Short and stocky, their faces flat and without expression, the soldiers looked more like husky country boys stuffed into ill-fitting khaki uniforms against their will. We were stopped several times by patrols and had to produce our identification cards, which I could swear most of them couldn't read. The Japanese officer who detained us, asked gruffly if we were American or Engrish. Unlike the Chinese who have difficulty pronouncing an "R" most Japanese cannot pronounce the letter "L." When we replied we were Germans, he dismissed us without another word. And as Max had discovered the day before, Allied offices and businesses were closed. Several foreign establishments had Japanese guards posted at their doors.

On the streets, Chinese people hustled along rarely looking left or right. Those carrying bundles were stopped by soldiers of the occupation forces; their possessions were searched and often pilfered regardless of their owner's protests and pleas. Traffic was light that day and moved swiftly with a lot less noise than usual. Maybe it was just our mood, but I thought the city was subdued and wary.

Dockside on the Bund, Japanese soldiers were strung out in single columns, guarding the harbor. The Hong-Kong Shanghai bank was closed. Fortunately my father had missed going to the bank the previous week, and had a few hundred dollars in the house. Mutti, beaming from ear to ear with her see-I-told-you-so smirk on her face, retrieved my knee socks containing her savings from their hiding place. "See what I meant, when I said I didn't trust a bank in Shanghai? I'll make you a wealthy man yet," she joked, pleased with herself.

"Just wait, Irene," Vati defended himself, "things may settle down sooner than you think, and the banks will open again. They may confiscate Allied accounts and assets, but not monies from the refugees. But if you feel better, I'll close my account when the banks open again. That's just as well. We pay for our materials and the coolies wages with cash anyway. I'll just turn our share of the income into American dollars, and get another set of our daughter's knee socks. They seem to make good safety deposit boxes." It was his turn to tease.

Contrary to his faith in banking establishments my father never saw a penny of his money from the Hong Kong-Shanghai Bank again. Commercial Allied businesses were not the only victims of Japanese aggression. Americans, Englishmen, Dutch, French, all the enemies of Hirohito's empire, were rounded up and placed in hastily constructed camps at the edge of the city. The Langfords were among the first to be gone, and I was desperate to find them. I hoped I would be able to visit them. School was closed. The Sisters were still at their convent, but rumors had it that in spite of their religious status, they would not be left alone to do their work. They, too, were headed for camp.

"How quickly one's world can change. The whim of a king, the quirk of a leader, the wild idea of an empress, and it's … Off with your head. Yesterdays' friend, today's foe," Kurt Vogel philosophized.

"That's life," my father cut in with his precise and unromantic logic. "The most important thing is that — whim or no whim — we don't lose our head. We don't give in. We've all talked of going to

America. That's our goal, our destination, regardless of the detours we have to take. Let's plan on persevering."

I remembered a line from an English poet: "To strive,to seek to find, and not to yield." My father could have written these words.

    ❦   ❦   ❦

Except for visiting with each other for afternoon tea or a casual luncheon, our household and our friends more or less ignored Christmas 1941. It was just as well. On December 25th, the news was bad: Hong Kong, the British garrison had surrendered. Who'd be next?

We all gathered at the Levysohns on New Year's Eve — no hats, no streamers, no confetti. The beat-up gramophone with some of the records the boys had dragged along with them from border to border for two months in Europe, set the mood for the evening. Lovely compositions from the old masters of melody set us free of worry for a while, and the conversation turned to dreams, ideas and ideals. At the stroke of midnight, Paul popped the cork on a bottle French champagne, and everyone around the table offered a toast to the year 1942. My father was the last to raise his glass, "To peace. To us. Le chaim!" Simple words that broke the gentle mood. Reality set in full force. What would the year bring? Would there be peace? No one could foretell the future. And that was just as well.

    ❦   ❦   ❦

As the days of the new year marched ahead, they carried with them a sense of complacency, a feeling of false comfort. The Japanese occupation forces ignored the Jewish refugees. Mutti continued with her sewing activities, Vati and Mr. Yung carried on the painting business, and my father deposited his modest savings into an old sock of his. I taught English to General Yi's three "sisters" four afternoons a week and had the time of my life. I had fun!

With the Levysohns we attended a few concerts by the Shanghai Philharmonic Orchestra, got swept away by a lovely performance of *Swan Lake* at the Ballet Russe, visited with our friends in Hongkew where we saw a performance of our refugee theatre group's *King Lear* in English with a German accent. I spent a great deal of time with the Levysohns, played badminton with the

Chi girls, listened to Paul's piano recitals, walked in the park with the boys, and loved Olga's hearty East Prussian cooking. Whenever we had some mad money, Heinz, Wolf and I went to Cafe Deedee and filled up on piroshkies.

I was lucky to have such good friends. Heinz was a bit stodgy, loquacious and sort-of-engineer-minded, but Wolf was a light-hearted, funny and charming young man. He was of slight build, had the friendliest light brown eyes, and a thick head of brown hair combed straight back. Like his father, he played the piano, did fine pencil sketches, but was not serious about pursuing his talents. Paul, being a perfectionist, played the heavy critic, which apparently discouraged Wolf from practicing the piano. Heinz was a passionate photographer and only the shortage and inflated cost of film kept him from shooting everything that came in front of his lens. And there was a lot to photograph.

The Levysohns were one tight, loyal and fun-loving bunch. They attracted people into their circles like magnets, welcomed their visitors and cherished their friendship. Mutti complained teasingly that I spent more time with them than with my parents. That was almost true. But it wasn't just the atmosphere that drew me to them. I really liked Wolf. In four years, I decided, I would marry him. I wondered if he thought about it too?

For a while our lives went on outwardly undisturbed, and we were lulled into a counterfeit mode of purely selfish content. On the other hand, none of us was too certain about the next day, not to mention the distant future. We knew what we wanted so badly, but we also knew that nothing would happen to make our dreams come true until the war was over; until there was an end to Hitler.

There was no way I could find out in which camp the Langfords had ended up and I was devastated not to be able to see Janey. Maybe I could help, if I could only find them. Mutti and I took a walk to the convent, to see if things had changed. But no such luck. The building was locked; the Sisters were gone. Gone where? I wanted to know. A Portuguese lady whose girls had attended the school, said that the nuns had left over night for the interior to join another convent of the Sacre Coeur sisters. I missed them all. I had lost another part of my life when the days at the convent school ended. I lay awake a long time that night thinking of the sisters and my schoolmates. I prayed for their well being on imaginary rosary beads. Maybe their God would hear me.

The year 1942 may have appeared innocuous as far as our daily life was concerned, but we tasted bitter reality when we read the Shanghai newspapers as they followed the war in all parts of the world. If correctly reported, the news was devastating:

In February Japan's war machine captured Singapore; in March the Japanese sank the *HMS Exeter* and overran the Dutch East Indies. In May, American forces surrendered in Bataan on the Philippines. This was the hard news. Then there were rumors on the heels of rumors. Almost daily Japanese sources reported the sinking of America's Seventh Fleet. We heard about their advances on land, as well as their conquests on the sun-drenched islands in the Pacific. Some of what we heard may not have been true for that particular day, but sooner or later, fact caught up with fiction. Like their German allies, Japanese forces were on the roll. We were scared. Was it be possible for a puny little nation like Japan, and for the overly inflated ego of Germany — a country half the size of Texas, to win a war against the whole western world? America, included?

"I won't permit myself to entertain that thought," my father pounded his fist on the table. "Further more," he almost shouted, "I know America is going to win the war. I haven't met many Americans, but I know this, it is not only a big country, but it is a strong country, as tough as the people who built it. I just wish we had left for America when we had the chance in 1936. But I was a blind as a bat when it came to foresight. We kept saying that Hitler would go away, that his threats were pompous boastings and that the German people would not go along with his crazy plans. Well, we were wrong. So wrong!"

On and on he went, until Mutti finally put a stop to it, as only she could.

"Remember your own words, Martin: it all comes to pass, it doesn't come to stay."

"Well said. I'll eat my own words. No dinner for me," he joked feebly.

I knew America would win the war; my father willed it.

❧   ❧   ❧

Several days later, Max returned home from one of his visits to Hongkew. He spoke about the grim conditions that continued to exist in the shelters in spite of the frequent financial contributions from the United States and from wealthy Shanghai residents. So many refugees simply couldn't cope with their new life and its challenging conditions. Perhaps they were just tired and had given up. On the other hand, there were the entrepreneurs who started businesses, restaurants and offered all kinds of services. Modest and inadequate as they may have been, their undertakings flourished and provided their owners a living.

"This war just has to end soon," Max said. "I don't know how long our people can survive. It's got to be terribly depressing to live in a six-by-nine cubicle, separated from the world by tattered sheets. No privacy, no life. What is to become of them?"

A deep frown worried his forehead and he made a prediction that increased our foreboding: "I have an uneasy feeling that we're not going to be left to ourselves by the Japanese for long. It stands to reason that they are going to be influenced by Germany's systematic Jew-hating policy. I believe they are not anti-Semitic, but with enough pressure applied by the Nazis, that too can change."

Max's words were an accurate analysis of a situation we all dreaded to admit might come true sooner than we cared to think about.

❧   ❧   ❧

By late summer General Yi's three sisters who had long confessed their concubine status to me, had acquired a good smattering of English. I insisted that their sentences were grammatically correct, would not let them pick up pidgin English, and made it a rule that at each session they learn ten new words. With childlike glee, and after much searching for the right one, the girls each selected an English name for themselves from a long list of suggestions: Sister One called herself Connie, Sister Two became Madeleine, and Sister Three opted for Anna. Through Madeleine, who was the quickest to learn, General Yi conveyed his pleasure at the progress his sisters had made, and predicted that in six more months, they would be fluent in English, and French classes could begin.

In between lessons we turned into four giggly girls, played croquet in the garden and ping pong and gin rummy when the weather kept us indoors. The sisters loved to gamble, show off their jewelry, freely spent the General's money and displayed an unbridled passion for American cosmetics and French perfumes. Accompanied by bouts of laughter — their dainty hands coyly cupping their ruby-red mouths — the sisters discussed the most personal and intimate details of their times spent in the General's bedroom — no shame, no show of jealousy, no hands-off-this-is-my-man attitude.

I kept on learning.

One day an older Chinese lady burst unceremoniously into the sisters' pleasant sitting room where we were reading. I had caught a glimpse of her several times on my way to the east wing, but had not bothered to ask who she was. She was dressed in a showy bronze-colored brocade gown, dripping gorgeous gold and jade jewelry and sported a slick, tall hairdo that towered above a cold and angry face.

No sooner had she entered the room when she started to yell and scream at the three sisters who had jumped up from their chairs and with their heads bowed and eyes trained to the floor, let the barrage of anger pass over them. On and on went the furious lady, yelling and hissing and sputtering all the while spittle trickled down her chin. Suddenly, she stepped towards the girls, and one, two three, slapped each one a hefty smack on her cheek, let go with one final colorful string of curses, turned on her high-heel leather pumps, and stomped out of the room. I just stood there with my mouth open.

"Hey, girls, what was that all about?" I shrieked.

Before any one of them would answer, they broke out into uncontrolled laughter, holding on to their sides. Tears ran down the faint red bruises the older woman's harsh hand had left on their silken, ivory cheeks. Mascara ran in fine trickles and smudged their glowing skin.

"No matter! No matter!" Connie finally caught up with her breathing. "That I-Tai-Tai, General Yi number-one wife. She has bad temper. She does not like us. We are young and pretty, she old and ugly. But she I-Tai-Tai. She has two sons for General Yi, very important. But she gets angry at us; we have a good time. No matter, she old and ugly. All her friends are I Tai-Tai, they also old and ugly." Anna, the more scholarly one, went to great length to explain the way the Chinese household works — the pecking order of the wives and concubines. It seemed rather complicated.

Totally undisturbed by the incident and still chuckling to themselves, the sisters returned to reading their lesson for the day from *Little Women* — which we would discuss the following day — just like Fraulein Amanda used to do.

Though the east wing of the big house was somewhat remote from household activities, I couldn't help but catch a glimpse here and there of Chinese men in military garb stepping out of chauffeur-driven automobiles. They were greeted with deep bows by General Yi at the impressive entrance to his villa. Occasionally, Japanese officers arrived, dragging their show-off sabers along the marble floor of the great hall. I could never figure out why these overly showy sabers were longer than their bearers' legs. It looked so silly!

The visitors spent hours around huge teakwood tables in one of the large rooms in the west wing. Also important-looking foreigners in well-cut European suits came to the villa. They arrived in shiny limousines attended by chauffeurs in unadorned, dun-colored uniforms and peaked caps on their heads. When I observed the drivers visiting with each other at the side of the house where they parked the cars, I realized they were all packing weapons. Who were these people? Who was General Yi?

When I asked the sisters what kind of business General Yi and his guests were doing, the usually chatty girls clammed up and offered no more than: "Very busy people, very important people, make big business. Very high class! Everything is big secret. General Yi do not tell poor, lowly girls."

I'd find out. I was curious.

I cornered Max and told him at great length about the goings on at Villa Yi. He immediately had an answer, or, as he qualified, at least an opinion.

He said he thought our General Yi was connected to the new

puppet government of Wang Ching Wei, which was in cahoots with the Japanese military government. He went on to explain that the country had been run by war lords for a long time, and as of late by the scheming, self-serving Generalissimo Chiang Kai Shek. He admitted not knowing much about the situation, but promised to find out.

If anyone could qualify for the job of investigating reporter, Max Selig could. I begged him not to tell my parents, for they would surely be concerned about my safety. I was having a great time, earned some serious money for just a kid, and didn't want to quit my job. The three sisters expressed their fondness for me with lovely surprise gifts, included me in their games, and made me feel most welcome. I liked them very much. We belonged in two different worlds. We had nothing in common beyond the time we spent together and there was no permanency in our relationship; I just liked them; we liked each other.

By the fall of 1942, Max had discovered a little more about General Yi, and confirmed his earlier assumption that the man was deeply involved with the puppet government of Wang Ching Wei. Whether Chinese politics would affect the well being of the refugees in Shanghai, Max could not venture a guess. He assured me, that he would continue his digging. The scholar in him demanded to know more. I was only curious as far as my relationship with the General's household was concerned. China's internal politics were quite complicated, and I wasn't really that interested at the time. Ever since my very first day in Shanghai, I never lost the odd sensation of living a dream-like experience — that I was just a casual visitor — a sort of uninvolved observer to my life in China. My past lay in Europe, my future in America, and the present was merely the passage that led from yesterday to tomorrow. I kept myself somewhat detached from my surroundings — not looking for roots in China soil. I had places to go; far-away places. That feeling never left me.

The rumors from Europe that disturbed and frightened us to the very core of our being, was that Jews were being shipped by the trainloads to concentrations camps in the "East." Snatches of unspeakable brutalities executed by the SS against Jews reached our breaking hearts. Little did we know the horrible truth that lay behind these rumors. But those who had suffered incredible pain and shameful indignities at the hand of the Nazis, like my father, like Max and other friends, interpreted the situation differently.

"If I were an orthodox Jew," Mac confessed, "I would sit shiva for the Jews of Europe." He was referring to the ritual of sitting in "sackcloth and ashes" for eight days mourning the dead. There were no words to lighten the load. Every time we talked or even thought about the fate of the Jewish people under Hitler's thumb, the hollow, empty-eyed face of death stared back at us.

More rumors made their way through Hongkew. We heard that a high-ranking member of the Gestapo, a Colonel Josef Meisinger, had visited Tokyo to discuss the Jewish refugee situation there. He was now in Shanghai conferring with Japanese government officials about all of us. That was not good news. Next, whispers came to us that several Jewish community leaders had been taken prisoner by the occupation forces, and were held at the infamous Bridge House. Rumor or fact? Which was it?

"Behind every rumor there is a fact," Mutti stated with unequivocal authority.

The rumors of impending doom spread like wildfire through the Jewish community which had only one question: "Had they come this far, only to be persecuted by a new Hitler? Had they gone from the frying pan into the fire?"

Fresh panic set in. Max brought us the tragic news of several suicides among the refugees, and reports of an outbreak of aggressive behavior by Japanese soldiers — unheard of until then. Occasionally, bunched together into small groups, soldiers broke down doors, smashed their way into refugee houses looking for radio receivers, U.S. currency, and in the process often destroyed the few pitiful belongings of these unfortunate people.

Living in the French Concession gave us the illusion of immunity from the Japanese, simply because none of their troops cluttered the streets, as they did in occupied Hongkew. We sort of blended in with the White Russians, Portuguese, Germans, and members of other "friendly" nations who made their homes in the quiet streets of this pleasant part of the city. But would it last? Was the constant thought that loomed in our minds like thunderclouds darkening before the storm.

❧ ❧ ❧

The three sisters informed me that the General was planning a dinner for several honorable foreign guests, and wanted not only to serve a "foreign" meal, but also display an appropriate and elegant table setting. His orders were for me to plan the menu for thirty, check the household's supply of dishes, crystal and silverware, and purchase what was needed to set a table "fit for a king."

Mutti helped me with the menu, provided the necessary instructions for the preparation of the meal, and made out a shopping list. Accompanied by Wong, the head servant of the Yi household, I looked through cabinets, drawers and vast storage shelves in the attic. To my surprise I discovered a fabulous horde of beautifully embroidered table linens, crystal goblets, wine glasses, brandy snifters and enough English bone China and silver to set a table for sixty. The owner of Cafe DeeDee whom we met while stuffing ourselves with his famous piroshkies, was most helpful in having his Chef Wah Chu translate to Wong Mutti's recipes and serving instructions, as well as my mother's shopping list

The day before the dinner, and under the watchful eye of the household staff I was permitted to enter the hollowed halls of the west wing to set the table. The dining room was huge, dark and burdened by heavy furniture and heavy paneling. The tall windows were dressed in heavy, burgundy velvet drapes that puddled on the floor in fat folds shutting out all light. But by the time snowy linens, glowing silver and sparkling crystal, a scattering of carved ivory birds, candles and bowls of fresh flowers graced the long table, the room looked inviting and a lot less pompous.

The next day, the kitchen was a madhouse and several times I was sent to taste a dish, a dressing or a sauce. We had kept the menu simple and the General's kitchen staff had no problem following Mutti's translated instructions. When it was all over, I was told by the sisters, who had not been invited, that the dinner had been a great success. But no matter how many times I asked who the foreign guests were, I received the same answer I heard before: "Very important people; big important talk … very high class … very important business…."

In spite of their passion for gossip, and their chatty ways, when it came to the general's "business," they kept their mouths shut — while I was dying of curiosity. I wanted to be able to give Max something more to go on in his research.

No such luck! I resigned myself to the possibility of never finding the secret of Villa Yi.

☯   ☯   ☯

No sooner had the heat of summer and the glow of fall disappeared, than strong winds roared across the Whangpoo river and winter set in with its customary damp and bone-chilling manner. The news from Europe continued to weaken our hopes for a quick end to the war. Hitler's war machine swallowed one country after the other, bombed England so relentlessly, that we worried and wondered how long the English could hold on. From the Pacific came daily reports of Japanese victories. Our enemy's radio stations consistently announced the sinking of the American fleet, the destruction of British Navy vessels and "Glory to the Empire." How much of it was true was anyone's guess.

Max had a friend in Hongkew who ran the risk of hiding a wireless in his house, and was able to receive British news and at times reports direct from America. No longer rumors, many of the devastating war reports were true and the future haunted us all — except my father. He defended the ultimate victory of the Americans without a single breach in his faith.

☯   ☯   ☯

The three sisters and I celebrated a little bit of Christmas with an authentic English Tea and an exchange of keepsake presents for each other. Connie who had been practicing the piano for quite a while under the guidance of a White Russian teacher, acquired sheet music with some of the most popular Christmas Carols and played for us. The girls had learned the words to a few songs and their sweet voices rang clear and true. This was their first "American Christmas."

"I like Christmas," Connie contributed. "And I like Baby Jesus, his mama and his papa. Is funny though," she added thoughtfully, "every year you celebrate same baby, he never grow up." We all laughed. I wasn't offering any further explanation.

The Levysohns passed on the word that Mrs. Chi invited us to her house for high tea on Christmas Eve. The Chi household was always busy and bustling with the comings and goings of the Chi boys and girls and their friends. We were so glad to be included. White chrysanthemums and greenery filled an array of hand-painted porcelain and silver bowls that were scattered all through the house. A magnificent crystal vase with dozens of long-stemmed white roses and lacy ferns sat on the grand piano. A tall bamboo bush decorated with silvery ornaments served as the Christmas tree. Candles warmed the room — their flickering glow softening the ragged edges of our troubled times, and sent me straight into the pockets of my heart where I kept the memories of Marienhall. Everyone tried valiantly to create a festive mood, but in the end, Paul sat own at the grand piano and played heavenly selections of familiar melodies — straight from the old masters. The evening turned pensive and wistful, and, oh yes, a bit sad.

"So many men have created so much joy and beauty, and so many others have created so much pain and ugliness," Elizabeth Chi said softly to the room in general.

"Without knowing joy and beauty, good men couldn't combat the pain and ugliness," Olga Lansing replied to her hostess in a whisper loud enough for all of us to hear.

New Years Eve was spent with our friends in the house at Place de Fleurs. The evening was wrapped in nostalgia. Everyone contributed memories of times gone by, of sparkling celebrations and poignant moments. At midnight, we toasted the brand new year as we had done each year before.

We said goodbye to 1942. It was over.

Chapter Seven

1943
The Year of the Sheep

*I*n late January, right in the middle of a lesson with the three sisters in General Yi's west wing, we heard a big commotion coming from the front of the house and rushed to the windows to see what was going on. Six automobiles roared into the huge circular driveway and screeched to halt with their doors flying open. At least twenty-men in military garb poured out of the cars, their boots striking harshly on the pavement. With guns drawn, they charged up the steps of the marble terrace, heading for the front door.

Next we heard shots being fired. Anna grabbed Madeleine and Connie by the hand, yelled at me, "Come! Come quickly." Anna made a mad dash for the nearest bathroom and locked the door behind us. She threw a big bath towel into the tub, and jumped in, pulling the two girls in behind her. "Get a towel, Ursula, throw it on the floor right here by the tub, and get down."

Another barrage of shots screamed through the house; we heard the sharp popping sound of rapid rifle fire, and then suddenly — dead silence. A few seconds later, voices shouted, women screamed; more shots rang out, followed almost instantly by the sharp clatter of heavy boots down the stone steps in front of the house. Cars raced their motors, doors slammed, wheels squealed on the driveway, followed by the heavy clang of the big iron gates that guarded the entrance to General's Yi's sanctuary. Silence.

Shocked, I looked at Anna for directions. "What happened, Anna? Who in the hell did the shooting?" I stammered shaken and excited.

"Later," she said, as she climbed out of the tub and followed by the three of us tiptoed into the sitting room. Anna put her finger on her lips. "Shsh, shsh," she cautioned. "You stay here. I come back," she ordered and slipped out of the room.

Connie and Madeleine looked a bit pale, and were still shaky. They held each other's hand and Connie said, "Anna is brave, much courage. She is not afraid of anything."

We heard noises and agitated voices coming from the center of the house, but no one ventured to the door. Anna was the oldest of the three, and was very much in control of her part of the household. I jokingly called her the I-Tai-Tai of the east wing.

A few minutes later, Anna reappeared. "Don't worry; big trouble is over," she announced. The general was safe, one of his assistants and two servants had stopped a bullet, but were not in danger. She looked at us as we clustered around her, when a big grin changed her face and she reported gleefully, "I-Tai-Tai got scared, she run and fall, break two front teeth." Connie and Madeleine chirped in their delight about the misfortune of their enemy.

"Old and ugly I-Tai-Tai now two front teeth missing," Connie sang. I couldn't help but laugh as well. Apparently, I wasn't above enjoying a touch of revenge myself.

Anna got serious again and turned to me. "I ask boy to get rickshaw for you right now. Boy paid rickshaw. You go home. Don't come tomorrow. I shall send boy with message when it is good for you to return."

For the first time in all these months we have been together, the girls walked up to me, put their slender arms around me and gave me soft, fluttery kisses on the cheek. I was touched by their unusual show of affection. Anna smiled sweetly as we parted. "We are better friends now. We have been through battle."

"I hope there won't be any more battles." I let out a low whistle and rolled my eyes to the ceiling. "Goodbye for now, and take care of yourselves. Send for me soon. I'll miss you."

On the ride home I was debating with myself whether to tell my parents the truth, or invent a little white lie. I could say that the sisters were going to honorable grandmother's funeral and would send for me when they returned. I decided on the latter. I also would not tell Max. He had already warned me to be careful. He'd probably tell my parents, and that would be the end. I knew everyone meant well, but I wanted to make some of my own decisions, try myself out.

Living in one room night and day with my parents was a necessity. At the same time, I lived under a microscope. Sometimes I could swear my mother not only knew what I was doing, but what I was thinking. She would look at me, her dark eyes searching my face, as though invading my thoughts. Gerda Cohn had been fully aware of my need to be alone. I was never alone, I was always with someone. She came to my rescue and often when they visited with my parents, would suggest I take my book upstairs. I could read there without being distracted by their talking. At other times, she insisted it was her turn to have my parents visit in their quarters, giving me a chance to be by myself.

I found out that I liked my own company. I liked solitude. I liked the sounds of silence. I could try out a dance step, and not be questioned. I could hum and sing without being informed., "You're singing off-key." I could try on dresses and do a variety of things with them without hearing, "That looks silly … that is too long … too short … too bright … too tight … too.…"

I could read a favorite passage from a book out loud, recite poetry in any voice I chose; be as dramatic as I wanted to be; make faces in the mirror; try holding an unlit cigarette like a movie star … practice a grand entrance on a make-believe stage; descend a non-existing sweeping staircase in a ballgown with a non-existing train — and discover Me. I could be anybody. When I was alone and the room was quiet, I could hear myself think. I could sit down and write, without being told: "let me see what you've written when you're finished."

It wasn't that my parents were nosy, it was just that we had become a sort-of "one-unit," where everyone's activity became everybody's activity. We acted as a threesome, when I wanted to be a "onesome." It wasn't that I had any deep secrets, I just wanted them to be my own. For me, the end of the war would mean a room of my own. Privacy was such a stuffy word, I always thought. Like using the bathroom with the door locked. But I finally understood the breadth and the depth of privacy. It was a big word full of meaning and promise. Privacy meant time spent unobserved — moments of aloneness to take out my thoughts and my feelings, examine them, "separate the chaff from the grain and keep that which was worth keeping." I liked that.

Two days later, Boy arrived from the sisters with a note, asking me to return to the General's house. Was I ever glad.

       ❧   ❧   ❧

As I approached the big iron gates of the House of Yi, I realized that the graceful grill work had been covered from the inside with sheets of dull, black metal, blocking out the world. The handsome tall brick wall that enclosed the grounds had been topped by mean-looking, three-foot tall curlings of nasty barbed wire. In response to my banging on the gate, a tiny square in the iron-clad armor opened, two dark eyes scrutinized me. I heard the big bolt release and Wong, the daytime gatekeeper let me in. He grinned a welcome "Hello" and adjusted the wide leather strap of his rifle which was slightly taller than his slender frame and threatened to slip off his narrow shoulders along with the heavy ammunition belt. He looked like a little boy playing war. Next to him stood a new man also armed to the teeth. Wong made the introduction. His name was Li Yen; he came from Nantao.

Well! Maybe big trouble wasn't over after all, I thought, as I walked up to the house. My concerns were confirmed when two armed guards opened the front door for me. The new additions to the household staff looked positively menacing as they gruffly pointed me in the direction of the east wing — as though I didn't know.

The girls greeted me like a long-lost relative and Anna volunteered the briefest information regarding the shooting at the Villa Yi, starting with a saying she had learned only recently.

"All is well that ends well," she proclaimed. "General is fine. He is very angry about the trouble. He say he fixed the problem. Other people make a big mistake; they lose face. And," she added with an impish grin blossoming on her face, "I-Tai-Tai has two new front tooth. No," she corrected herself, "two new front teeth. The dentist made them too big. Now her new teeth can fit a horse."

"I-Tai-Tai still old and ugly," Madeleine chirped in, bouncing up and down on her tiny feet, "but now looks more like a pony."

I disregarded their attempt to gloss over the shooting. "If the trouble is over, then why are there two men at the gate now, two new men inside the house, all armed to the teeth? It tells me, that General Yi must be expecting more of the same," I challenged.

"No, no," Madeleine replied, her little hands fluttering like tiny birds in flight, "you don't worry. General say men and guns are just for face."

"Well, but who is after him? Who are his enemies and why?" I kept prodding.

I might as well have consulted the three monkeys — see no evil, hear no evil, speak no evil. That's exactly how the sisters behaved. As always, Anna took the lead, before the other two could utter a word.

"Not important, dear friend, and please, not worry. General Yi is a powerful man and has enemies. Somebody tried something foolish. He thought he could scare him. Lose face! Our General no scare easily. So, please do not be fearful. It will not happen again. We don't bother him with unhappy talk. The General is a busy man. When we see him, he is tired. He does not tell us anything. All we know is that it is politics. China politics, very complicated. Is also business, big business with very important people."

"Have I heard that before?"

"Look," Connie said, determined to change the conversation with the opening of a lacquered box that sat on a small table next to the brocade-covered sofa. She held up a large pendant carved from a flawless piece of Imperial jade. "General Yi made Anna a present for being so courageous and strong of heart."

Anna looked pleased and added that the General had given Connie and Madeleine also a pendant. Connie's new treasure was a beautiful coral leaf set in fine gold band, and the third sister showed off an intricately carved chunk of rare lavender jade.

"Surprise!" Connie shouted.

"Shut your eyes," she ordered, stepped close to me and slipped something around my neck. "Ready! Open eyes! Look in the mirror! Your present from General Yi. We told him you plenty brave too, and he asked Anna to pick a gift for you."

She held up a large hand mirror in front of me and the reflection revealed a gold chain from which dangled a carved pendant — a piece of deep-toned, highly polished coral.

"You like?" Madeleine looked anxiously at my face.

"Of course. I love it. I'm overwhelmed. I want to thank the General." I was stunned. As much as I poked around in the stores, I had never seen such a fine piece of coral. I was certain the sisters had a lot to do with that. It might even be from them. I knew I'd never find out.

"The General is very busy. You write him a note. We will give it to him," Madeleine suggested.

I gave up. Some things never change, I pondered as I looked at the lively faces of the three beautiful young women who lived in a golden cage that offered leisure, comfort and security. They honored the traditions of their world. As long as the General lived, they were in a safe place. Even though they eventually might be replaced with a younger version — as often was the case — they would remain a member of the household forever — honorable concubines who would help train their younger replacements. When I talked to Max about the Chinese custom of wealthy men having concubines, he replied that he believed the Chinese companions to their rich masters enjoyed a much more prestigious presence than the European mistress. "Read up on it," he suggested with his pleasant grin.

I was going to do that, but I didn't know whom to ask to recommend a title. It would have to wait. It really wasn't that important.

I had always joined the sisters in their merriment when one of the silly, pranks they loved to play on each other and on the servants with great regularity was successful. But that was only until the day I was their victim.

I had told them that Mr Yung and my father were planning to entertain several important customers at a dinner to be held at Tsu-chen Li's Golden Jasmine restaurant. I asked the sisters to teach me how to order four of my favorite dishes in Chinese — Peking Duck, Mandarin Fish, Beef and Bamboo shoots in a ginger sauce, and

Sour/Sweet Pork. The girls giggled a bit too much, I thought, as I carefully wrote down the names for the dishes phonetically. The three sisters were having a good time, probably chuckling about my pronunciation of some of the difficult syllables.

The night of the dinner arrived, and as we took our places at the big round table at the Golden Jasmine, I announced proudly to Mr. Yung, that I had learned the proper Chinese names for my favorite dishes, and may I please order?

No sooner had I rattled off my order when the waiters roared with laughter and were joined by our Chinese guests at the table. When every one kept on laughing, holding their aching sides and wiping fat tears from their cheeks, I wondered just what I had said to result in such hilarity.

Finally, Mrs. Yung took pity on me, pulled me over to her side and behind her cupped hand, put her mouth to my ear and still giggling furiously, whispered the awful truth.

According to her, I had ordered male and female genitalia in a wide range of preparations — from fried, chopped, sauced, diced, pickled, gingered, to braised, steamed and God-knows what else. My cheeks flamed hot red, I buried my face in my hands, and hoped for a hole in the floor to open and swallow me.

When I told Mrs. Yung that the three sisters had taught me how to order, she laughed out loud, and still chuckling and speaking in Chinese, explained to our guests and their wives, how General Yi's three naughty concubines had played a joke on me. Our guests thought it a remarkably clever prank, cheered for the three sisters and assured me that I was not to blame. It was quite all right, and not to worry. Not to worry.

My parents weren't at all sure what had gone on, and I would make up something "funny" to explain it all away — later. And as far as the three sisters were concerned, I decided to tell hem that Mr. Yung had pre-ordered the sumptuous meal, and I never had a chance to show off my vast Chinese "culinary" vocabulary. That would fix their wagon.

        ❧   ❧   ❧

Between my visits to the Levysohns, going to the movies and on photo-taking walks with both brothers, spending most afternoons with the sisters, I began to think that Shanghai wasn't so bad after all. I had a lot more freedom than I would have had at home. There was no Fraulein Amanda to shadow my every step, nor to direct my thoughts. I was five-foot eight, and passed for being a lot older than my fourteen years. Always concerned with "marrying" me off at one time or another, Mutti kept reminding me to stop growing or else I wouldn't find a husband. I wasn't worried. I already knew I was going to marry Wolf Levysohn, and become part of that grand family. But, just to please my mother, and with a little help from nature, I stopped growing.

I enjoyed myself. The only worry and dark moments I had were the times when I thought about my beloved uncles and aunts in Germany, Janey Langford and her family, and the kids from the convent school, the latter tucked away in some horrid Japanese prison. We heard that the camps for the members of Japan's enemy nations were beyond primitive, with deplorable sanitary conditions, and terrible slop for meals. People were ill and despondent. Max promised to see what he could find out at the Swiss Consulate and if there was a possibility to smuggle some food into camp. Nothing ever came of that because before our good intentions could be put into action, Hitler's long arm caught up with the Shanghai Jews. A proclamation that changed our lives appeared in the newspaper on February 18, 1943;

> ... Because of military necessity Stateless refugees will be restricted to an area (description of boundary streets followed) in Hongkew ... all stateless residents presently residing outside the area mentioned, shall move their business and/or residence inside the above prescribed area by May 18, 1943. Any person who violates this proclamation and interferes with its enforcement shall be liable to severe punishment...."

The proclamation was signed by the commander in chief of the Imperial Japanese Army and commander in chief of the Imperial Japanese Navy in the Shanghai area.

The proclamation put the Jewish community in an uproar — buzzing, conferring, debating, meeting and disbanding, arguing and agreeing. The order was like a bomb going off, exploding into a million fragments of anxiety and cold fear. Everybody sought answers. Just what lay behind the conveniently termed expression, "military necessity?" What did it really mean? How strong was Germany's chokehold on Japan? What had turned our "friends" into our enemies? But more than anything, where would this lead? What will "they" do next? Obviously there was a lot more behind the Japanese-German alliance than we knew.

Vati was the one who gave voice to our dilemma. "Somehow we repeated the same pattern that failed us in Germany. We went about our way, living the I-leave-you-alone-you-leave-me-alone policy. Wrong! I'm learning that uninvolvement with daily circumstance, that our ignorance-is-bliss attitude and not looking beyond political shenanigans, demands a big price. I clearly remember when we heard Hitler's first threats against the Jews. We all tossed them aside and lulled ourselves into sleep with words like ... Oh ... nothing but threats ... Hitler just needs a whipping boy ... our Germans won't stand for it. this is the land of Goethe, Schiller and Beethoven. The Jews have nothing but the best for their country at heart ... What? Me, read *Mein Kampf?* Of course not! Insane drivel of an insane mind. And we liked our words, and we lived by them, and only God knows how many thousands have already died by them.

"We need to find the meaning behind the proclamation," Vati thundered. "This may just be step one in the Japanese/German plan to further control us, to ... to ... do ... God knows do what with us. What then is Step Two? How do we find out? What can we do?"

Max who had been visiting in Hongkew when the proclamation made headlines agreed with my father. During the last few weeks Max had spent a great deal of time with Joseph Schiller and met with some of the leaders of the Jewish community. He also saw a lot of his friend, Michael, the owner of the shortwave radio, whose last name he never mentioned. I even began to speculate if Max was a spy for the Allies.

He told us that while rumors were rampant, some of them had a frightening ring of reality to them. It was true that the Japanese war machine was not only holding its own, but was still advancing and the Allied forces were retreating. To say that the mood in

Hongkew was bordering on despair and hysteria was putting it mildly. It was not overlooked by the Jewish community that the word "Jew" was not mentioned in the proclamation, but in spite of that omission there was no doubt that the message was directed at the stateless European Jews. Neither White Russian nor Shanghailander Jews were affected by this edict. It all boiled down to the fact that the upcoming internment — and we had to call it that — was instigated by pressure from the Nazis.

Mutti put down her sewing for a moment and said, "Isn't it wonderful that we, as bystanders to a war that's not going our way, are still optimistic?" Smiling with irony, her dark eyes shining, she added, "That's so un-Jewish." We all shared her laughter for a moment.

"Let's be positive. That's the right attitude," Max said. "Lets go room-hunting in Hongkew. It won't be easy, it won't be fun, it won't be good and it won't be cheap. How is that for being optimistic?" Max directed his bad-little-boy grin at Mutti and bowed his way out of our room.

No sooner had he left, than my parents took out their "saving-deposit" socks to which I had added my earnings, counted the money, noted the amount in Mutti's little accounting book and then in unison combined their horde. It became a joint account, Vati chuckled. They discussed the move which of course would be costly. Chinese rental policies were different and strange. Before moving into a place, one had to pay "key money" which had nothing to do with the rent. It was a one-time fee that gave one access to a house, a room or an apartment. Max had mentioned that approximately 8,000 people were going to be looking for a place to live by May 18, 1943. The Designated Area, according to some, was less than a square mile of land, where apart from the 10,000 or so refugees, 100,000 Chinese already had made their home.

Key money would go sky high. Shanghai was the breeding ground for unscrupulous opportunists. We dared not delay the chore of househunting until the last minute.

Resisting the change, I hoped that we would move at the last minute. I wanted to hang on to my job with the three sisters, and Vati, of course needed to work as long as possible with Mr. Yung. No one had any idea of just how limited our comings and goings would be once we were stuck in Hongkew. Some people already referred to the Designated Area as a ghetto. Vati wasn't going to move his business; there was nothing to move. Mr. Yung maintained a small office in a downtown building for his other activities from which he also conducted the affairs of the China Art Painting and Decorating Company. My father was going to ask him to just carry on, and would let him know after May 18, how restricted his movements were going to be. Until then, he planned to paint a lot of Flower Houses, opium dens and gambling halls. What a clientele!

When I explained my situation to the sisters, ending with the fact that after May 18, I would most probably no longer be able to come to the House of Yi, Anna spoke up immediately, and I might say, endlessly.

"No, No. You don't go to Hongkew. General very important man, very big taipan. He knows many important people. He can fix so you stay right here. You don't go. You stay right here in this house. You live with us. Japanese government does not know you. You hide right here."

I was surprised at the fervor with which Anna responded to the situation. I was grateful for her good intentions, but I also knew I wasn't going to stay with them. No matter what came along, I had to be with my parents. But if things got too rough, I was glad to have a place to hide — how safe, I didn't know. My bright and shiny sisters were quite the ladies.

One thing was certain, Anna, Connie and Madeleine came closest to being the living counterparts of the pictures in my China book. When the three of them traipsed through the villa's beautiful gardens, long silk gowns slit up high on their slender thighs, every black, lacquered hair in place, when they rested on the tiny red bridge that arched gracefully over the water lily-covered pond to feed the koy fish, they made my pre-conceived visions come to life. Catching a glimpse of them sipping tea in the pagoda-like gazebo tucked against blossoming jasmine was an exact copy of the picture on page 99. The China I dreamt really existed.

That evening, Mutti was quiet and pensive. She looked sad. I fixed two cups of hot tea and curled up on the couch next to her. I had learned from my British friends that a fragrant cup of tea was the first step to creating harmony out of chaos, to heal from spiritual injuries, and to come to terms with the end of the day. I knew from the look on her face that she was deeply troubled.

It all came out. "Don't tell your father, but I wish with all my heart we didn't have to live in Hongkew again. It is so ugly; it is painful just to think about it. I remember everything. I can still smell the filth."

We talked for a while and she calmed down. By the time Vati came home she didn't have a trace of unhappiness left on her face or in her voice. That night, my parents decided to start looking for a room in Hongkew.

Chapter Eight

March 1943
The Year of the Sheep

*H*ouse hunting in Hongkew was delayed by more than three weeks because Mutti became ill with a serious intestinal disorder, typical of Shanghai's climate and its less than desirable health conditions. Lucy recommended a physician who used to have a general practice in Frankfurt once upon a time, and who was practicing medicine on Avenue Foch. He prescribed an expensive Swiss medication which was supposed to put a stop to the problem. However, Doctor Mittelfeld warned her to be extra careful in handling food. "Once you have had this condition, it weakens your intestines and becomes your Achilles heel."

That sounded scary. The prescription medicine was only available at a fancy pharmacy in the French Concession and cost an equally fancy fortune. On top of that the pharmacist was doubtful if another shipment would ever reach Shanghai again. After all, there was a war going on. "Your mother will have to watch her diet," he recommended, and ticked off a list of don'ts that was longer than his arm. I was really worried. How could we get the things for her that she could eat? One more reason to pray for an end to the war.

In the meantime, the Levysohns had rented the lower floor of a row house in a lane on Tongshan Road, which consisted of a large room that opened up to the typical twelve by twelve foot courtyard, a much smaller room — just big enough for the boy's narrow beds and a small wardrobe — a storage area under the stairs, and a tiny cement-clad, cold-water bathroom with the standard, square cement japanese bathtub. In the dark of night and at the cost of a small fortune, according to Paul, he had an illegal toilet, a real W.C., installed. Vati sent four coolies and several buckets of paint over — no roller designs, please — to freshen up the place, and I helped the Levysohns move in at the end of April. At the same time, Max and Kurt announced they had taken a place in a nearby lane and would settle in as close to the deadline as possible. That left the Cohns and us to find rooms.

Once again we made our reluctant pilgrimage to Hongkew. Max of course had been right. Housing was at a premium and unscrupulous brokers — in this case mostly Russians — helped to vastly inflate rental prices. Mutti walked around with her handkerchief clutched against her mouth and nose as we trudged from lane to lane, looking at rooms that weren't big enough to accommodate a midget without luggage. Larger rooms that came with a water closet were not only few and far between, but were priced out of sight. Vati didn't know how he could make a living in the Designated Area, nor was he sure Mr. Yung would continue the painting business. What modest monies we had might have to last a long time and my father was hesitant to spend half of it on key money.

We made our house hunting trips to Hongkew three more times, spent hours walking back and forth through lanes and crowded streets. With each outing, Mutti became a little more depressed, and I realized how fortunate we had been to have lived in a pretty part of the city for a while.

On the fourth trip to Hongkew, we stopped at the Vienna Cafe for tea. We sat down at a small table next to one occupied by a nice-looking couple deeply engaged in conversation. Before we had our tea served, we overheard them saying that if only they could find decent, refined people of good background they would take "that space" in a minute. The price was certainly right, they nodded in agreement. It was apparent, that they too, were looking for quarters in Hongkew.

Curious, Vati turned to them and with a wicked smile on his face, stood up, and in a theatrical voice, he said:

"May I introduce myself and my family. My wife Irene, refined, my daughter Ursula, decent, and I am Martin Blomberg, good background — country estate and all that — also decent, looking for housing. How is that for a recommendation?"

With a grin, a twinkle and a grimace of embarrassment, the petite, dark-haired lady rose to her feet, did a half curtsy in front of my father and said, "We are the Lowenbergs, Manfred and I am Helene — fairy decent, I believe. We found a large room on the second floor of a row house, that has been divided into two rooms. We want to take the larger one. The drawback is that the dividing wall does not reach all the way up, and stops short of the ceiling by about two feet. So, we'd be fortunate to find people with whom to share our life. Fifty percent of privacy is gone." With a deep sigh, she described the other drawback. It was the bathroom, which was primitive, in other words, a honeypot, a sink, no tub, no hot water. What else was new?

The Lowenbergs joined us at our table — a scene reminiscent to that of our meeting with the Schillers at the Wayside Shelter on our first day in Shanghai. It turned out that our new acquaintances were a charming, witty and sincere couple — originally from Koeln (Cologne) in the Rheinland — who knew the Levysohns as well as our other friends, the Herrnstadts. Manfred and Helene had emigrated to Shanghai about the same time we did, accompanied by their only son and his Viennese wife. Hans Lowenberg conducted a large dance band in one of Shanghai's popular dance halls and his wife Martha, sang with the band.

I was all ears. Heinz and Wolf had taken me to a dance hall only recently. Chinese loved American dance music and built huge places, the size of a dozen tennis courts, to accommodate the enthusiastic crowds. The giant dance floors were lined with tables twenty deep which were attended to by an army of white-clad waiters. Clustering near the entrance to the dance floor, like a large bouquet of flowers, waited the official dance-hall girls who for the price of a ticket, purchased at the door, dipped and twirled, waltzed, foxtrotted and tangoed with the patrons who did not bring a date. The girls were well groomed, attractively dressed young ladies, mostly Chinese. The members of the big dance bands and their leaders usually were Filipinos. After paying a modest entrance fee, you chose a table, ordered a drink, and danced. The music was great, and the boys had taught me quite a few steps, a fact I conveniently forget to mention at home. Sometimes that was easier. Grownups could be so strange. I would find out where the young Lowenbergs performed. It would be great to know the artists.

My parents had listened closely to the Lowenbergs, looked at each other questioningly, gave a slight nod, and shortly, led by our new friends, headed out to inspect the room. The lane on Chusan Road appeared fairly clean that day, the house was a typical rowhouse — two rooms downstairs, two rooms on the second floor. The two downstairs rooms were rented, to what later turned out to be a noisy, sloppy Polish family with three, shrieky, quarrelsome little children. The bathroom — depressing with its dark grey cement walls and floors — was tucked under the staircase that led to our floor and on to the roof garden. (The latter had no kinship with the term "garden.") The staircase was open, and the bathroom ceiling was constructed from several window panes set in a wooden frame. Anyone on the upper staircase had only to glance down and become witness to bathroom activities in progress. Not a sight to seek.

The large upstairs room had been made into two rooms with the help of a plywood wall that did not reach the ceiling. The larger half was the one with the standard big window, the smaller part measured twelve by eleven feet and had only a little window that looked out at the open staircase that led to the roof. The view also included a view at the door to the still vacant small room, directly below the so-called roof garden. As it turned out, the Cohns would rent it the next day.

My parents decided to take the room. The Lowenbergs had found their decent, refined people with good background, and we had found a place before we ran out of time. One look at Mutti's face told the real story. We were right back where we had started off in Hongkew, and she was miserable. Her eyes had that dull, hushed look that robbed them of their life and broadcasted anguish and misery.

"How long can it last, Mutti?" I whispered. "we've done it before, we can do it again. I'm four years older now, and I can do a lot more. Remember what Vati said: nothing lasts forever." I pleaded with empty words, with a promise I couldn't fulfill — just more words. She looked at me with a forced smile, and shrugged her shoulders in a gesture of helpless resignation.

Unfortunately Mutti's withered sense of humor had left her too depressed for her to appreciate the scene that played out in the landlord's "sitting" room while we negotiated and dickered for reduced key money and a lower rent. For years, the recollection and the retelling of the event brought gales of laughter and tears into my father's eyes and mine. Actually, it was unbelievable, but it happened.

The landlord, a man of about forty or so, (profession unknown) lived in the adjoining house with enough family members to start a soccer team. Mr. Ling Lo, dressed in a traditional black long gown and a small round silk cap on his head, was seated in a grandiose high-back, ornately carved teakwood chair. Kids cluttered around the room, women walked in and out and gawked, while a scruffy cat paraded around proudly carrying a huge rat in its mouth. The house reeked of garlic, ginger, humans, fried tofu, and a heavy dose of a thickly sweet incense clouded the air. Throughout the "Hello" greeting period and the lively haggling, Mr. Ling lo remained seated. The bartering completed, he wrote some figures on a piece of paper and pushed it across the table to my father.

The agreement was brief: Key Money $ ... Rent $ ... Date ... You sign here ....

In fragmented English he explained the conditions of the rent payments ... "Long you pay, long you stay. I sign. You sign. Please. Thank you."

My father reached for his fountain pen to put his name to the simple rental agreement, void of legal prattle or fine print, just as Mr. Ling Lo emitted some strange and strangled noises. His hands gripped the handsome arm rests of his regal chair, his face turned taut and reddish. Suddenly, he let out a resounding grunt, followed by a deep sigh of satisfaction. His face relaxed and the room filled instantly with the unmistakable stink of human feces. It finally dawned on us, that the man sat on a commode — a chair containing a chamber pot — and was in the process of completing a human function usually conducted behind closed doors and without an audience. As if on cue, one of the women rushed to his side, handed him a wad of crumpled newspapers which he grabbed as he half rose from his throne to cleanse himself.

By then Mutti, her hand covering her nose and mouth, her eyes widened with shock and disgust, made a wild dash for the entrance and literally threw herself out the door. Father and I were transfixed, frozen to our chairs, wavering between fascination, disbelief and overwhelming repugnance. Then, I started to laugh and I couldn't stop. Vati at first shook with silent mirth, but finally broke lose and we both roared — none of which disturbed the man on his throne from completing what he set out to do. He paid no attention to our outburst; he knew that nakonings (foreigners) were strange!

His cleaning process accomplished, Mr. Ling Lo rearranged his clothes, rubbed his hands together, cracked a smile, pleased with himself, scrawled some picturesque characters on the agreement and applied his personal "chop" (seal) for authenticity to the paper.

Gingerly, between two fingers, Vati received the document, counted out the money under Ling Lo's eagle eye, and still trying to breathe through our mouths, we bowed our way out of the house. Before our hasty departure, we had agreed that we'd move in on the fifteenth of May, rent would begin that day. If I knew my Chinese people by then, Mr. Ling Lo would probably rent it out by the day until we appeared on the scene.

Outside, Mutti was standing in the middle of the lane, with tears running down her cheeks, looking at the two of us still laughing our heads off.

"What in the world was so funny?" she asked, choking back a sob. "This horrible, crude, filthy man was going to bathroom right in front of everybody … I … I … I have no words for that. I don't want to live this way."

Vati put his arms around her and tried to calm her down, which was difficult, because he was still chuckling, while trying in vain to convince her to see the humor of this impossible situation.

"Other lands, other customs," he tried to rationalize with her. She would have nothing to do with anything he proposed. "Let's just stop talking about it," she finally said, "I'm sure I'll forget about it — maybe in fifty years."

Back at the Place de Fleurs, we told the Cohns about the Lowenbergs and about that small room available at our new Chusan Road address. Vati and I had promised my mother not to mention the Mr. Ling Lo "incident" at any price. The very next day, our friends took off for Hongkew and upon their return reported that they indeed had rented the place.

"I'd rather live in a hole in the wall next door to you and Martin, than in a bigger place with strangers," Gerda hugged my mother and me. "From what we have seen, quarters are tight everywhere, especially in those houses where we can afford the rent," she continued. "We'll make it cozy." Cozy it would be, there was no doubt about that.

Gerda said she would hang her kitchen things on the outside wall at the bottom of the stairs — unprotected by a roof over head. Robert would put up several narrow shelves to store a few pots and dishes, and one for cooking on the charcoal stove. In reality the latter was just a large flowerpot with a grid in its middle to hold the coals — and, voila! a kitchen al fresco.

"Where will you cook when it rains?" I asked;

"I won't cook. We'll have a piece of bread and a cup of tea, or," she joked putting on airs, "we'll just dine out on pâté, caviar and hold the roast duckling for a sunny day." I told her that I hoped she would invite me along.

Mutti ignored our chatter and looked around our comfortable quarters, "I guess all we can take with us, is one couch. There isn't room for two. We'll take Ursula's cot, the wardrobe, the storage chest, the small round table and three chairs. Martin can trade my couch for one of those easy chairs that folds out into a narrow bed. I'll make these curtains smaller to fit the window and sew a cover for that box-like thing that squats next to the window." She was referring to the enclosed part of the lower staircase, that jutted into our small room and would serve as a spot for cooking.

In a monotone voice, she continued to discuss the dismantling of our small household and made plans for selling off everything that our Hongkew room couldn't hold. I had not seen her this despondent for a long, long time. She refused to respond to any cheerful remarks or attempts to lighten the load. I wished it was all done and over with. But, knowing my mother, I was certain that she would pull out of her dark mood, especially when one of us was down. She always came to our rescue, and in the process lost her own set of woes.

A week before our move, I had to tell the three sisters, that I would only be around for a few more days. As fate would have it, they were leaving for a month, taking the train to Nanking and Tsieng Tao to visit their families. The General had some important business up North and they would accompany him part of the way. That would give me time to settle in and find out what it would take to leave Hongkew. We had heard that passes would be issued for those who could produce proof of employment outside the District, but we didn't know any details yet. Nor did we know how long it would take to receive such a permit. I had prepared the necessary document and Anna saw to it that the General signed it and affixed his personal chop. According to some of the stories that Max had carried to us from Hongkew, a Japanese camp commander was in place, and it was rumored that his acts of chicanery were already in full bloom. We would have to wait and see.

In the meantime, Anna, Connie, Madeleine and I said farewell to each other. I was touched by their concern for our well being. First, Anna handed me a large envelope with my fee for the next six weeks, even though I wasn't going to work. Being "important," the General always paid me in American dollars, which I kept folded tightly in the false bottom of three Coty face powder boxes. Under the new Japanese occupation law it was illegal to possess U.S. currency, and if caught, one became subject to punishment and the dollars were confiscated. I cherished my nest egg, which had grown big enough to Mutti's delight to last for six months rent. Inflation was racing across China's fragile economy, and we exchanged American dollars for local currency only if we could use up the amount the same day. Dollars were worth more than their weight in gold, which, by the way, also was illegal to possess.

As the moment came to say goodbye to my friends, Anna's face clouded over and she became terribly serious when she addressed me.

"Dear, honored friend and teacher, you must promise us to send word if you need us. General Yi is an important man; he can help. He knows plenty important Japanese taipan from Tokyo. Maybe he can help your friends too. You come back to this house, you live here. When you can leave your place, you come back and teach us more English every day," Anna insisted. "And, we send Boy to let you know we have returned, and he find out how you are." Anna sighed deeply.

"Why you don't pay cumshaw to big Japanese officer. He let you stay in your house," Madeleine interrupted Anna. "All people take money. In Shanghai you can buy anything with plenty dollars, the General say."

None of the three young women, really understood the seriousness of the Jewish refugee situation. They did not understand the Hitler regime, the German-Italian-Japan alliance, the threats to our lives, the whole political mess, including the war that raged in Europe and in the Pacific. They believed we could have bribed our way into staying in the French Concession. Perhaps they were right. Bribery, cumshaw, was the way things were done in a lot of places in the world, and especially in China. Money talked. I knew a little about that from my wild and eccentric grandfather, the Old Baron, who, according to my mother, bribed the devil himself to buy his way into Heaven.

But this was different. I tried to explain to the girls that bribery was not unlike paying blackmail — once you started, there would be no end to it. You pay off one official, and he gets transferred. You pay the new one and, so it went. Another thing the girls didn't comprehend at all was money. General Yi was one of those wealthy Chinese with access to a river of gold that never ceased flowing. The sisters were fun girls, whose only concerns were to remain in favor with their benefactor and to keep themselves puffed, powdered and pretty. They were by no means stupid, but their interests were limited and their intellectual needs easily satisfied by reading poetry by Longfellow. Only since I had entered into their lives, had they learned a few things about the big world outside their world.

Madelaine handed me a small silk-wrapped bundle. "Is from us, for Dah Pietze (big nose)" she joked. "Is for your good luck, how win-chi. You must leave present wrapped in sacred silk to keep good luck inside, just for you. When you feel bad, you take it out, hold it in your hand, and make a wish to Kwan Yin. Good luck come to you. Now you look, please."

The bundle revealed a small, exquisite piece of rose quartz. It represented the Goddess of Mercy, Kwan-Yin, beautifully carved down to the last most miniscule detail. Wrapped separately in silver-threaded gossamer silk, there rested a large pendant, a replica of the Chinese character for good luck. An artist had captured the thick strokes of a fine calligrapher in rich gold and polished it to a high gloss.

"Each time you look," Connie chirped in, her voice thin and bird-like, "you have good luck. Sometimes, you just hold it and pray to Kwan Yin. She can make good luck come true for you." She added that the fabrics were the work of a special weaver in Peking, who wove sacred silks in the temple of the Thousand Sleeping Buddhas.

"All his silks are offered to Buddha for heavenly response. Weaver burns best incense to Kwan-Yin and sends special prayers while he weaves fine cloth. General Yi's family have a piece of cloth woven with pure gold threads. Very expensive," Connie purred, relishing the luxury of the thought.

I had written each of the sisters a "Thank-you" letter in my best handwriting, on some exquisite handmade silk and bamboo stationary, expressing my gratitude for their friendship and their generosity. I would miss them dearly, but I hoped to eventually be able to return to the House of Yi.

Anna clasped the three letters to her heart. "We keep your letters always, and we learn how to write nice words. We write to you, and send Boy with letters." It was all childlike fun and a new adventure for them. The sisters were truly still children, playful, loving and carefree. They were naive and innocent in ways that made me older than their combined years.

I took off before it all got too teary. I hadn't realized how much of my life in that year had played out around these young women, and how much I had learned from them. I marvelled at the unique relationship that had blossomed between three dainty Chinese concubines and one overgrown Jewish refugee — a teenage girl with a big nose.

The Shanghai Bund, 1939

Everyday traffic in downtown Shanghai

Transporting a load of lumber

One of Hongkew's Jewish refugee shelters

Our friendly water merchant

The outdoor barber shop

On the street ear-cleaning specialist

The learned village scribe

A Hongkew "read-on-the-spot" commercial lending library

Paper scavengers peeling off bits of
advertising posters

Selling individual strands of embroidery yarn,
walking on bound feet

A "Cotton Tail"

Portable 'fast-food" restaurant

Hongkew's "Fuller Brush Man"

Outdoor dining on a hot day

The outdoor "men's
room" for everybody

"The" Coca Cola sign at the sweet shop

The every-day
"Honey Pot"
Event

Chapter Nine

More of 1943
The Year of the Sheep

On moving day, Heinz and Wolf appeared promptly at eight o'clock as arranged. They were a breath of fresh air with their big grins as they jokingly flexed their muscles in mock anticipation of lifting tons of goods. My parents were glad to have our friends' help, and responded to their wonderfully funny ways with big chuckles, making life easier, at least for the moment. And we did as Vati always preached: "Enjoy the moment, it's all you have!" Plenty of sound wisdom, those clever words … but were words the remedy to everything?

In no time the creaky, old cart that Mr. Yung had rented for us along with two creaky, old coolies, was loaded with the few pieces of our household, which fitted into each other like a jigsaw puzzle. Roped-in for safety, the two coolies, accompanied by the two brothers riding in a rickshaw trotted off — Hongkew-bound. Obviously, we could not have let the coolies charge off on their own; we would have never seen our things again.

We said goodbye to Amah who was inconsolable at our leaving.

"So solly you go. Japanese bad. You need Amah. Amah move to Hongkew next week, and come to house take care Missy Cohn, take care Massa Selig, and take care you. Young missy, you no be bad, Amah come, take care you." If I knew anything about Amah, I knew she would keep her promise — or as Vati put it, she would keep her threat.

I looked at our empty "apartment" for moment, but before I could gather any maudlin thoughts, Mutti walked by me briskly, grabbed my arm, and pulled me out into the lane where Vati was already seated in a pedicab. All of a sudden she was a regular Miss Cheerful. "Let's go, avanti, avanti," she laughed, and waved her arms about.

"Never look back, or you'll get a stiff mind and a stiff neck. Something new is waiting for us, even if it's called Hongkew. Let us go!" She acted like the master of a wagon train I had seen in an American western film in a Shanghai movie house. All she needed was a horse, a hat, yell "Wagons, ho!" and she would have qualified. That display of bravado was quite a change from the woman so recently locked in depression.

The sun was already stinging our skin and the air was muggy and full of wet cotton. Our rickshaw slowly gathered speed as we rolled out of the area we had liked so much and which had given us a semblance of our old world, even if it was contained in one room instead of a spacious old manor house in the country. Vati and I planned to return to the city the next day and meet with Mr. Yung to work out things with him. My father wanted to have an idea of what to expect from the business when he was not able to do his part for a while. Mr. Yung had been true-blue in his relationship with my father, but people change. Time and circumstances often make different demands even on those with the best of intentions. We needed to talk. On my portable Swiss typewriter which I had bought with the first money I earned from General Yi, I prepared the official document as proof of my father's employment with The Shanghai Art Painting and Decorating Company. to which Mr. Yung had applied his signature and his chop. We'll see if it works.

On our way to the International Settlement, Mutti prattled on like a waterfall, chatting about this, and that and nothing. Vati was deep in thought, and I was trying to hold on to two sewing baskets, a pillowcase stuffed full with groceries and myself. A pedicab rickshaw was not the steadiest form of transportation, nor was it fast. We had a long way to go between our Place de Fleurs and Hongkew.

It wasn't just that the air was hot and oppressive, but the feeling and the mood of the city itself was heavy and apprehensive. What would happen next? How could one anticipate and prepare? The dun-colored figures of the Japanese occupation forces hovered like thick, yellow smoke over the streets. Shanghai felt like a naughty child trying to behave. The Bund was patrolled by several groups of Japanese soldiers, the ships in the harbor flew the white flag with the red sun. The absence of the familiar Star Spangled Banner and the comforting colors representing Great Britain left me sad and worried. I wondered what happened to "our" boys, my heroes of the Fifth Marine Corps. I wondered how my friends, the Langfords, the Sisters of Sacre Coeur, my other class mates were faring. I said a quick prayer for them. Oh, if wishes were horses that beggars might ride.

The Garden Bridge was now solely guarded by our conquerors; the British boys were long gone. A short, squat soldier stopped our rickshaw, asked for papers, scrutinized them for the longest time, and finally handed them back to us with a guttural grunt and a hiss through his gaping front teeth. Another one of Hirohito's best, just off the farm, but pretending to be able to read English. Face! Can't lose face!

Back in Hongkew nothing had changed. The street scene was made up of mangy dogs, defecating kids, and men urinating against walls. Mother kept her eyes trained on her lap, pretending — I didn't know what. We arrived at our lane on Chusan Road where the offensive stench of recently cleansed honey pots still lingered on the hot and sticky air. Out came Mutti's hanky and stayed there until we passed through the narrow door of our new home.

The Lowenbergs invited us to their room to wait until our things arrived. Their place was cozy and pleasant. Like my mother, Helene had the gift to make something out of nothing. I was learning!

After the second cup of tea, we heard the front door open, and a voice shouted up the stairs: "Anybody home? The moving van is here!"

"A moving van?" Elizabeth gasped. "You have a whole moving van full of things?"

Mother laughed out loud and assured our new neighbors that the "van" was actually a cart pulled by two coolies, and the voice belonged to Wolf Levysohn. The coolies hauled our things upstairs, were paid off, and in less than an hour our few belongings were in place. Mutti and I dressed up our room by tossing several pillows on the couch and the sleep chair, put up the curtains, hung three handsome prints on the wall, (there wasn't room for any more) rolled the Oriental rug over the shabby wooden floor, placed a floor lamp in a dark corner, a table lamp on the wooden box, and stored our three empty suitcases under Vati's couch. Done.

"Because of military necessity" we had to cut our already miniscule household possessions in half in order to fit into a twelve by eleven foot space, for which my parents had payed an exorbitant amount of "key" money. We had to move into an area of less than a square mile which, according to some sources, was already filled to bursting with more than 100,000 Chinese and Japanese citizens. Most of the Jewish refugees called the District a ghetto. I had always been under the impression that a ghetto contained Jews only and no one else. Well, whatever one called it, we were definitely confined to an area — military necessity or not.

Vati stretched out on the couch, Mutti sat in her new chair-bed when I announced that I was going to make a cup of tea. I set out cups and saucers, brought out a few of Mutti's butter cookies, and reached for the hot water kettle. Stop! Mrs. Lowenberg overheard our conversation, and across the open space sailed her advice.

"The hot water man is just across the street, take ten pennies with you and buy some bamboo tokens, so you have them around. One ladle of boiling water cost one token; be sure and check that the water is indeed boiling. Next door to the hot water man, is a shop where you can buy a charcoal stove and fuel. The wiring in this house is not very good and we only use a hot plate in emergencies. Besides our landlord charges dearly for the use of electricity. I start my charcoal stove outside on the steps that lead to the roof, and in good weather, I just cook there."

"Thank you, Helene," Mutti replied, interrupting the flow of information with a wicked smile on her face.

I sat down for a moment and looked at her and then pointed to the open space of the room divider.

"We're going to have to lower our voices, and watch our noises," I rhymed, trying to be funny. "This brings back our life with the Schillers. Remember how careful were were, and how thoughtful we had to be?"

Mutti just nodded, and said in a mid-size whisper, "I'm afraid this is going to be a little different, my dear. Just from the few moments I spent with Helene, I can tell you that she is one spoiled lady. I wouldn't expect too much thoughtfulness from her. Not because she is not nice, she's just occupied with herself." Mutti did have an uncanny instant insight into people and her assessment and predictions were usually right.

"Why did you agree to sharing a room with them?" I whispered back.

"First of all they are good people, secondly, we too have our faults, and lastly, we were running out of time. We had to get settled. If things change, or if it becomes unbearable and difficult, we'll move. You know how little we possess, and how quickly we can load and unload our few things. It's not that we're moving a twenty-room mansion."

I nodded, grabbed my mother's coin purse, picked up the water kettle and our net shopping bag and went out on the street.

Chusan Road was just another one of Hongkew's unattractive, rowhouse-lined streets, with adjoining open store fronts that made the block look like a gaping mouth without teeth. The shops, being part of the owner's living quarters were standard, had no doors, and were boarded up at night with heavy wooden shutters. On the sidewalks and in the gutters, kids played, dogs squatted, vendors haggled, beggars begged, barbers shaved, vendors cooked, people ate, men urinated, women gossiped — street life was in full bloom. I bought a clay charcoal stove, ten pounds of charcoal, two straw fans and went next door to the hot-water man.

The shop was shrouded in steam that rose in thick clouds from two huge iron cauldrons encased in a cement housing. An exposed opening in front of the vats revealed hot-glowing coals that kept the water boiling. Raised wooden planks ran the length of the space on which a tall man, topless, his chests and arms glistening with sweat, was dispensing hot water from a big copper dipper. One dip filled a large tea kettle and cost one penny. I purchased twenty-five tokens. The man looked like a pleasant soul, and in my ratty Shanghai dialect I told him we had just moved in across the street, and if his water was good, I would be around a lot.

A big grin crossed his face, he steepled his hands, bowed, wished me good luck and refused payment for my first purchase.

My chien-chien, (thank you) was gracefully accepted. I had made my first friend in the new neighborhood. I hurried across the street and back to our house, only to discover that Gerda and Robert Cohn had arrived with their few belongings and were trying to fit everything into the little room under the roof garden. We hadn't expected them until the next day.

Mutti made a pot of tea, and it was like old times, except our quarters had shrunk and our voices were turned on low. Our first day in the Designated Area was about to come to a close. When Mutti and Vati were settled in for the night, I stacked our three chairs on the small round table, wedged it in between the wardrobe and the short end of my father's couch, opened my cot and placed it at an angle into the room — as close to the wardrobe as I could get it. Every inch counted. It was only nine o'clock. The Lowenbergs were still up and eventually I fell asleep with Helene's soft voice reading poetry to her husband.

The next sounds I heard were the infernal dry rustlings of cockroaches skittering on the floor in our room and outside in the narrow hall, and the occasional sharp squeak of a rat scurrying on the stairs. In the semi-darkness of the night, lulled by a false sense of privacy, I drew my magic curtain against the troubled Now and returned to my cherished Yesterdays — gentle, harmonious and beautiful.

The soothing sounds and comforting images of home, ended abruptly, when I came awake to the low, guttural grunting shout that heralded the arrival of the honey-cart coolie, collecting the contents of the lane's honey pots. Helene had informed us the day before, that someone from the landlord's household would be cleaning out our "barrel of laughs" for a small monthly fee. Great! Blessings come in all shapes and forms. I remained in my bed until my parents woke up. I then turned away from them to give them a chance to get dressed.

After I folded up my cot, popped it in its designated corner and stored the bedding in the chest, I headed for the Levysohns. There was no sense in waiting for the use of the bathroom, the downstairs lady and her three children were having their morning session, all at the same time. I hoped they cleaned up after themselves. Otherwise, poor everybody! I could see a series of problems looming ahead, and I knew they would start over the use and misuse of the bathroom.

The Levysohns lived only a block and a half away rom us. That was great, or as Olga proclaimed in her funny Berlin/English accent: "It couldn't be betta." It took me no more than three minutes to get to their lane on Tongshan Road.

Built against one wall of the arched entrance — and taking up half the space of the first lane — sat a large box-like, rough-hewn wooden structure which contained a tiny you-name-it-we-have-it shop. Behind a barred window, not unlike a bank teller's cage, a Chinese woman sold cigarettes, matches, herbs, sewing threads and needles, small toys, chewing gum, pickled pigs feet, marbles, chopsticks, cobwebs, writing pens and brushes, ink, Chinese comic books, candied fruits, amulets against evil spirits, and several hundred strange and unidentifiable items. By its location alone — observing the coming and the going of people in and out of the lane — the little shop with its owner had the aura of a central information-communication station. I would have to improve my Chinese vocabulary before I could become privy to local gossip.

The lane was stinky and dirty — true to form. The garbage containers overflowed and the trash literally simmered and shimmered, and moved in the hot morning air as hordes of bluebottle flies soared and settled, swarmed and landed, feasting on the foul refuse of the lane's inhabitants.

At the last house in the third row of the lane, Olga greeted me in her chatty, up-beat, noisy way, put her arms around me and waltzed me into the big room.

"Voila," she announced, "it couldn't be betta!" Her irresistible enthusiasm, her genuine never-wavering cheerfulness were catching, and provided a soothing balm for ruffled souls. I admired the familiar setting of their quarters which had the same pleasant and comfortable atmosphere as their place at the Chi estate. One thing had been added to my great surprise, a tiny pump organ, its ivory and black keyboard gleaming against dark wood.

"It's no grand piano," Paul laughed, "but it plays true. I am certain Schubert, Beethoven and Mozart won't mind. And for me, it's almost heaven."

Paul stood about five-foot-two inches tall, "towered" over his wife by at two inches, but was a giant in heart and mind. Always dressed impeccably, he was a man of stature. Olga was quick on her feet, had an instant smile and a sunny disposition. Short, dark hair framed her pixie-like features; her big brown eyes were warm and mischievous. When I was through admiring the little organ, she grinned, and told how she had traded a curling iron and two heavy skillets for the Ersatz piano.

"I traded iron for ivory," she announced proudly, "and now we have music."

That pretty much described the needs of many of the Jewish refugees. Music, art and books where the inspiration to help them rise above their misery. By getting lost in the jubilant notes of a Beethoven symphony, dreaming with Schubert and Mendelsohn, living for a moment in the pages of literature, we fed on food for the spirit, even if food for the body was sparse. I had always thought that these things were simply the trimmings and knick-knacks that one "just had." I knew differently now. Fortunately for us, books were available for pennies, thanks to the Chinese casual practice of "pirating" foreign works without a thought to the rights of the publishers. What a country; every time we turned around, we discovered something new.

Loyal and totally dedicated to the the Levysohn family, Lee, their house boy of three years, had to take care of missy, and moved with them. He made his sleeping quarters under the stairs, and was as happy as a puppy that came in from the cold. His father was cook at the Austrian Embassy, and Lee had learned to make a mean Wiener Schnitzel and spoke English with an Austrian accent. He had helped with the move to Hongkew and had set up the "kitchen" at one of the two big windows that looked out on the standard, tiny courtyard. It was a "deluxe" arrangement — one hot plate, one charcoal pot, to which Olga laughingly referred as her "advanced two-burner model."

One thing was sure about the Levysohns, I would always find a generous serving of laughter, a cup of hot, spicy tea, a second helping of music, animated conversation and the best of company. And of course, there was Wolf. I had not changed my mind about him. I was going to marry him ... one day. Happy, dreamy thoughts! That would have to last for a long while.

Wolf and I took off to acquire a cat — not because I wanted a pet — but because we had to control the rat population. In Shanghai one didn't have to look far for a kitten. Short of throwing them way, killing them and dumping the newborn in the garbage, there was always a kid on the street trying to dispose of at least of one of the most recent litter to refugee customers. For a few coppers, I settled for a pitch-black kitten, with a short, zig-zig tail and stone-grey eyes, after having patiently listened to the young salesman's pitch:

"Missy, missy! Look-see! Cat no got flee, plenny clean, no sick; you see, catchee plenny lats." He kept rolling the fur back on the little fellow, to prove his kitten was flee-proof. To be on the safe side, I purchased some flee powder, stocked up on mosquito-repellent incense and a Japanese powder guaranteed to kill bedbugs and cockroaches. instantly, What a calling card for city life!

We walked the perimeter of the Designated Area to famil-iarize ourselves with the streets, and check out where our district ended. We didn't have far to go and soon ran into nasty looking barbed wire barricades which clearly marked our boundaries, each guarded by a pair of Japanese soldiers. Checkpoints had been estab-lished for overseeing the comings and goings of the refugees.

Off Tongshan Road, at the edge of our district, the local prison with its tall, shard-studded brick walls squatted like a mute and foreboding fortress. Across the way, was the big market where butchers, bakers, produce vendors, fish mongers and purveyors of the local delicacies, staples, dry goods, and most curious items displayed their wares. Scrawny chickens, tired, stringy cuts of pork and beef, long-necked ducks, pigs' bladders, hearts, lungs, and other innards still dripping blood, all dangled from hooks at shoppers' eye level. Between the flies on the meat, insects and bugs on the vegetables, mangy dogs and scab-covered kids begging for scraps, and the handling of food by dirt-stained hands, it was easy to loose one's appetite.

American canned goods were available at exorbitant prices and made a rich and tempting display. One can of sliced pineapple, to use my mother's cost-comparison method, equaled one month rent. The purchase of one pound of Maxwell House coffee would have blown the budget for the duration.

Pedestrian traffic on the streets was brisk and the array of merchandise was astonishing. The line-up of street vendors had grown since Jewish refugees joined the locals, and from their propped-up suitcases offered everything from European clothing, thin blankets, to odd pieces of crystal, porcelain and table linens, to underwear, someone's bridal gown, curtains, velvet pillows, to prayer shawls. Everything was saleable, every scrap had value, every bent nail brought a price.

From a half-naked street urchin I bought a handful of flowers for Mutti. I learned quickly not to do that again. I discovered that these little con-artists simply plucked the blossoms from the thick stem of a hollyhock, affixed them one at a time to a toothpick and stuck them on some greenery. Needless to say, not connected to moisture, these colorful flowers wilted away in no time. Little thieves!

The early summer heat was oppressive. The street odors were overpowering as thin streams of urine slowly dried on the hot pavement, peanut oil sizzled and the greasy smell of frying tofu cakes and fish mingled with all the other cooking smells. A girl, perhaps nine or ten years old, naked except for a tattered strip of grayish cloth around her middle, was vigorously pulling scraps of paper — remnants of weathered, peeling advertising posters — from a wall, and tucked them into her basket. As she reached high above her head, the rag on her waist rose with her stretch and exposed her bare bottom. A piece of stained cotton wadding protruded from the middle of the child's rear, which was her way of stopping the constant trickles of diarrhea from running down her legs. There were many children like her walking around in that pitiful condition. The refugees had named them "cotton tails." What a world!

I had a lot to think about. A lot of things worried me. I needed time to myself. It would have to wait until bedtime, when the darkness pulled its covers over the world around me, and I could pretend to be alone.

Chapter Ten

December 1943
The Year of the Sheep

W e've been in Hongkew for seven months, and much has happened. I named the black, little kitten Piezek, and I didn't know why. I liked the sound of it, and so did he. He grew up to be quite the hunter and did his share daily to reduce our lane's rat population. Mutti hated going out on the street during the day, so Vati and I did our shopping — what there was of it. Inflation was outrunning itself, but due to lack of proper storage and cooling, we could only buy what we needed for the day. If stored more than a few days, rice and flour became infested with insects, sugar turned into a moist, gray mass, bread and baked goods mildewed and everything else rotted away.

Good news: Amah found us, and true to her promise, piled in with some family members in Hongkew, (which wasn't difficult for her) and split her time between our postage-stamp size room, the Cohns and our two bachelors. Nothing made Amah happier than to boss me around, impart her wisdom, while I played her willing victim. Her favorite subject was my future husband "He mo betta be savvy and plenty lich; no wantchee old men, too tired, no fun. You catchee Amelican man, plenty lich, plenty land."

I agreed and she smiled content to have made her point. But when I once asked her how come she had no husband, she let fly with the longest speech ever, and left no doubt in my mind about her real feelings for the opposite sex.

"Amah have husband befo'. He no good. He no work much. All he do makee jig-jig, play mahjong, loose money, smoke pipe. He no good. He go sing-song girl house. He beat Amah. He...." On and on she went repeating herself in her most colorful and descriptive way.

Amah insisted on going to market with me which turned out to be a lesson each time for which I was grateful. She knew her way around and taught me a few tricks. She haggled until she got her way, or else, she walked. She pinched and tweaked, she smelled and punched, she checked the scales, she scolded and complained, and she drove even the sturdiest bargainers to defeat. She made sure I would follow her example. I did.

☯   ☯   ☯

In our new location, I made a new friends, and I lost a friend. I met new teachers, among them an Oxford-educated Buddhist priest; I saw a lot of Wolf and the Levysohns, took jujitsu lessons and in between all the misery, I managed to have a good time. But first things first.

Mr. Yung's father died and he had to go to Chungking to help run the family business. The Shanghai Art Painting and Decorating Company ceased to operate, except for the few jobs in progress, and the occasional painting contract my father was able to obtain and complete. Getting permission to leave the Designated Area wasn't all that easy.

The Japanese occupation forces appointed two dedicated men as "camp commanders." One was the calculating and dangerous Okuro-san, and his counter part was the slightly mad and only mildly dangerous Goya-san. Barely five feet tall, the latter referred to himself as the King of the Jews, which gave him the right to torment them. He had some misconceived ideas of being a concert violinist; forced refugees to accompany him on the piano as he tweaked and squeaked his violin, and was often seen strolling the streets, playing his renditions of Schubert, Mendelsohn or Mozart.

The man was a study in unbridled delusions of grandeur, enhanced by his fondness for petty cruelties.

The Japanese military government had contrived a method with which to control the comings and goings of those refugees who had proof (made-up or real) of employment outside the Designated Area. This control consisted of a blue or pink permit and matching circular pin the size of a nickel, engraved with the Japanese character for "Jew" — the latter to be worn in plain sight on one's clothing upon leaving the district. The blue pass was good for one month, the pink one for a week. Printed on the back of this identification was a rough map of Shanghai, and marked with crosses was the shortest, most direct route its bearer had to take to work and back. Also indicated next to the map, were the hours its owner was permitted to be absent from Hongkew.

Random Japanese controls checked foreigners on the streets of the occupied International Settlement and the Concession Française with great regularity. If a refugee neglected to wear his pin and had no other ID to offer than his pink or blue card — that spelled trouble. If caught on a street not indicated in the prescribed route — more trouble. Even a brief twenty-four-hour stay at the infamous Bridge Prison was one more exercise in human misery that one could readily do without.

Obtaining a pass was another story. Hundreds of refugees lined up outside the building that housed the Japanese administration where Okuro and Goya sat on their thrones. We stood for hours, for days and as long as a week in the broiling summer sun or the bone-chilling winter mist, waiting for our turn to see our honorable camp commander. The first time I faced the mighty Goya-san to apply for a pass after spending eleven hours in line, he perused my papers at great length, looked up at me, hissed a few Japanese words through his front teeth — beads of spittle settling at the corners of his mouth — and then yelled in his heavily accented English, "No pass for you. You are a dirty girl. You make dirty love to dirty men. You are very dirty." He slammed down a wooden ruler on his desk, and pointed to the door, his face taught and furious.

Astonished by his idiotic remarks, I had a hard time containing my laughter. After all, I had been called names by Nazi experts. But I was annoyed by the obvious practice of psychotic bullying, and went right back in line. By then I had met some of the people who waited patiently with me, heard their stories, and was touched by the raw fear some of the men expressed at the prospect of having to face our crazy camp commander. Why wouldn't they be terrified? These men were bruised and scarred, and their memories were alive with the indignities, cruelties and acts of brutality they had suffered at the hands of the Gestapo's SS and other assorted Nazi bullies. These men had a deep distrust and instinctive fear of dictators and tyrants. They were terribly afraid.

I remembered Fraulein Amanda's lecture to me on fear:"Fear is a terrible thing; it robs you of your own power, it weakens your beliefs that good things can happen and it feeds the evil in your enemies. Never, never act from fear," she advised, "you'll lose every time."

But our fear was real, and none of us standing in line had good memories when it came to being dealt with as a Jew.

Two days later, I stood again in front of the desk of the ridiculous Goya-san. During the long hours of waiting, I had turned my mind back, way back, to the beautiful pictures and grand moments of the past that occupied my nights. I was full of good things when my turn came. The magic must have worked. The "King of the Jews" barely looked at me, gave a cursory glance at my papers, and in a few moments, I had my blue pass, the offensive identifying button and all. Sayonara, Goya-san!

The three sisters had sent word to me that they had returned from their trip north and were anxious for me to pick up where we had left off. The reunion was wonderful. We played and hugged, and laughed, and talked on and on. Happiness lasted for six more weeks, when they tearfully informed me that General Yi's very important business required him to take up permanent residence in Nanking immediately. They were to leave within the week. In order not to go through another teary parting scene, I simply skipped the last two sessions with them. I sent a note with Lee, saying my farewell on paper. It was easier. That was the end. I never saw them again.

It had been a unique time for me, and I knew it had been fun for them as well. I gained much insight into Chinese traditions, the

Oriental mind, and learned some practical wisdoms. The pretty pages of Fraulein Amanda's book on China had come to life for a short while. My gratitude and the memories live on.

I kept renewing my pass several times more with Goya-san — witnessing only occasional outbursts of madness by the king — so that I could accompany my father on his excursions outside the district. I will never forget the time I stood in line behind Vati waiting for our turn to see our camp commander for pass extensions. It was winter, and a fine curtain of moisture eventually soaked us to the skin and chilled our bones as the hours dragged on before we made it into the front door of the building. Tall and straight, Vati stood before Goya. Suddenly the little man popped out of his chair, ape-like, he jumped onto his desk and proceeded to hit my father on the head with a wooden ruler. It was a ridiculous scene. Suddenly, Vati grabbed the descending ruler and stopped the next blow dead in its tracks. The ruler clattered onto the desk.

"No! No more!" Vati said in a low voice, never taking his eyes off Goya-san who slowly lowered his arm. Surprise and shock registered on his flat features. The room became as silent as a tomb. The people in line behind us barely breathed, and I could smell the fear in the air. Someone emptied his bowels into his pants. Between awe and fear, I stood stone-still. Why did one always anticipate the worst?

But nothing happened. Taken aback, surprise registering on his his face, Goya slowly slid back into his chair, and without looking at my father, started to ramble about...."Jews ... they don't know how good I am. I am their solution, I am their king...."

He stamped my father's papers without looking up, and with a vicious gesture, he brought down the stamp on mine, and the next, and the next in rapid succession. The line had never moved so fast. My father's face bore a faint grin for the rest of the day. He winked at me as he said, "This time it worked. I think I took him by surprise. But I wouldn't try it again soon," he confessed.

My hero! We didn't tell Mutti. The incident was sure to make the rounds among the refugees and she would hear it eventually — whatever the version. My heart was still with that poor man whose fear had soiled his pants. He must have been mortified, embarrassed and ashamed. Fear was the enemy.

Wolf's brother, Heinz, was beaming when he introduced his new girlfriend to us. How exciting! Her name was Margo Hausmann. She was a nineteen-year-old beauty, and a senior member of the corps de ballet at Ballet Russe in Shanghai. That was so glamorous, so romantic. A ballerina in our midst; how different! Her thick, copper hair was pulled back tightly from a lovely, sensitive face that was dominated by expressive dark eyes, finely arched brows and high cheekbones. Originally from Berlin, she lived with her parents just one block down on Tongshan Road in yet another lane. Everybody fell in love with her warm smile and her shy and gentle ways.

Margo and I had a great deal in common. We were each an only child, and our parents depended on us for a lot of things. However, she confessed that her mother was a rather difficult and demanding woman who complained bitterly about their fate, and blamed her husband daily for not having done better — in every way. There was little laughter and harmony in Margo's life, and the "house of Levysohn" gave her the kind of joyful camaraderie and caring she never had at home.

Depending on the season, Margo rehearsed during the day and danced several nights a week. Heinz met her at the edge of the district, where she arrived on the streetcar after an evening performance. Sometimes Wolf and I went along, and we either stopped at the Vienna Cafe if we were flush, or ended up at the Levysohns where we sat around the big table drinking tea. We never went to Margo's house. Her mother was not pleased with Heinz, nor did she like Wolf and me. She had bigger plans for her daughter, Margo confessed. She wanted her daughter to associate with moneyed people — some wealthy Arab or Persian, a merchant, or better yet, an Egyptian prince perhaps. Anybody with money.

My other new friend was Eva Ruben, who lived with her parents a few houses down from us. Eva's father had spent several terrifying weeks at Dachau, and the three of them had made it out of Dresden just a week before World War II broke out. Eva was seventeen and worked a few hours a day in a cafe; her mother had a job in a bakery, and her father joined the ranks of "China traders."

Like most of us, the Rubens barely made ends meet, and a big chunk of their earnings went for the rent. We all paid a heavy price for not living in a Heime.

Eva was a slim, petite brunette beauty whose thick hair with its golden highlights framed a piquant face with a full mouth and curious, amber eyes. Her family who had been successful spice merchants in Austria, were self-involved, removed from the Oriental world they abhorred, and had no idea what to do with a child. Until emigration, Eva had been raised by nannies and governesses, and usually was given what she wanted.

She was a lively sort with a quick sense of humor, and more mischief in her soul than was good for her. I loved being around her, and together we laughed and giggled at the most impossible possibilities. Eva was extremely clever with her hands. She knitted, embroidered and sewed, all of which she did with great imagination and deliberate care for detail. Mutti had taken up her sewing activities again, and often paid Eva to do some of the fine hand-finishing work.

Eva and I spent a lot of time together, trying to act our age, but somehow our "age" had been lost along the way. We didn't know how to behave like carefree teenagers. The demands life made on us robbed us of those young and carefree years, and we acted just like all the adults around us — worried, fearful and concerned with daily events and a veiled, uncertain future.

Our conversation invariably turned to Hongkew, the war, the Japanese and speculations of what the future might hold. We did not have those "young adult" years of normal proportions. We were not allowed the luxury of groping for maturity and "grown-up" attitudes and responses to crisis were expected of us. There were no holidays, no special events, no vacations by the sea or in the mountains; no school dances, no sports, no games. We had to entertain ourselves; and the best entertainment were books and people. We grew up with grownups; we grew up old, and whether we liked it or not, we learned from them.

We didn't play with our cats out of fear of catching a terrible disease they might have brought home from hunting rats. And we played the same games as the Chinese children. We too, caught cockroaches, put them on a string, drew a "start" line with a piece of chalk on the dirty pavement, and "raced" them to a chalk-line finish. If some kid didn't like the way one of the "racers" behaved, he just stomped on the offending cockroach. So what! There were more where they came from.

The biggest treat we could think of in our circumstances, was to have enough money on any given afternoon for a cup of tea and a pastry at Vienna Cafe. Eva, Margo and I often pooled our "spending" money, carefully and figured out if this was the day to go out for tea. If not, we'd try again another time. Life may have been extraordinarily difficult, but at the same time, it was quite simple. We were learning to take what the day offered, and for the unattainable, there were always the dreams.

                    ❧   ❧   ❧

The war was in its fourth year. Europe was burning. England was heavily bruised but alive. Ever since February, when the news reached us that Germany's Sixth Army had surrendered at Stalingrad, Max was beside himself with joy, and literally bounced up and down like a kid at Christmas.

"I knew it! I knew it! Just like Napoleon. It's a good thing for the world that Hitler didn't take history seriously. This is the turning point of the war," he exclaimed, over and over again. He was right.

With every reported advance by the Allied forces, our spirits rose, and hope blossomed anew in the dingy lanes of rowhouses in the Designated Area. Even though Japanese broadcasters proclaimed victory in the Pacific daily, and assured their listeners that America's Seventh Fleet had been sunk once again, we knew differently. We celebrated a bit here and there, and we prayed for an end to this global insanity.

In Spring news reached us of the uprising and eventual liquidation of the Warsaw Ghetto. We had no idea how many Jews perished, and in our wildest dreams could not imagine the horror, the tragedy and the devastation the Warsaw Ghetto Jews experienced. On the other hand, we were plagued by constant rumors that the local SS planned to get rid of the Shanghai Jews. I could only think of Mutti's theory that behind every rumor was a truth. Hitler's arm was long and indeed reached far.

"What a century we live in," Mutti mourned. "What a complete failure for humanity. We've moved back into the Middle Ages."

Even though there were moments were we had a vague inkling that our suffering was more like a large dose of discomfort compared to what was going on in Europe, it was human nature to respond to what we experienced routinely. People were hungry, people were ill and despondent. We were soaked through and through with sweat in the humid, life-draining days and sleepless nights of summer. We were tormented by mosquitoes, bedbugs and cockroaches; rats came up from the city's foul sewers spreading disease. Equally hard were the wet and cold winters and the lack of adequate heating and clothing. Refugees had sold their heavy European garments for food, and many could be seen walking the wintry streets wrapped in threadbare blankets.

Many mornings after a freezing night, the pitiful remnants of a pitiful existence lay lifeless in front of some merchant's tightly shuttered doorway. As soon as the dead body of the rags-clad corpse was discovered by the shop's owner who did not want to be responsible for the cost and trouble of a burial as demanded by tradition, he rolled the body over to his neighbor, who rolled the unwanted dead over to his neighbor. And, on and on — like a piece of trash carried away by a determined wind — the last remains of a life were rolled down the street until the poor corpse reached the corner and dropped into the gutter. After all, it was Buddha's will. Eventually a cart from the local "Blue Cross" picked up the bodies and wheeled them to wherever they were to be buried. Sometimes corpses were piled so high on a narrow cart, that the coolie pushing it couldn't see where he was going. Life was cheap. So much for local color. The Jews in the Hongkew Designated Area faced their own battles.

The Japanese occupation forces were not raised in a Swiss finishing school, and directed their rowdy and rough behavior at their foreign captives. Never having been fond of Caucasians to begin with, these soldiers gave free rein to their antipathies. House searches increased; properties were destroyed and people were terrorized, their fragile minds ready to crack. Why did people treat each other like that? I asked my friends, I asked Paul, I asked my parents. Shoulders shrugged, eyes clouded over, heads shook. No answers.

A multitude of problems had to be faced every day. Like the head of Medusa, no matter how many problems were eliminated, a whole set of new ones waited to be born. People's health demanded attention, babies had to be delivered and cared for, surgery was needed, and special care for our elders begged for attention. Dietary requirements for individuals went unfilled, teeth remained unrepaired and rotted. Even with enough dentists around, the shortage of instruments and medical supplies, restricted treatment to emergencies only, and made practicing medicine a joke. Doctors treated their patients with methods that were carryovers from the Middle Ages. No matter how skilled our physicians, how eager to help, how dedicated to humanity, without tools, their skills failed.

Poor diets, a horrible climate, deplorable sanitary conditions all contributed to our intestinal problems. A daily greeting between our people usually included a concerned: "and how many times did you go ... yesterday ... today?"

Paul observed correctly that we had all become "stomach and gut" — the first was growling and empty, the latter growling and running. As almost constant bouts with diarrhea weakened our whole system, other problems evolved. My mother had been diagnosed with "sprue" — a tropical intestinal disorder — that she had treated successfully with a prescribed Swiss medication. But the scarcity of the product and the galloping inflation raised the cost of daily dosages beyond our reach. What would happen to her? How long could she live without medication? How many more like her faced the same problem? Another enemy was amoebic dysentery — a nasty condition that required drugs that were as scarce as hen's teeth. People died.

The constant struggle to secure financial support for our pitiful community never ceased. Jewish leaders sought relief from local sources, the International Red Cross, and Jewish relief organizations in America. Max and Joseph were involved with community activities and knew what was going on. When we met at the Schiller's place, the two men talked about nothing else.

"Conditions are getting worse," Max stated, "people are hungry, they are sick, they live in hopeless despair. It's been going on for more than four and a half years; the years carry the load, and the load is getting too much."

"Yet we have some restaurants, there is theatre, there's music. We even have an occasional opera," Lucy interjected. "A lot of people manage to earn a living. Some of the people who are so badly off here, were welfare cases in their own home towns. Some of us had enough get-up-and-go to look for a way to make a living."

The debate heated up and lasted the rest of the afternoon. Nothing was solved, but just being together in friendship gave substance to our lives.

Life at home was difficult as well. Our number one problem was the sorry affair that called itself a "bathroom." Three children and nine adults occupied the house and had to take turns in some fashion to use the facilities. My parents and I made the least demand on the cement cave. We had been cordially invited to visit the Levysohns delux W.C. whenever we were in the neighborhood. This may not sound like much, but it was the gift of gifts.

"I can't wait to have a marble bath and matching W.C.," Vati joked. "we could invite the Levysohns to share our luxurious setting and repay them for their hospitality," his face broke out in a boyish grin.

"How low we've sunk!" Mutti laughingly joined in. "Never mind coming for high tea — but come use our bathroom!"

But of course there were the middle-of-the-night emergencies, the hasty retreats to the biffy during the day, not to mention the getting ready for the day. We tried schedules, we tried as-you-go, we tried it all. Nothing ever worked. One "honeypot" barely addressed the daily deposits of twelve people. Carelessness on the children's part and unbridled sloppiness practiced by their parents made the situation unbearable. Insults flew as freely as crows in a wheat field. Mutti tried to be the peacemaker, but couldn't change the situation. To add to the existing difficulties, Gerda accidentally dropped a heavy pot lid onto the glass roof of the bathroom during one of her cooking sessions, and shattered three panes to smithereens. The landlord promised to replace it ... tomollow. But tomollow never came. However, the rains did come, and we went to the bathroom with an umbrella. Next!

What with our room divider not reaching the ceiling, it quickly made for familiarity — the kind that bred contempt. No matter how nice the Lowenbergs were, no matter how friendly and social and how much fun, their intimate habits could not be retained behind their own three-and-three-quarters walls, but overflowed into our lives. At the same time, our close neighbors were witness to our sounds and sighs. Mutti, the most thoughtful and considerate person on earth, made my father and me toe the line of silence. The forefinger of her right hand was forever pressed against her closed lips, her eyes pleading to lower our voices, quell our laughter or refrain from clanking around in general. (At least we didn't use a chamber pot, like … you know who!) Next.

Cooking presented another problem. I usually started the charcoal fire in our oversize flower pot in mid-morning, and kept fanning the coals to get them hot. Mutti and I took turns squatting Chinese-fashion on our haunches, fanning the coals to keep the food cooking. Careful, or not, with clock-like regularity we passed out from inhaling the fumes of the burning charcoal. First, a heavy, lazy-like dizziness would slowly spread over us from head to toe, and soon we lost consciousness. We were out for several minutes. Revived by a hefty whiff of ammonia, we resumed our cooking chores — only to pass out again. Our meals consisted of rice, or potatoes, a vegetable stew with strange transparent noodles, or a thick soup. Once a week we had a few ounces of meat, and ever since Mutti made peace with some of the local fish, seafood (maybe just riverfood) made it to our table.

Endlessly, we rinsed the rice to remove all those little bugs that invaded our meager supply. In an attempt to eliminate all traces of the human fertilizer the farmers used in their fields, we scrubbed the vegetables and potatoes in permanganate until our hands turned purple. Mutti was a good cook and managed to make the plainest dish tasty and appetizing. As soon as our meal was done, she wrapped the pot in a blanket and placed it into the storage chest that held our bedding. It kept our dinner warm, but our sheets and blankets no longer were fragrant with a hint of lavender sachet — they smelled more like cabbage and steamed rice. I didn't bother to learn how to cook. I swore I would never, ever, cross-my-heart-and-hope-to-die eat any of that food again. Ever!

No matter how sparse the meal, Mutti set the table with a treasured piece of white linen, which she hand washed weekly. With a clumsy, black-as-night iron, equipped with a thick, wooden handle, its belly filled with glowing hot coals, she pressed the linens silky smooth, often leaving her with nasty burns from exploding bits of coals that landed on her arms and hands. She cut two large damask napkins — which had mysteriously escaped with us — in to four equal squares, and patiently hand-hemmed them with tiny, even stitches to increase our supply of napery. Bits of tough, weedy greenery that grew in the plaster cracks below our window, or leaves from a bamboo plant that poked a few slim shoots through a fence on the street, were carefully plucked to share a small crystal vase with two slightly faded, pink silk roses rescued from a long-forgotten ball gown. Mother insisted that food tasted better when the table looked pretty. And we needed a lot of "pretty" to face daily the tired menu of yesterday and the day before.

My mother was truly the center of our world. With her never-flinching approach to life's struggles, and her unbeatable combination of strength and Jewish resignation, she mended our brittle souls with great regularity. She kept a tight rein on our fears and apprehensions and talked of ... when we go to America ... when we ... when this is over ... when ... when ... all will be well. Like my father, she did not believe that complaining changed our predicament, but would only dig us deeper into the black hole of our despair.

She never let up on her display of good manners, and tenaciously held on to traditions — fragmented and incomplete as they may have been. They were the disciplines and reliable customs upon which our lives had been given substance, and she knew how important a sense of continuity was to everyone. She took apart the last of her two evening gowns that had made the journey with her, and turned them into more common garments — underwear for Vati, blouses, slips and nightgowns, table clothes and napkins. All of these things Mutti sewed by hand, while my father was out and about scrounging for "opportunities," which translated into a piece of German sausage, a pound or two of moldy rice, or even two ounces of grey, wet sugar.

By the end of 1943, Vati was no longer contracting for paint jobs. He did what a lot of others did, he traded goods — all kinds of goods, ranging from salami to soap. He knew several people outside the district who liked him, and who bought "things" from him. Brokering goods was a fascinating operation in Shanghai and went something like this:

Father knew a man, who knew a man, who knew a man, who had ten cases of flints to sell. Father now had the "goods." He then went to a man, who knew a man, who knew a man, who knew several men ... who wanted to buy ten cases of flints. The deal was consummated. My father never met the seller or the buyer, nor did he actually confirm the existence of the ten cases of flints. Six people shared the commission, with the one who instigated the activity getting the lion's share. These transactions took time — Oriental time — and were few and far between. But somehow we managed to keep going.

Vati rarely lost his sense of humor nor his "social" soul, which found expression by the way people were drawn to him — they just loved him. To the little Chinese children he was that lanky, laughing nakoning who always had a tiny bit of candy or a few pennies to distribute among them. He laughed with them, made funny faces, skipped and two-stepped on the trash-littered sidewalks to their great delight. From him I learned that adversity loses its power when met with divine indifference and lots of laughter.

"It's alright to act a bit of a fool," Vati explained, "just as long as you know you're only fooling yourself." Simple, simple man with a heart full of gold and wisdom.

I did some work at one of the refugee shelters, continued my jujitsu lessons, helped a lady with her book work, and occasionally volunteered my time at the hospital. The latter was not for me. I bled along with the patients, couldn't stand the sight of wounds and threw up a lot. I finally ended up keeping order in the meagerly-stocked supply room and the linen closets.

Around the first week in December, I started to have terrifying dreams. In the dark of night, behind my closed eyes, I saw endless masses of grey and colorless people crowded closely against each other in a place without walls. Their upturned faces were contorted into masks of fear, their big hollow eyes were pools from hell. From their open mouths emerged howlings of such gut-wrenching terror that I came awake to my own silent screams that took away my breath. Tears cascaded down my face as I struggled to erase the nightmare. I wondered who these

people were, and why they came to me at night — night after
night. Masses, thousands of faces I didn't know, faces that
changed with each dream but never lost their look of having seen
Armageddon. How much longer would these dreams last? I
wanted to go back to Marienhall, to my yesterday-world of
gardens and sun-lit ponds, of torch-bearing chestnut trees, of
flower fairies and gentle breezes, of magic frogs, furry kittens and
rainbows. Even dreaming became difficult. The images lost their
brilliance and their promise. My picture book turned grey and flat.
Fortunately I had my friends.

Gathering at the Levysohns occurred almost daily, and
became part of my life. Margo and Heinz were seeing a lot of each
other, but never speculated on the future. We were simply young
people with unspoken plans — the present was too volatile, too
demanding and the future was light years away. The future would
have to wait.

Paul had kept his job with the Swiss Chemical Company, and
employed Heinz as his assistant. Wolf worked in the firm's caffeine
factory. In spite of the money the three men earned, inflation
reduced their incomes to less than half the value before they could
bring their earnings home.

Spending money on "fun" things was out of the question. We
spent our free time visiting with friends in their tiny quarters, but
most often we just stayed at home. Paul and Olga thrived at having
young people around, "The more the merrier," Olga insisted. She
had a baking-form gadget for producing simple pound cakes on her
charcoal stove, experimented with all kinds of toppings and icings
which she proudly offered our grateful gang. Mutti was glad I had
found friends I enjoyed, but Vati wasn't thrilled about my serious
thoughts about Wolf. I suppose he had other plans for me — most
parents do.

Max and Kurt often joined our group in the evening and
brought with them the latest news and stimulating conversations.
They always managed to bring a few cookies, a bag of peanuts or
sack full of sweet, sticky dried fruit. Olga made countless cups of
tea and we were off and talking up a storm. The war — facts,
rumors and gossip, true or false — was at the center of our interest.
Next conditions in our Designated Area came under discussion, and

always hovering at the edge of "truth" were the rumors of SS activities directed at the fate of the Shanghai Jews.

"What could 'they' do? How can 'they' get rid of 18,000 people? We would fight back," Wolf protested.

"Fight back with what," Max challenged. "With a night stick from the Pao Chia?" Max referred to the auxiliary police with limited authority that more than three thousand refugees were forced to join. Every member served a few hours a week, which was not an unwelcome form of self protection for our people in the District. Needless to say, our Pao Chia were under close scrutiny by Japanese and hired Russian police, who came down hard on anyone who failed to report on irregularities, or neglected to turn in the offender. Outfitted with an armband and a night stick, Pao Chia members patrolled the streets and lanes of our Designated Area. Most of our friends pulled their share of policing duties.

Kurt was still in charge of entertainment. He knew what play was in production, what music could be heard where, and how much was admission. Both he and Max confessed to missing the days at Place des Fleurs, and visited us as often as they could catch us. We were so fortunate to have these wonderful people in our lives. I came to realize that life was not about events, life was about people. I have learned to treasure friendships and to recognize what it takes to be a good friend. Then came a brief opportunity for me to meet more people of great thoughts, strong ideals and a passion to pass on their knowledge.

For a short while a small empty godown (warehouse) served as a twenty-four-hour come-and-go-as-you-want schoolroom where never less than ten subjects were being taught and discussed at the same time. There were no chairs or desks. There were no charts, no maps, no blackboards, no textbooks. We brought along a pillow to escape the hard, cracked cement floor as we sat at our teachers' feet. We listened for as long as we wanted — or as long as he lasted — to his subject of choice. A Napoleon aficionado talked about French history; a former throat surgeon explained his trade, and shared his passion for the music and history of Beethoven and Bach with his audience. A Russian history buff, a devoted Anglophile, a master of mathematics, chemistry or biology, all held court in their fields of interest. An engineer expounded on bridge-building, Shakespeare and other literary greats. One never knew who would be there the next day, and for a few heavenly weeks I spent every waking hour in the company of these volunteer teachers. I knew, I would never get enough. In those few weeks, we learned more than a structured university classroom could offer in a year.

The godown was sold, and once again filled with goods. "Most probably ammunition," Max suggested. "Not good." Well, what else was good.

In the meantime, to Amah's delight I had completed my course in jujitsu. "Young Missy now plenny strong, plenny quick; makee chop-chop with bad men."

Although Mutti made all sorts of noises that "roughhousing was not for a young lady," I knew she was secretly relieved that I had learned to defend myself — not that I would ever need it. Or so she thought.

Amah still popped in several times a week, even if there was little to do, and less money to pay her. But she had an answer for everything. "You no wolly pay Amah. Bamby young Missy mally lich man, Amah come live with young Missy all-time. Young Missy have plenny dollah; Amah no wolly."

Always spotlessly clean herself, smelling of fresh jasmine soap, green tea and incense, she was a treasure beyond measure. She was all life. She was loaded with mischief, full of ancestral myths, ancient beliefs, silly superstitions, local logic and loyal friendship. Amah taught me a lot.

Among a few friends, we shared an edition of Shakespeare's plays, selected one to perform, picked a part, took turns reading and memorizing our roles, and put on a performance at the Levysohns. We would never make the stage with our rendition of the Bard's work, but it gave us a purpose and we had a great time in make-believe.

Not to be outdone, Paul and three of his acquaintances formed a quartet, and at least twice a week played their music for anyone who cared to listen. When the room filled with sounds of the great composers, sorrow and misery faded. The familiar melodies diminished the ugliness we faced daily, and confirmed that harmony, beauty and dignity existed. We would catch up with those qualities again; I was certain.

And that's how we spent Christmas of 1943 and New Year's Eve: in a circle of friends, with the music we loved and with the restored vigor to our dreams of a better future. Once again we toasted the new year, carried forward the balance of all the things we had wished for before that hadn't come true — a victorious end to the war. Peace on Earth.

Chapter Eleven

1944
The Year of the Monkey

"*W*hen we are certain that things can't get any worse, they usually do," Olga quipped in an unsuccessful attempt to lighten the dark. She was referring once again to the frequent reports of small groups of Japanese soldiers crashing their way into refugee homes repeatedly, and in the process of searching for American currency and hidden shortwave radios, broke furniture, tore up things and generally demolished a residence no matter how humble. Others reported nightly encounters with drunken members of Hirohito's finest. Confrontations ensued and fortunately the soldiers were often too drunk to be able to cause harm, nor were they swift enough on their feet to pursue their prey.

"You have to remember," Max lectured, "that the Japanese people can't drink. Secondly, look at Japan's occupation forces in Shanghai right now. They are not the same well-trained army that took over the city on December eighth. Those guys are long gone; shipped out to fight the war in the Pacific. Just look at Hirohito's soldiers. They look exactly like fourteen-year-old country bumpkins in ill-fitting uniforms, poor shoes, and outdated rifles — straight off the rice paddies.

"This is the first time these kids have seen something other than the four walls of their huts and the inside of a rice bowl. They gawk at foreigners and are carried away by the power of authority they have over us. They go crazy! They are a crude and cruel lot. At the moment, they're here to just watch and guard, but, if they'd ever had to defend Shanghai against an American invasion force, they wouldn't know their heads from a hole in the ground. Their ignorance matched by their arrogance will be their defeat."

"Maybe they're dumb and arrogant, but there are a hell of a lot of them around now," our friend Joseph Schiller interjected. "They have doubled the guards at our checkpoints, they've encircled the jail with enough troops to foil a prison break. On the riverfront, they're three-deep at certain areas on the docks, and downtown Shanghai is heavier patrolled than ever before. Those dirty, diarrhea-drab uniforms are all you see everywhere in the city; wherever you go. I heard more soldiers are on their way."

"I doubt, that," Max said thoughtfully. "According to several broadcasts from an Australian chap somewhere in the Pacific — one of the many volunteers who watch naval and troop movements — the Japs are in deep trouble. Instead of trying to recapture each and every island, Allied forces play hopscotch, skip one island and attack and recapture the next. It has been a highly effective strategy and has caused great losses for the enemy, who has no idea which island will be the Allies' next target. The Empire of the Sun is losing one island at a time, one ship at a time."

"And not a day too soon," Olga piped in, as we all raised our tea cups and toasted the news. She disappeared for a moment, and returned with a pair of lady's knee-high rubber boots. She reached into one boot and retrieved a big bottle of fine Scotch. "When we really know the tide has turned, and the enemy is on the run, we'll crack this one," she promised. "And," she continued, "since no lady can walk on one foot," she reached into the other boot with a grin, and brought a twin bottle, "we'll crack its mate when the damn war is over."

More applause. I realized that curfew was only thirty minutes away, and I'd better be going. Heinz had left to pick up up Margo, Wolf was on Pao chia duty, and everyone else was deeply involved in conversation. I threw Olga a kiss when she looked in my direction, and slipped out of the room. I only had a two-minute walk at a fast trot to my front door, and was familiar with every crack in the pavement.

It was a rainy, chilly February night. The streets were empty, except for the occasional passing of a rickshaw or two. I could hear the wet slapping sound the coolie's feet made on the rain-slick pavement, and the faint splashing noise when he landed in a puddle. I was less than twenty feet from the entrance to our lane on Chusan Road, when a drunken Japanese soldier careened towards me on unsteady legs at a death-defying clip only a drunk could manage and still remain on his wobbly feet. He made some wild, roaring sounds as he collided with me, recovered and grabbed me in a vice-like grip. I thought he was trying to steady himself, when his foul, liquor-laden breath assaulted my face, as he pushed me violently against a shuttered storefront. With one quick jerk, he brought up his knee and kept me pinned with it. One hand got busy with the buttons on his pants and the other grabbed for me. A nauseating wave of hot panic rushed over me for just a fraction of a second. No! No! This was not going to happen to me.

No time for panic, time to act. In a lightning flash, the instructions of my jujitsu teacher guided my right arm to bend at the elbow as I brought it up to my chin. I tightened the muscles and tendons in my hand until it was hard as a board. Just then the soldier's rifle slipped off his shoulder and clattered to pavement. Surprised by the noise, he turned his head away from me to see what happened — just enough to expose his protruding adam's apple. My arm flew away from me.

I struck out — short and hard — with all my strength, and connected with the soldier's throat. I heard a sickening crack, a gagging gurgle, he released his grip on me, folded into himself and sank to the ground like a puppet whose strings had been cut. I stood dead-still for a moment or two. My heart raced and a deep sob lodged somewhere in my throat. Gingerly, I edged myself away from the wooden shutters and the soldier's crumpled figure, stepped aside, and without a glance back, started to hum a tuneless tune, and walked briskly into the lane as though I didn't have a care in the world. Whatever that surge of energy, that "second breath," that "divine assistance" was that moved my legs and kept my stride steady was beyond my understanding. Maybe I would be able to sort it out later ... maybe I would not remember ... maybe ... never?

My parents were visiting across the stairs with the Cohns. I announced my return, and made a mad dash for the bathroom. I sat down on the small wooden stool my mother had donated to the dubious comforts of the facility, and started to shake and moan at the same time. I knew I had killed a man.

I had killed a man. No! Impossible! No! I was just a kid; I didn't have the strength to kill a man. I didn't have a gun, or a knife, or an axe. Just my bare hands — one hand. One "empty hand." I just gave him a good chop with the flat of my hand, and he fainted. No! He's probably back on his feet and long gone about his way.

No! I buried my face in my hands so that I could catch the sounds of my moaning in the hollow of my palms. I welcomed the fine rain that sprayed in through the big hole in the glass roof. It felt fresh and clean. I had no idea, how long I sat in that smelly little cement toilet on that hard wooden stool, when Mutti's voice broke through my wandering mind.

"Ursula, are you all right, child? What takes you so long? Someone here needs to use the bathroom. Are you coming out?"

I knew I'd better find my voice. "Coming! Just a second." I had not brought a towel, but I ran some water, rinsed my hands, shook off the moisture, unlocked the door, and stepped out.

"Why, child, you didn't bring a towel, your hands are all wet. And why didn't you use the umbrella, you're soaked," Mutti chided gently and followed me up the stairs to our room. Vati had tucked himself in for he night, but said hello, made some joke about my sitting in the rain, and asked what the topic of discussion had been at the Levysohns.

Somehow I managed to tell him who had been there, and what we had talked about. He looked at me a bit searchingly, I thought. Was my black deed making me look for things that weren't there? But it did seem uncanny that of all nights, he asked who had walked me home. When I told him that the brothers had been absent, and that I had left while everyone was still chatting away, and came home by myself, his eyebrows climbed up on his forehead and he raised himself on his elbows.

"I don't like that. I don't like that at all. You're not ever to do that again, or you'll be staying home a lot. Understand?" his voice rose to match his level of irritation. "These are crazy times," he said hoarse with anger, "we're in a strange land. You know by now that the streets are full of thugs and enemy soldiers, and you … you … you, a young girl, walk around in the dark by yourself. Where's your head? Who do you think you are? Hercules?"

I promised I would never, ever to do it again. I wasn't lying either. I had not nearly come to peace with the events of this night, and I knew as soon as the lights were out, and my parents were asleep, I would fall apart.

And I did, after a fashion. To begin with, I went over every move I made after I turned into Chusan Road. I replayed the encounter with the drunken soldier over and over in my mind. I heard again the crunching crack when the hard edge of my hand connected with his throat. I had broken his windpipe. I had killed a man. I had killed….

I started to cry silently. I wanted to find some one I could ask for assurance, for forgiveness. Someone important, whose word would mean something. I didn't know to whom to turn.

Behind the wall, the Lowenbergs were preparing for bed. Soon, I heard Helene's soft voice as she started the nightly ritual of reading poetry to her husband. What a lovely thing to do, I thought. I tuned out all noises in my head, dropped a heavy curtain on the crumpled figure on the wet pavement and was grateful for the shortcomings of the dividing wall that let the healing words of poets flow straight into my heart.

And then the night closed in and a gentle light led me back to Marienhall, to the safe and peaceful gardens of my childhood.

      ❧   ❧   ❧

Like most every morning, I awoke to the low, grunting shouts of the honey-pot collector on his approach into our lane. It was still dark. My first thoughts brought back the events of last night. Would that man still be on the sidewalk? If he wasn't there, he might have walked away. Great. What if he had been found by his comrades and carried away? I would never know. Perhaps there would be some gossip among the people on the street. Perhaps I would hear something? Enough. I would have to put the whole thing behind me. No guilt, no shame. I could have been raped and murdered. I could have been hurt for life. What was there to forgive? For starters, I could do that for myself.

Later, when I walked across the street to buy hot water for our morning tea, I glanced furtively to my right. A few people were going about their business. The crumpled figure of my assailant from the night before was gone. I kept telling myself that the man most probably regained consciousness and walked away. But I knew better. One didn't "pass out" from a hard chop on one's Adam's apple. Passing out was for blows on the head. I had cracked that soldier's windpipe ... I had k....

I would not have to puzzle the outcome any longer. In a matter-of-fact tone of voice, with a quirky set to his mouth, the hot-water man told me that a dead Japanese soldier had been found across the street early in the morning.

No, he didn't think anyone knew what had happened, "All-time soldiers make trouble for everybody. Now his time for trouble. Bad people, bad joss," he concluded philosophically, pouring the boiling water into my kettle. I walked home in a fog.

Bad joss! Bad luck! It would have to do. Each day I forgave myself a little more and soon, the event became a fleeting one-picture vision that faded and lost its color as time went on. Finally, it became a dark memory that moved into the deep recesses of my soul. May it rest in peace. There was so much else going on.

Max reported in March that funds from the Joint Distribution Committee (Joint for short) had finally arrived, and at least food for one meal daily would be available for more people. The milk fund for the children and the requirements for the sick and elderly would get a boost as well. A lot of people already received a daily ration of bread and one hot meal which they picked up around noon at one of the shelters. We were still trying to make it on our own.

The cost of electricity had soared, and we cut back the use of it even more. The list of lacks went on and on. I had outgrown and outworn my bra as well as my shoes. Fashion was replaced with practicality. We rarely gave clothes a thought, and wore what we had. All Mutti ever cared about was neatness. She kept on top of every little spot or tear, and fixed and patched and reworked our garments. She had magic in her hands, orderliness in her soul and needles and thread in her heart.

"You always have to look your best," she contributed, "or else you might forget who you are. It's all right to be poor, but it's not all right to be sloppy."

Bargaining had become a source of survival, a way of life. Mutti traded her work for a piece of fabric or a garment in good condition which she altered to fit our needs. She accepted a freshly baked pound cake in exchange for altering a dress or jacket. Vati still traded soap for salami, an old hammer for charcoal, a leather notebook for five pounds of rice. Each day the list of trading goods changed. An age-yellowed lace collar brought a pound of flour one time, and an old cigarette case was traded for tea and peanut butter. Sometimes when he came home with the results of a day's work, and I saw the light of challenge in his eyes, I almost believed he enjoyed the game.

However, good food was available on the black market — among the choices were American coffee, Dutch cocoa, canned fruits and vegetables, sardines and other items. I could only imagine how the godowns must have been filled to the brim with imported goods at the outbreak of the war. Someone was making a fortune. Inflation had already sent the price of local goods up and out of reach, and only Rockefeller and the Maharajah of Ranjhipur could have purchased a can of pineapple or a pound of coffee. We learned to make "apple strudel" dough out of water, vinegar and flour, and concocted an Ersatz filling from a grated sweet potatoes and lime juice. A plate of fried potatoes and onions, more often than not, was dinner. Rice was prepared in a hundred different ways, and the occasional piece of meat took on qualities reserved for Beluga caviar.

What we lacked in "stuff" we made up with people. My father attracted them like a magnet attracts metal. He had a special talent for making friends and keeping friends. Like a collector of fine art, he brought his finds to our eleven-by-twelve "apartment" — but no more than two at a time. They came from all over the globe, told us their stories, enriched our world, and brought us their gift of friendship. Mutti was the reticent one, but always welcoming and gracious, she warmed up to her guests quickly.

"The world is full of wonderful people," I heard Vati say once, "and I know them all." From him, I learned about friendship.

Then there were the people I encountered on the street, in the lanes, at the market and at friends' homes. Among those who made a difference in my life was round-faced, roly-poly, middle-age Rosa Goldberg.

To find some questionable relief from the steamy, hot and breathless air of Shanghai's endless summer days, Rosa Goldberg would place her three-legged stool in a shady spot in the garbage-cluttered, stinking lane, seemingly oblivious to its rivers of urine, heaps of feces and trash. Friendly and outgoing, she knew most of the inhabitants of our lane by name. She greeted us with a cheerful smile, a warm twinkle in her deep brown eyes, and in her "Jewish delicatessen" accent dispatched us on our way with one bit of wisdom or another. Her message to me never varied.

Each day as I passed her on my way out of our lane, she stopped me, reached out her hand to grasp mine, pulled me to a stop at her side, looked up into my face and asked," "So! What does Mrs. Goldberg tell you to do everyday, little girl?"

Knowing her game well, I shook my head, voiced a quiet I-don't-know, and waited.

"Well, darlink, Mrs. Goldberg will have to tell you again. Now, listen and remember what I'm tellink you," she instructed. "Go out and make a miracle today, God's busy, He can't do it all."

Her face beamed up at me, her hand let go of mine. With a friendly parting pat on my backside, she sent me on my way giving me a purpose for the day and meaning to my young life for as long as I shall live. She handed me wings to fly, opened my eyes to a world that needed miracles, and gave me the assurance I could do God's work.

To this moment, every day of my life, each time I leave my house, I hear the raspy, heavy voice of Rosa Goldberg calling to me, and I remember to "go out and make a miracle; God's busy, he can't do it all."

What a lesson to learn. No text book, no classroom curriculum could have done a finer job. Rosa Goldberg was in her early sixties and had emigrated to America in 1935, to join her brother in Chicago who ran a thriving delicatessen. Disturbed by news about her family in Germany, she decided to go back to Stettin and "fix" the problem. The year was 1938. One thing led to another and she delayed her return to the United States until it was too late. She made it out of Germany by the skin of her teeth, and like the rest of us, found a haven in Shanghai. I spent many an afternoon in her crowded, tiny room that smelled of dried roses and toasted apples, listening to her stories, laughing at her whimsical ways and storing her bits of wisdom in my heart.

Then there was Yuan Lin who opened doors for me I didn't know existed. I happened to meet him at the market one early morning when I was shopping for a few vegetables. I noticed a man leaning against an empty stall, dressed in a dark gray robe held in place by a wide sash of the same fabric, bare feet in rough "coolie" straw sandals. He was tall for a Chinese, but his handsome face was definitely that of an Eurasian. He kept closing and opening his eyes, as though to clear his vision. He just did not look well. I'll never know what in the world possessed me to stop at his side and ask in English, "Are you all right?"

The man opened astonishing turquoise eyes, and replied in a clipped, perfect British accent, "Actually, no. Not really. I feel faint and my vision keeps blurring. Rather annoying, I should say!"

Surprise must have registered on my face, because a smile brightened his pale features, as he responded. "It's all right, young lady, I'm not a British subject on the lam. I'm a Chinese Buddhist priest with a degree in economics from Oxford. My name is Yuan Lin — Chinese father, English mother. Both dead, I'm sad to say. Otherwise, I'm whole and hearty, usually in splendid physical condition. Perhaps just a bit hungry at the moment."

It dawned on me that he must be a monk on his walk, on his pilgrimage. A man who had chosen the way of poverty. He was probably at the market to beg for food. I realized that there was something pulling at my insides, something so strong and inexplicable that I obeyed its urging..

"Why don't you follow me. My best friends live just around the corner. They'll feed you." Not waiting for a reply, I headed out of the market and walked toward the Levysohn's lane. I didn't look back, but I could feel his presence and heard the soft swish of his straw sandals as his feet connected with the pavement. Olga answered the knock on the door, and true to her ready-for-anything spirit, didn't raise an eyebrow as I introduced Yuan Lin and explained his need for food.

In her charming way, in her broken English (she had a terrible time learning any foreign language), she invited him in. "You sit, please, I fix to eat."

We sat at the ever-inviting big round table that was covered with a colorful piece of tapestry, held down in the center by a singularly, beautiful cut crystal bowl Olga had managed to take along from home. While she prepared some soup and a cup of tea, my newly found friend elaborated on his back ground, and I translated here and there when Olga's face registered failure to understand him.

He was indeed an Oxford graduate who had returned to his home in Shanghai where his father, a banker, lived with his English wife. After the tragic drowning death of his parents and his disenchantment with the ways of the world — the politics, the economic measures and the general conditions in his homeland — Yuan Lin decided to chuck it all and entered a Buddhist monastery.

He admitted a bit sheepishly that he hadn't quite chucked it all, but had made his inheritance unavailable to him for decades to come. He had liquidated his parents' holdings and had established a trust fund in London, he could not touch until he reached the age of fifty — twenty years away.

"I have come to know and love the many things the material world does not offer. I know peace, and have a glimmer of understanding of the power of letting go. I am no longer poor of spirit. I may have mixed a bit of Western ideologies with Eastern philosophies, but it is that blending that expands the boundaries of thought, and let's me explore and experience both worlds. My spirit can soar on the sounds of the temple bells, and in the quiet moments, with the words of Emerson in my heart, I find peace. And that is what I am after — to embrace the best of two worlds. Only the best can raise mankind to a higher state of awareness and a more purposeful existence. Interestingly enough," he pondered, "it doesn't really matter in what camp you are; it's all the same."

In a voice soft with wonder and contentment, he talked on about the Eastern teachings, the Upanishads, the Bhagavid Gita,

Taoism and about his walk. He explained that he didn't measure his pilgrimage in miles, but in experiences and in his spiritual growth. I never said a word. I just sat there and drank it all in. Here was something new for me to learn, something for which I had been searching subconsciously. Maybe if I studied Buddhism and other Eastern teachings, I too could blend them with my Jewish-Lutheran-Catholic world, and perhaps come up with something — that "Great Something" to fill me from the inside out. I had been searching for "something," and my mother always said, that … "If it weren't out there, we wouldn't be looking for it … whatever the it was."

Yuan Lin leaned back in his chair, that painful look gone from his face. He had cleaned his plate. He rose from his chair, steepled his hands, touched his forehead with his fingertip as he approached Olga, bowed his dark head, and with a charming combination of East-meets-West, he thanked her for her generosity.

"I must not linger too long at a place where the comfort of body and soul are satisfied. My teachings tell me that comfort is not a fertile soil for growing spirit. I must go. Thank you. May you experience blessings upon blessings."

"Just a moment," I interrupted, "I want to see you again. I want you to teach me about the things I need to learn from your world. I want to know what it is like to soar on the sounds of temple bells. I want to…." my voice trailed off. I felt I had begun to whine. "And," I quipped quickly, trying to save myself from squeaking on, "we'll always feed you."

"Oh, but that is not necessary, Taoism teaches us, that we require little to achieve sufficiency. Like everything else, sufficiency is a state of mind. However," he added, a quick smile in his expressive, turquoise eyes, and placing his hand theatrically over his heart. "there is such a thing as a divine sufficiency, but there is also such a thing as a divine, but empty stomach. And since I am still a novice at the game of perfection, I shall have to consider that even a full stomach may lead to wisdom. It is hard to live in the fourth dimension with a third-dimensional body. It would honor me to return and discuss greatness."

Once more he bowed deeply before he left.

After he had gone, Olga and I sat in comfortable silence, sipping another cup of tea. She spoke first. "There is something special and grand about his modest demeanor," she mused. "I like his presence, and want Paul and the boys to meet him." I loved her for her receptiveness to exploring other worlds.

Outside the stink and noise of Hongkew greeted me. Gone was the serenity Yuan Lin radiated. No, may be not quite gone, I thought. May be just gone from sight. After all, he said that all and everything was a state of mind — the reality we created. There was so much to learn.

❧   ❧   ❧

Surprise! Jubilation! Celebration! June, 6, 1944. The Allies landed in Normandy. The second front was established. Max was climbing out of his skin with excitement. He couldn't sit still for a minute. He practically reenacted the scene of the invasion as he described how an armada of boats and floats, ships and barges, yachts, LSTs, rowboats and fishing vessels, anything that walked on water, had crossed the English Channel at dawn and landed on the beaches of Normandy. Even though the German army had been unprepared for this surprise landing, Allied casualties were high. While Max talked about the significance of this event and how it would lead to an Allied victory, I could only think of the casualties, the wounded, the dead. War! What a stone-age concept. Man was still swinging his club from the front porch of his cave while making angry noises. War! How utterly, utterly … stupid!

When I finally let go of my mournful thoughts, I joined in the festive mood. Paul opened the bottle of Scotch he had dedicated to this occasion, and there was no end to the round of toasts. I wished that our words of gratitude, our prayers and our good wishes would sail on the divine breath of the universe all the way to the fighting men on the bloody beaches of Normandy, and keep them from harm.

"God speed to all," Paul raised his glass in a final salute, sat down at his two-octave organ, pumped the pedals and the magnificent notes of Beethoven's Fifth Symphony filled the room from wall to wall, floor to ceiling, and I was carried away by the sounds of greatness. I understood what Yuan Lin meant.

❧   ❧   ❧

It was the middle of August. A typical Tiger heat — turned on high — blanketed the city. The air was as sticky and heavy as a steam bath. I couldn't stand the closeness of our room and decided to walk over to Eva's place, pool our money and go for an iced drink at the Vienna Cafe. I stepped out into the lane, and was almost knocked off my feet by the stench that emanated from the trash containers. The garbage collectors were on strike again and the cement receptacles overflowed, running over and dropping to the ground creating foul, oozing mounds of refuse. Someone had contributed a litter of dead kittens, the contents of chamber pots, and poking through the mess in mute protest was the tiny arm of a newborn baby. Dead! Clouds of fat, green flies feasted on the garbage, street dogs sniffed at the overflow, and a beggar women with the filthy remains of a canvas bag slung over one shoulder, was digging in the mess from hell with a wire hanger for something salvageable.

I pinched my nose shut and ran to Eva's house. I had not seen her for several days, and the last time we were together, she had been quiet, preoccupied and argumentative at the same time. I had not stayed very long.

Usually, Eva and I sat for hours in their tiny courtyard, swatting at flies and mosquitoes, speculating about what young people were doing on other continents, especially the kids in America. In the Hongkew District there was no place for teenagers to go, no place to play, no place to be young and carefree, no privacy, no swimming holes, no tennis — nothing. We wondered what Americans did for fun? What did they do on holidays? What did they eat, what did they drink, and did they go the movies?

We wondered what they wore. What was in? There we were in our faded, old, home-made and re-made outfits, about as fashionable as two scarecrows. We played a game called "What if we were in America today," what would we do? We might go on a picnic, see a movie, stop at a big department store to shop, have an ice cream at a drug store soda fountain, play tennis, go swimming … endless opportunities!

Eva answered the door, insisted it was too hot to move and poured us each a glass of water from their tiny ice chest. We settled into the two rattan chairs, fanned our selves with straw fans. Eva's mood had not improved, and she picked up where we had left off the last time.

Once again, she quarreled bitterly with her lot. I let her ramble on for a while, and then tried to joke with her, telling her that "after this time there comes another." In other words, be patient, make do with reality. Nothing lasts forever and better days will come again ... blah. blah, blah.... But words, wise or otherwise, were not what she wanted. Eva wanted "Things."

She just looked at me, shook her head, and told me the latest development in her life. She had been keeping company with a young Hungarian girl, Elena, who had acquired a Japanese "bene-factor" and enjoyed the fruits of her ill-chosen relationship. The young officer had access to a warehouse of things we had long forgotten existed. He brought her Swiss shoes, American canned goods, coffee, yards of fine silks and cotton fabrics accompanied by a handy tailor, American cigarettes, jewelry and books. The seventeen-year-old Elena was a well-fed fashion plate, and whenever we'd meet up with her she purred like the cat who swallowed the canary.

Eva and I both knew that Elena was not the only young woman who bartered her selfworth for stuff and things of no worth. Quite a few European girls and married women chose to improve their lifestyle by becoming "companions" to Japanese officers and businessmen. Some of us were not necessarily dispensing finger-pointing moral judgements, but simply understood that the price that had to be paid for a new dress, a pair of shoes or a meal at a restaurant came high. Young women had been disfigured by their "companions," physically hurt, and their spirits crudely battered and humiliated. These young women couldn't cover the pain with silk and silver. The scars would always be there.

But Eva saw no evil and heard no evil. She was all envy and longing, while some of our other friends and I considered Elena to be nothing more than a prostitute collaborating with the enemy. (Being a prostitute was more acceptable than being a collaborator.)

That summer afternoon, Eva announced to me in a hushed, voice, ringing with excitement, that she had had it! She was going to change things.

"I'm tired of my life," she announced to me. "I'm sick and tired of sitting around talking about grandiose ideas and shiny ideals when I'm hungry, sweaty and dressed in rags. I'm young and I want to have some fun. I want clothes. I want to go to a restaurant. I want the feel of a silk dress against my skin. I want a good perfume. I want to be admired by a man, I want ... I want ... I want...."

She swore me to secrecy as she confided that Elena was introducing her to a Japanese officer that evening who was looking for a companion. He was far away from home (weren't we all?) and lonely.

"You want to become a prostitute?" I was shocked, but not surprised. "You want to sell your body (how dramatic!) for a few meals and some clothes?" I kept after her. Although well informed about the technical aspects of human, sexual relationships, we were clueless about what to expect from intimate moments — especially one void of romantic aspects. However, we had heard some bone-chilling tales about diseases, perversion and mutilation that resulted from just such liaisons.

"Remember what we talked about at the Landerhoffs the other night?" I nagged, trying to make her see things in a different light.

Eva looked away.

The Landerhoffs were a wonderful couple in their early forties. Peter was a physician, his wife, Lore, a budding concert violinist, whose careers had been rudely interrupted, as had all our lives and aspirations. The couple devoted their time and their supply of roasted peanuts and jasmine tea, to bring young people to their tiny quarters to read poetry, spout Shakespeare, and discuss anything from the life cycle of the butterfly, to Lao Tse Tung, Greek philosophers, Voltaire and the Russian revolution. Lore and Peter challenged our intellect, fed our minds to overflowing, taught us the power of visions and gave us the opportunity to learn to think beyond our pitiful existence. Wolf and I went to their place almost daily, and referred to it as our midget schoolroom with giant teachers.

"When you meet that man tonight," I broke into Eva's closed face, "just remember what we talked about the other day. We agreed

that we defined our lives by the way we meet difficulties and how
we handle the hard knocks life hands out. Peter made us understand
that for every action, for every choice we make, there is a conse-
quence waiting in the wings. He reminded us that neither the body
nor the mind can grow healthy on a diet of sweets. Good times
don't make us strong, hard times do."

"Well," Eva got to her feet, "I've had all I want of hard times,
and furthermore," she added, tossing her magnificent head of hair
for emphasis, "I don't need approval from Peter, or you or anybody
else. My heart tells me what to do." Her face was tight, she was so
angry that she looked as though she had swallowed her mouth.
There was no arguing with her. I knew, she could be a real
hardhead. I was frustrated to no end.

"Good," I yelled at her, "just be sure to check in with your
heart one more time before you meet your Japanese Prince
Charming, before you...." I stormed out and slammed the door
behind me. I was scared to death for her.

The Tiger Heat lost its momentum, the air cooled down
enough to bring some relief, moods improved, and life seemed
easier. I didn't see Eva for several days, but finally gave in to
my inner nagging and went to her house. She opened the door
wearing the same old cotton skirt and faded shirt knotted at the
waist. well, I thought to myself, the handy tailor must not have
caught up with her yet. She smiled at me a bit sheepishly and
without saying a word, led the way to our perch in the
courtyard.

"Well," I challenged her silence. "What happened?"

She hid her face in her hands, dropped them again, sober
amber eyes looking straight at me, and said with a sigh, "Nothing.
Nothing happened. I changed my mind. I never went to meet that
man. My act of bravado and daring was just that — an act. I thought
about it a lot more after you left. I decided that getting into that kind
of a life was one memory I didn't want to have. You were right, I
really wasn't following my heart at all. I hadn't even asked. When
I finally did ask my heart, I was given the right answer. The heart
never lies."

We hugged and laughed, and celebrated the fact that we did
have enough money for two iced drinks at the Vienna Cafe —

maybe even a piece of day-old strudel on one plate with two forks. Life could be so simple.

❧   ❧   ❧

According to Max's secret source of information, the news from the war in Europe was encouraging. The Allies were advancing, and although Hitler was throwing everything he had against them, our friends were gaining territory. America's army was on the move. Better news yet, in October word reached us — in spite of Japanese propaganda denying the facts — that the battle of the Leyte Gulf had all but destroyed the mighty Japanese armada. Even the best propaganda and the most ambitious lies could not restore life to Japan's sunken fleet.

If America can sink the Japanese fleet and reclaim the islands of the Pacific, if the Allies are working their bloody way towards Berlin, surely we could stretch and reach and make do, and persevere until we'd meet our liberators. The tide had turned indeed. But the one thing Max, our strategist-psychologist-historian kept warning us, was that in the face of defeat and doom, the Japanese under Nazi influence, may still complete the plan to get rid of the Shanghai Jews.

"Desperate people use desperate measures. The threat of failure, the bitter disappointment of losing the war, the inevitable decline of power and loss of face, may drive them to do something that gives them a momentary shot in the arm — control and autonomy over a defenseless people."

He went on to say that we must keep our eyes and ears open, and let him know when we hear something that concerned Japanese activities of any kind. He was on my mother's side, and had come to believe that behind most rumors there was a kernel of truth — sometimes a big kernel.

❧   ❧   ❧

The winter of 1944 was bone-chilling, skin-shuddering misery. We went to bed earlier in the evenings and delayed getting up in the mornings. In these cold months our bathroom was an even sorrier affair, even though the landlord had finally replaced the broken panes in the biffy's roof. Cold, damp cement floor and walls, cold water to wash, cold air, cold, cold, cold. I thanked the heavens for the Levysohn facility.

Gerda still cooked outside her room at the bottom of the roof garden stairs, where her pots and utensils had turned a uniform brown with rust. She was bundled up to the teeth, and often had to use an umbrella while getting her fire started or watching over the cooking of a soup. We all did the kind of housekeeping that would never find a recommendation in Better Homes and Gardens magazine.

My parents finally gave in, as had most of our friends, and applied for a daily ration of bread and one hot meal from the community kitchen. After having been investigated, interviewed and finally approved, Vati and I took turns to stand in line at the soup kitchen every noon with our pot, picked up our ration and carried it home to Mutti's white table linens, and the little crystal vase with the two pink silk roses. The food wasn't the greatest but it was a thousand times better than the horrid slop the Japanese camps served to their emaciated prisoners — so we heard via the live gossip wire. Besides, complaining about conditions or "things" had long gone out the window at our house. Vati just sat there, ready to pounce on us. "If you can't change it, don't complain. If you don't have anything better, then this has got to be the best...." well said; often said; well learned.

Just before the year drew to a close, something strange happened — strange at first, but shattering, later. It had to do with Margo. She and Heinz saw a lot of each other. They met usually for a cup of tea at the Levysohns before he saw her off on the days she danced with the Ballet, and walked her home upon her return. The ballet company scheduled several additional performances and rehearsals during the winter season, and Margo went to the city more often. Sometimes Eva, Wolf and I walked with Heinz to the barricade to wait for her. We got along well and had formed a bond that went far beyond casual friendship.

So when Margo appeared at my place one afternoon in December, I assumed it was just another one of her visits before going to work. She invited me to to go our cafe hangout. We chatted about her part in the *Nutcracker* ballet. She had been advanced to stand-in for the prima ballerina, and could dance the part of Clara well.

"I'm really good. I don't wish for anything bad to happen to Nadja," she sighed, "just … may be a cold in her toes … just a one-night cold. I want to dance the lead so badly," she admitted. We had settled in with a steaming hot cup of luxurious coco and a large, fluffy cookie. Knowing how difficult her mother could be, I asked, "And, how are things at home."

Margo raised her eyebrows, whistled silently through her teeth, and said that things were so bad that she didn't want to talk about them, but went on anyway.

"My mother is impossible to please, you know that. I turn over every penny I earn. My father works for the community, he takes care of a man in a wheelchair; he doubles as a waiter, and trades things every chance he gets. Nothing is ever enough for her. I don't know who she thinks she is. We are all in the same boat, and she wants to live as we did in Germany. And she wants all these unnecessary fancy things, like silverware, linens, perfume … when everybody around us is fighting just to get food on the table. But not my mother! You name it, she wants it."

All of a sudden something in her face changed. She avoided looking at me, as she went on to say that her mother also complained about not having her around enough. She didn't like her being picked up every night by her boyfriend and his friends. "As a matter of fact," Margo continued, looking down on her plate with the cookie, "I promised her I was going to tell my friends not to pick me up at night for a while, but let her do that. It would keep her quiet. I'll tell Heinz when I see him this evening. I hope he won't be cross with me, but just for a little while, I shall have to see less of him. He'll understand; after all, we have our whole life ahead of us," she paused and with restless fingers, crumbled the rest of her cookie.

"Your mother wouldn't pick you up every night," I objected, "surely we can come to get you some times. You can let us know, when."

"Of course I will, but please, no surprises. I would just have to deal with her, and that's not pleasant. Oh, well, you know her," her eyes looked beyond me, and I had a sinking feeling that she was not telling the truth. Perhaps she was breaking up with Heinz, and that was her way of telling us. On the other hand, I knew she was extremely fond of him, and that they had made some serious plans for the future.

Margo sat down her empty cup, picked at the last bit of pastry, and said, "Ursula please understand," her husky voice pleaded. "Now, I've got to go. I have to get ready for tonight."

We left the cafe in silence. I walked her to her door, hugged her goodbye, and parted with a hollow feeling inside of me that things weren't right. My Chinese friends didn't call me Dah Pietze for nothing, I had a "nose" for lies.

Next day at the Levysohns, I casually mentioned, that I'd miss our nightly get-together with Margo and watched for a reaction from Heinz.

"Oh, it's only for while," he said. "You know what a witch her mother is. She'll get tired of climbing out of bed night after night to pick up Margo and chat about the day's events. And as far as Margo and I are concerned, we'll manage to see each other."

I let the matter rest for a while, but something haunted me about her. I finally talked Wolf into going to the bus stop one night several days later to see for ourselves if Mama would be there.

We arrived about five minutes before her bus. A dark automobile with a driver, and lonely passenger in the back seat was parked to the side of the barricade. The bus pulled up, two people got out — one of them was Margo. Light as a feather on her feet, she literally danced over to the waiting car, the passenger got out, held the door open for her, and slid in after her. The motor started, the auto drove away.

"I knew it! I knew Margo was not telling me the truth. That was a Japanese officer," I could barely breathe. Wolf's face was livid with anger. "God damn that mother of hers. Her stupid demands are making a whore out of her daughter — my brother's girl. I know how much he cares for her. I could slap that bitch silly," he fumed.

"But why would Margo give in? She knows better. Next, her mother may ask for a suite at the Park Hotel, a little trinket from the town jeweler, maybe … what next? That woman won't quit. And Margo knows what can happen." On and on we went in frustration and disappointment, fighting off the sinking feeling that often preceded tears.

We decided to say nothing to Heinz, and to return to the bus stop a few more nights. Then, I would corner her. We walked home in silence. There was nothing more to say. Fortunately Yuan Lin turned up the next day. He always seemed to know when things were wrong. He had appeared at my place, the day I discovered I had hepatitis, and would have to be lying around for several weeks. He overturned the unspoken reservations my mother had about him with his flawless manners and his gentle bearing. She was apprehensive about her daughter coming into close contact with what she termed an "exotic religious" influence I tried my best to explain myself to her.

"Mutti, I don't intend to become a Buddhist, a Taoist or take up Zen. I just want to learn about Eastern philosophies. I want to understand these people. I neither have to approve nor embrace Buddhism, but I do want to know what it's all about. You told me yourself that one can never learn enough about this world. And that's all I want to do. I want to learn. Please!"

With a vague gesture of defeat and no further discussion, she welcomed Yuan Lin into our home. Then I came down with hepatitis. One morning I looked into the mirror and the whites of my eyes were yellow. There wasn't much to be done, except rest. During the slow recuperation period from this lingering illness, Yuan Lin appeared regularly. There was little small talk with him, and that was just fine with me. I listened to him explain the finer points of his faith, debated Christianity, and read from the Upanishads and the Gitas. It was a most thorough introduction to the many different ways people from the eastern part of the globe viewed their gods and conducted their lives accordingly.

Every once in a while Mutti, whose English was still slow and hesitant, listened intently to our conversations, jotted down words, and later asked me to explain their meaning.

No matter what we discussed during his visits, at each parting, Yuan Lin steepled his hands, touched his fingertips to his forehead, bowed his head for a thoughtful moment, and with a warm smile lighting up his turquoise eyes, he always said the same thing: "Remember, it's all the same. There are many roads, but only one Destination. It's all the same."

I learned a lot more. I learned that peace is all about understanding Self and others. I also learned that I was not on this planet
to change the world. The work I had to do was me. I was The Work.
I was my own work.

❧   ❧   ❧

Hidden in the shadows of the dark of night, Wolf and I
watched several more times in silent pain as Margo ducked quickly
into the waiting automobile in the company of the same apparently
high-ranking Japanese officer. The few times the four of us got
together had taken on an imperceptible change of mood. Margo was
removed from us, subdued and preoccupied. Her warm, quick smile
was reduced to a bare shadow, her eyes were murky and sorrowful.
Contrary to the fun times we had spent together previously, she was
no longer a lively contributor to our conversation. One night Heinz,
whom we kept in the dark about her nightly activities, related a
story of a casual acquaintance of ours, who had not fared well at the
hands of her Japanese benefactor. My eyes met Margo's and stayed
intensely locked for a brief moment. She shrugged, and looked
away. She knew, that I knew. I said nothing.

"We are no one's judge and no one's jury," Yuan Lin
counseled. "Everyone on this earth is here by plan — his plan, her
plan. Karma. Everyone is fulfilling his destiny. Margo is on her
journey; that is what she has to do. Life is not easy for her now. Just
be her friend. She is not the enemy." Wise words. I listened.

The winter of 1944 seemed longer, darker and tougher than
the previous ones. Perhaps the length of our confinement, the
endless war, and all the things that continued to contribute to the
accumulated miseries of our daily lives, including serious health
problems, made the cold colder, the rain wetter, and made us less
agreeable. My father sold my bicycle which he had used more than
I to get around, and invested the proceeds in simple necessities —
mostly food and fuel.

The Levysohns had become my refuge. Mutti laughingly
referred to my daily visits there as "the place to run away from
home ... to." First of all, music always filled the room. Secondly,
people dropped in and brought with them their gifts and their
dreams. Self-made philosophers, literati, idealists, ideologists,

historians, musicians and artists produced lively debates that took us away from the daily grind and gave proof to the words that man cannot live by bread alone.

Since Paul and the "boys" still worked outside of the Hongkew District, and were in daily contact with several Swiss and Portuguese nationals, reliable news, pirate-edition books and even some long-forgotten food items, like cocoa, chocolate and a few ounces of coffee, found their way into the Tongshan Road dwelling. Also their big room, or as Olga named it, the "salon" was a lot warmer than ours, due to a windfall of fuel for the funny tin-can, clay-lined stove with its tin pipe that vented through a window pane.

Lee, the major domo of the household, claimed to have conveniently come across a broken fence and simply brought the scraps home. It took him six trips in the dark of night to haul his find to the house. The "goods" appeared a lot more valuable than just scraps. When I asked him to come clean with me about the real source of this precious fuel, he grinned mischievously and whispered, "Sshhh…only Buddha knows, and Buddha never tells."

He had that same look on his face once before when he arrived with a couple of chickens that did not come from the market. Then there was that little crate of eggs that had a mysterious history … a five-pound bag of rice someone had "given" him. His hands may not have been in the right place, but his heart certainly was. For all his sixteen years — he was something! He wanted to be an engineer and Paul and Olga talked about taking him to America … when … after … if….

Dysentery, suicide, surgery-gone-wrong, lack of "you-name-it-we lacked-it" robbed our circle of several good friends. Through all these unhappy happenings, Yuan Lin provided strength and solace, and a good dose of his own splendid medley of Christian-Buddhist-Judeo philosophy to help ease our existence. He fit into our lives like sunshine after rain. His European heritage, his clipped Oxford accent and his educated Western mind never clashed with his Eastern philosophies, nor with his choice of leading a life of poverty. There was a richness about him, an aristocracy of the spirit that far surpassed monetary wealth, and had absolutely nothing to do with social status. His presence was never obsessive or intrusive, nor did he overshadow those around him; he just was. And I wanted to be that kind of a presence. I wanted to own that clarity of thought, that knowing, that peace and wisdom. I had a long way to go. I still had a lot to learn.

❧   ❧   ❧

Christmas 1944 was simply an "also ran" — another day of cold and rain, of overflowing honey pots and boiled potatoes, fainting spells from exposure to charcoal fumes, harassment from the Japanese and at the end of day a treat — a cup of hot tea with one teaspoon of sugar. On New Year's Eve, the Cohns, my parents and I trudged over to the Levysohns with a pot of Mutti's "Magic Minestrone soup" for all. To our delight, Paul and his musical cohorts performed the Trout Quintet, Olga offered toasted spiced peanuts and glass of Paul's homemade plum "cognac," which was a far cry from cognac considering the fact that it was made from raw alcohol and fermented plums. Max and Kurt arrived bearing gifts of dried fruit, and a small bottle of Russian vodka.

Max toasted to the passing year with an enthusiastic: "Vive la France, vive Paris, and to hell with la guerre." The Allies had liberated Paris that year, and their armies had been yapping at the heels of the retreating German Army like bloodhounds after a scent. Great battles had been fought (how medieval), so many lives lost, so many lives shattered. Only my selfish half celebrated the victories. My other half wept.

"I'll put my hand in the fire, my head on the chopping block and give my soul to the devil, if I'm wrong about what I'm about to say," Max declared dramatically as he placed one hand over his heart. "I predict that before the first half of 1945 has passed, there will be peace in Europe. The war will be over. Hitler's Third Reich will be reduced to rubble and ashes, and he himself will only be a bad dream, a ghost who raped humanity and violated all that is decent and good in the world. He will be no more."

"Your word in God's ear," Mutti raised her teacup, tears gathering in her eyes.

The news from the European war had been encouraging. England had persevered. America had managed to step up her war efforts. Weapons, planes, tanks, ships, bombs, ammunition and supplies rolled off production lines in astonishing quantities and with awesome speed. Ragged and defeated, the German war machine had taken more than a beating in Russia, and with the landing of Allied troops in Normandy, had to battle two powerful armies on two fronts. For the first time since September of 1939, the war played out on German soil. German citizens were paid back in coin what their soldiers had dished out to France, Holland, Belgium, Poland, Russia and other countries. German cities were bombed daily, battles raged in forests and on farm lands, and big guns and tanks turned villages and towns to heaps of rubble. As far as Max was concerned, the war in Europe was as good as over; Hitler had lost. He went on to predict that the war in the Pacific was on its last leg as well.

The plum "cognac" must have had its effect, because the mood in the room tottered between enthusiastic and maudlin and on to cheerful and teary. For lack of citizenship and ownership of a national anthem, Paul and his musician friends softly played God Bless America, God Save the King, the Marsalleise, and for good measure ended their medley with a rendition of Home on the Range. We kept the noise way down, we did not want to attract a Japanese patrol.

In order to save precious fuel, and not be caught on the streets late at night, we set the arrival of the new year ahead by three hours, and at nine o'clock toasted the coming year.

"Let us drink to peace, to friendship, and to a fresh start in America," Paul's voice rang out.

"If we wish long enough," Vati added, "it's bound to come true." His hazel yes glowed with optimism, the deep lines in his face softened. He expected nothing less.

Happy, happy 1945!

Chapter Twelve

1945
The Year of the Cock

My dreams about Marienhall, about flower fairies, magic frogs, party dresses and golden days were permanently replaced by those grey, formless faces with their accusing eyes who tormented my sleep night after night. Their mute cries for help grew louder, more insistent. Help for what? "Who are you? what do you want?" my silent voice shouted back at the phantoms of terror. There was never an answer, but slowly, the faces would move in closer and closer against me, threatening to suffocate me with their sheer weight of despair, until I would wake up, gasping for air, my arms flapping about to ward off the onslaught. As I lay on my coat trying to catch my breath a desperate sense of loss and a feeling of hopeless pity engulfed me. The faces would not go away and haunted me with an intensity that drained and terrified me. Each night, I cried myself back to sleep.

It was a hard winter; perhaps spring would take my phantoms away and bring back the flowers and the magic. But long before spring could intervene, a new nightmare dared the daylight. It was still bitter winter when Margo died and broke our hearts of glass. I wondered if spring or any time could mend us. Margo's death was a tragedy that could have been prevented — a fact that made the healing of our wounds even more difficult.

Wolf and I hadn't seen our friend for several days. Heinz explained that she was tired from the season's heavy dancing schedule, and added that he had a date with her for the coming Sunday — just two days away. Something nagged at me, and out of the blue I decided to just walk in on her. Her mother answered my repeated knocking on the door, and when she opened it, I could have sworn that that woman turned into a fire-breathing dragon.

"What do you want," she hissed, blocking the staircase that led to Margo's upstairs room.

"Why, Mrs. Sabor, I don't want anything. Why are you angry with me. All I want is to say hello to Margo." She had never been particularly charming to me, but this behavior was more than strange.

"Margo is very ill," she replied, her voice hoarse with strain, "she can't see anybody. Please leave. I will let you know when she is better." She reached for me as though to propel me out of the house.

I avoided her grasp, slipped around her, loped up the stairs and opened the door to my friend's room rather noisily. Margo tried to raise herself halfway from her fancy lace-appliqued linens, her dark hair a mess, her cheeks flaming red, and pointed to her throat with one hand. She was trying to make herself heard, but all that came out of her mouth was a terrible rasping croak; exhausted she fell back against her pillows, eyes closed, her breathing labored.

I rushed to her side. I touched her face and throat. Margo was burning up. To my question if she had been seen by a doctor, she just shook her head "No."

"I'll be right back, darling. Please hang on. Please! I'll get help."

Mrs. Sabor was standing at the doorway of her daughter's room, fuming. "Get out. She is ill, and I can handle it perfectly well. I don't need anybody. This is my child. I know what to do. Don't you dare come back!"

"Like hell, I won't," I cursed. "you haven't had a doctor for your child. What kind of a monster are you?"

"I am a nurse," she shrieked. That was news to me! "And I know what's good for my own daughter. I won't have any interference. Get Out!"

"Where in the hell is Margo's father? If he has eyes in his head he would see she's dying," I yelled.

No more words. I pushed by her, raced out of the house, down the lane, onto the street, heading for the Levysohns. Luckily, Wolf had just returned from work.

"We've got to get Margo to the hospital. She's terribly ill. Come...."

Without another word, we tore back to the Sabor's place. The front door still stood open. Up the stairs we rushed, and came face to face with Margo's mother who immediately started to shout her objections at us. We paid no attention to her, pushed her aside, and not too gently at that. Wolf took one look at Margo, wrapped a few pieces of bedding around her, picked her up and with me clearing the way, accompanied by the horrible shrieking and cursing of Mama, we raced out of the house and all the way to the hospital without stopping.

Some refugees on the street stared at us, but the Chinese people never gave us a second glance. Within five minutes we were at the hospital, found a doctor, a bed and waited.

"Your friend has diphtheria," Dr. Eisenberg announced. "Her temperature is beyond measuring. Why didn't you bring her to the hospital sooner," he charged, grey eyes angry and sad. "Yesterday, we could have pulled her through. It's too late now. Her throat is closed, the infection is ravaging her system, her fever is literally burning her up, she...."

I quickly explained that I had discovered her condition only fifteen minutes earlier, and brought her to the hospital on the run. "Her mother is a terribly strange woman, and did not call a doctor. She claims to be not only a mother who knows best, but said she was a nurse...."

All the explaining didn't make any difference. All the words were useless. We stood at Margo's Spartan bed in this makeshift hospital in the Shanghai ghetto, listening to every labored breath she took, held her slender, hot hands in ours, and with the doctor at our side, we watched her die.

Dr. Levy put his arms around our shoulders, and pulled us in against him in a loving gesture. "There was nothing you could have done, or we could have done," he assured us. "It was too late. Too late." How often did he have to say these few devastating words to how many people? I didn't want to be in his shoes.

He let go of us, and just as he slowly pulled the sheet over Margo's still face, her parents burst into the room. Mrs. Sabor threw herself over her daughter's body, screaming and howling like a wounded animal. Her husband stood at the foot of the narrow hospital bed. There was no life left in him; he was a study in grey stone. Wolf and I left in silent sorrow. We had to go home and tell Heinz.

When we got back, Yuan Lin greeted us at the door. He always knew when to appear. I wanted to know how he knew, and I wanted to learn how to do whatever it was he did. But that would have to wait for another time.

With his hands steepled, his eyes large and measureless fathoms deep, he bowed his head in silence. "Her Karma has come full circle for this journey. She has completed what she came to do. Buddha's will. Let her go in peace. Her peace will bring peace to you."

Words, words, words. More words. I was battling the could-have-would-have, why-did-it-happen phantoms and it was a fight I could not win.

I would have to learn to let go.

Yuan Lin stood by me in silence, and somehow his serenity became mine.

"Death does not diminish her. What she was to you, she will always be. She left her gifts behind for you to have. So many questions in life go unanswered. So many puzzles remain unsolved — and that is the will of Buddha. The will of the Creator," Yuan Lin's soft voice was a balm to our broken spirits.

"Oh, yes," Heinz interrupted, his grief peppered with sarcasm, "good for her, good for Buddha. But I wasn't through with her, nor were the rest of us. And, furthermore, how do you know she was done with her life? She hasn't danced all the roles she wanted to dance. She has not loved long enough; she hasn't lived enough. She hasn't laughed … cried … seen … felt…. All you are saying are words to accommodate a senseless loss, and whitewash, and explain away death."

Yuan Lin's face remained serene and still; his eyes looked beyond pain. Undisturbed by Heinz's outburst of raw rage and despair he said, "Of course you feel cheated. Your pain of losing Margo is part of your Karma. If this sounds too simple, too accommodating, then it is in this simplicity that life expresses itself."

We talked for a long time. Words flowed back and forth, debating the fundamentals of our existence, trying out ideas, questioning and quarreling with fate

Long after he was gone, and longer, his presence remained in the room. Yuan Lin's departure from our sight did not diminish him, and as for Margo, she was still as big as life in our hearts. But Heinz was inconsolable and beside himself with grief; Olga and Paul were speechless with sorrow.

Then something strange and unexpected happened. Mr. Sabor appeared at the door, small and grey, uncontrolled tears sliding down his cheeks. He wanted to say something, but words didn't come to him. He just stood and sobbed, while I attempted to convey words of condolence which never reached him. Finally, he raised his arms sky high, shook his head in a pitiful gesture of helpless anguish, dropped his arms to his sides and in barely a whisper I heard him say: "May God forgive me." Without a glance at me, he turned around and slowly walked away. I watched his tragic figure disappear in the rain-darkened evening, went back into the house and returned to the shadows of our own sorrow.

So much to learn. So many hard lessons. So much Karma.

I didn't go to the funeral, instead I spent the day with Eva. We held our own memorial, our own celebration of the human spirit. We cried and we laughed and challenged the wisdom of unanswered questions.

꙰   ꙰   ꙰

As if life weren't complicated enough, Eva got tangled up with a handsome Polish Talmud student with soulful, brown eyes, curly black hair, dreadlocks and all. The young man went to Schul to study God's law all day, debated it with his cronies all night, and treated women like the Creator's mistake at worst and as "also-ran" at best. Moishe Chernowitz was his name, and, smitten as he was with Eva, he worked hard at making a traditional, orthodox Jewish woman out of the free-thinking, free-roaming, Berlin-raised girl. Eva, who had rarely seen the inside of a reformed synagogue was trying to reinvent herself. All of a sudden she wouldn't go to our hangout, Little Vienna, because the place wasn't kosher. Moishe wouldn't eat at her house for the same reason. The Sabbath was so holy, Eva was not permitted to do the simplest chore until Saturday sundown. There were morning prayers and evening prayers to be observed, and more importantly, a shutting out of her old world, which included her friends.

But she was so hung up on that dark-haired, curly-bearded, long-coated Yeshiva Casanova, that all her energy was directed at making herself into a kosher, orthodox yente. Her parents stood by and watched this attempted transformation with great anxiety, but somehow I managed to find humor in the situation. I knew Eva well enough and predicted that Moishe's laws were going to be the ruin of the great romance. Observing the laws of the Talmud were difficult enough in normal times, but almost impossible under Hongkew circumstances. However, Yeshiva Jews stuck together like glue, and were heavily supported by the Yeshivas in America.

"So you want to shave your hair," I started bickering with my good friend, "wear a wig, and each time when you're through menstruating, you go to the women's mikveh to get dunked under and prayed over by the rabbi. You have to submit to your husband in every way — the Law says so. You'll have a ton of children, spend your life in a dirty house, cook kosher, be a second-class citizen, sit upstairs in the synagogue with all the other poor women, speak Yiddish, and never have a thought of your own. And, there's more. I'll read up on it," I announced uncharitably.

"Don't even get it into your head that he might become a reformed Jew," I added quickly, "You're crazy, he won't change, you have to become orthodox. It's another world."

As Yuan Lin said a hundred times, "If you leave the Universe alone, it will fulfill itself." Well, he was right again. Eva started to rebel here and there against the extreme limitations of conduct Moishe had set for her, and the demands he claimed the God of the

Jews made on women, which caused a strong friction. But in the end it was Moishe's Yeshiva and his congregation, all of whom rejected Eva for not having been raised a "true Jewish woman" and viewed her an unfit companion for their member. Simple. End of romance.

Bruised and disappointed, Eva sought solace among her friends and an occasional cup of tea accompanied by some delicious non-kosher pastries at Little Vienna. Young hearts mend quickly, Buddha said.

"Well," she admitted, "this is the second time I was saved from making a colossal mistake." she looked at me chagrined, "I hope you'll be around the next time."

"Oh, I'm just here to annoy you," I laughed, "All you have to do is check in with your Self. You've got all the help you need." Surprised, I heard myself use Yuan Lin's words. Perhaps I was learning something, after all.

February was blustery, chilly with a bone-eating veil of moisture, and it matched our mood. We were still nursing our grief over Margo's death, questioning the wisdom of Yuan Lin's Buddha, and generally practicing melancholy, when out of the blue more disturbing news reached us.

Mr. Hesse, a gentleman with whom Paul often walked home from downtown Shanghai after work, appeared at the door in a rather agitated manner. Repeatedly wiping non-existing perspiration from his brow, he finally managed to tell Olga that Paul had wandered one block off his prescribed route. He had decided to take a shortcut that afternoon — one he had taken several times before. Playing the role of an important conqueror, one lonely Japanese officer made a big to-do out of it, and hauled Paul off to jail. In his hurry to deal with this major crime, he failed to ask Mr. Hesse for his pass who would have found himself in the same predicament, but who had hurried on to Hongkew instead.

We all knew we had to get Paul out quickly. People had been "lost" in jail and we couldn't let that happen. First a call went out to Mr. Schettli, the director of Paul's company, who immediately turned up at the jail demanding his employee's release. At the same time, Olga sent Lee to the prison with a bottle of boiled water and some food that met Paul's strict dietary requirements.

"We now have a jailbird in our family," Olga sighed dramatically, attempting to make light of the situation. Fortunately, Mr. Schettli was a Swiss citizen with the persistence of a cuckoo announcing midnight, and enough built-in blarney to pass for Irish. Loyal beyond the call of duty, Paul's boss remained at the prison until the next afternoon, when his persistence (and perhaps a fistful of Swiss francs) paid off. Paul's was released only twenty-four hours after his arrest. No harm done.

Paul's description of the condition of Shanghai's prison were frightening, and everyone was eternally grateful to have him back in such a short time. He had been put in to a crowded, stinking cell with several filthy, lice-infested Chinese bums, sore-covered beggars, several lepers, a few assorted mean-looking Russian thugs, and one confessed murderer. Bathroom facilities bore the stamp of Shanghai's lack of interest in sanitation, and Paul spared us the details.

Olga immediately brought out a fistful of bamboo tokens to buy enough hot water for a bath in the cement tub for her husband to wash off his prison stay. Heinz, Wolf, Lee and I equipped with buckets and pots — some of them borrowed from the neighbors — lined up at the hot-water man. Lugging those heavy buckets full of boiling water was no easy chore, and I wished I had learned the art of suspending the load from a bamboo pole. However, once in the lane, I met Mrs. Goldberg who spurred me on with with some of her delicatessen logic and eased the load. I directed a theatrical grimace of pain at her to which she responded quickly:

"Look at it this way, darlink, you'll feel soooo good when you can put the buckets down, and you won't remember how heavy they were." What wisdom!

Needless to say, I was the last one in the house. Olga dumped a generous dose of permanganate crystals into the steaming water which turned a deep purple, which in turn would leave a hue of violet on the skin of the one taking a bath. After his hour-long soak, we referred to Paul as our "blueblood." He just grinned; he had had a bath. I was trying to remember what a hot bath was like — the luxury of fragrant bath crystals, the rich, silky foam of a lavender soap and heated, fluffy towels that wrap from head to toes. That time will come again — in America.

At home, the mood was fragile. Due to her intestinal problems, Mutti's weight was about to beat my 110 pounds. She was painfully thin, and I was worried silly. Vati, always slender and tough, had dropped a few pounds as well. His face was deeply lined, yet his skin stretched tightly across his high cheekbones, giving him a gaunt and hollow look. He jokingly commented that when we moved in our sleep at night, it sounded more like bones rattling in a sack. It was no wonder, our diet was less than nourishing. Instead of saying "Good night" as we tucked into our beds, we wished each other a resounding "Stay well." Health was so important. Living in such close quarters, forever around human feces, decaying corpses and rotting things in general, it was a wonder we didn't drop like flies. Vati, never discouraged and always full of optimism, kept us energized with his never-fading optimism.

"If we made it this long, we're going to make it all the way. Just think 'America,' think Empire State building, Coca Cola, the Statue of Liberty, Golden Gate Bridge, think San Francisco ... think ... United States of America." How could we resist?

Faithful Amah popped in to check on us and to help with our "household" which was a joke. Mutti had to leave our "apartment" for Amah to clean because there wasn't room enough for two. Amah helped the Lowenbergs, the Cohns and our two bachelors, and carried friendly gossip as well as messages from one to the other. Her greatest delight, however, remained bossing me around.

"How come you no mally yet? You fifteen, getting plenty old. Pletty soon, no lich man wantchee you. You mo' careful, you too skinny, no lich man wantchee skinny woman...." On and on she went, scolding, chiding and advising. I loved her giggles, her theatrical shrieks, her jumping-for-effect gymnastics, and her blissful mischief. She made life a lot more pleasant.

The news from Europe was great. Allied forces were pushing their way deep into Germany, and Max's predictions for peace by June became more than a glimmer of hope. On the other hand, I wondered about the possibility of the end to the war in the Pacific.

"Don't forget the terrain where the fighting is taking place," Max, always the authority, explained. "you're not talking about farm land, or rolling hills and grassy valleys. The Allied forces are fighting in the muck of insect-infested, dangerous swamps and jungles. Those romantic islands, that tropical paradise, are most probably the original hell holes of dengue fever and jungle rot. But I also believe," Max continued, "that with the end of the war in Europe in sight, troops and equipment will become available, and most probably will be thrown against the Japanese. The Emperor's Blitzkrieg has gone sayonara. No matter how tough, no matter how resourceful the Empire of the Sun may be, Japan cannot hold a candle to the power and the spirit of America. We're on our way ... and bless the Day...." he ended triumphantly, discreetly wiping a few suspicious drops of moisture from his eyes. That was just about as emotional as I ever saw our historian. We all cheered his sentiments, and as usual my mother recommended his words to God's ear.

Soon the first reports of the fire bombing of Japanese cities by the American air force made the rounds among the Hongkew refugees, and sent our hopes up another notch. It meant that American planes were close enough to reach Japanese soil — either from airplane carriers or from islands near the the Japanese mainland. That certainly was progress. We began to talk about plans for after the war — when it's over. We talked about America.

Then came the day when we heard the screech and wail of an air raid warning siren and ran for cover. However, there was no cover, no air raid shelters. Shanghai had few basements because the presence of ground water close to surface discouraged digging more than a few feet deep. We discovered the next day that American bombers had dropped their load on an area across the river. One American plane had been shot down. Now the war was truly coming into our neighborhood.

"It's the damnedest feeling," remarked Paul, "here our friends are bombing our enemy to bring about the end of the war, but they could kill us in the process. Life's little tricks!"

We all came to live his words as the bombing raids gradually increased in frequency and duration. We could hear the sharp ack-ack of anti-aircraft guns and caught occasional glimpses of B-24 and B-29 formations streaking overhead. How close would the bombs come to Hongkew? Surely the American Air Force was aware of the existence of our "ghetto" stuffed with thousands of friendly refugees. I didn't know wether to cheer with joy or shake with fright. So, I did a lot of both.

Max had heard rumors that our Japanese hosts were going to dig in on the Bund in anticipation of an Allied invasion, and were going to force our refugees to do the digging. I couldn't figure out how a five-block long ditch could hold back the heroes of Iwo Jima, Borneo, Burma, Tortuga and the rest of the places with strange names. Paul had brought home a good pirated-edition atlas, and we spent hours pouring over our world from Europe to Asia and on to America. We memorized island and rivers, oceans and peninsulas, mountain ranges and lakes, and made a game out of testing each others' knowledge of geography

Our entertainment and fun times centered strictly on reading, committing Shakespeare plays and long poems to memory and giving impromptu recitals. We even sank as low as the little kids and held occasional "cockroach races."

During the nasty spring rains of early March, I got into deep trouble. With my shopping bag in hand, I was on my way to market, when I heard a pitiful chirp-like wail coming from the nearest garbage container in our lane. Against my better judgement and being an "Old China Hand" who knew the rules, but propelled by my insatiable curiosity, I went to investigate. I carefully lifted the rusty iron lid that was haphazardly dropped over the opening of the garbage bin, and looked straight into the dark eyes of a new-born baby, squeaky sounds coming from its tiny mouth. No doubt it was another unwanted baby girl. But she was alive and complaining bitterly.

Oh, dear God! What to do? I knew about Buddha's rule (save me-take-care-of-me-forever) but I lived by another rule — a rule where life was precious, where life had value and meaning. There was no more time for reasoning, no more self-debating. I could not overrule my heart. I could not drop the lid back into place on the garbage bin and go on to market to buy potatoes. I knew those dark eyes and that tinny, pleading wail would accuse me forever, take over my days and invade my dreams.

I took off one of my shoes and used it to cleared away the filthy garbage that had been dumped on her tiny body. The baby seemed perfectly formed and was a healthy-looking, chubby

Chinese girl-child. She was streaked with dried blood and part of the umbilical cord was resting on her tummy. I pulled out the pieces of old newspaper that lined my shopping bag, gingerly I placed them over the small body, lifted the baby out with both hands, and placed it carefully in the bag, trying to protect her wobbly dark head. No sooner had I done that, when, as though by magic, Amah appeared on the scene, shrieking, squabbling, bouncing up and down, and flapping her arms about like the wings of a big, black crow that had been robbed of a morsel of food.

"Young missy, you go clazy, you no gotchee savvy? No wantchee worthless girl-child. You wantchee be mama? You no got lich husband, you baby you-self. You go puttee baby back, light now. Amah plenty mad."

"Amah, I take care of it, you go see big Missy," pointed to our house and took off for the hospital with my shopping bag full of baby, disregarding her shrieks of protest that followed me.

At the hospital, the same kind doctor who had tried to save Margo's life greeted me, and acted almost like Amah. "Oh, my dear, not another girl-child," he wailed dramatically — but at the same time he cooed and fussed over the baby like a dotty, old grandfather. Girl-child had stopped crying and was sucking vigorously on her tiny fist. A nurse appeared at Dr. Levy's side, carrying a small basin filled with water, took the baby out of the shopping bag and proceeded to give her a bath, making soothing, lovey-dovey sounds. A hospital volunteer arrived with bottle in hand, and "Little Worthless" greedily took her first taste of food.

It turned out that the people at the hospital weren't exactly new at saving worthless girl-child types, and had established contact with several Portuguese orphanages who took the little babies into their often overcrowded facilities. These wonderful nuns raised the unwanted and trained them to do fine embroidery from the time they could hold a needle in their hands and had learned the colors of the yarns. Table and bed linens, handkerchiefs and towels were embroidered in delicate patterns, and quickly found their way to stores and exporters. This activity provided the money to support the good work of the convent. The nuns taught classes and educated the girls until they were ready to go out on their own. The young women remained under the watchful eyes of their surrogate mothers until the nuns were satisfied, their "children" were on their way to a decent life.

When the baby was scrubbed clean, fed and sound asleep, Dr. Levy pronounced her hale and hearty. "It's a miracle that she is still alive. I can't imagine what that little soul must have gone through being half buried in garbage. Or, may be, she didn't know." He shuddered visibly, as he gently stroked the fine, black hairs on her tiny head. "She needs a special name," he added wistfully, "something like 'Promise' or ... 'Endurance' ... or...." his voice trailed off in a sigh.

Shanghai, the garbage can. When would it all end? Or would it?

When I arrived home from the market, Amah was sitting on the stairs waiting for me — her eyes still fuming a bit.

"What you do with girl-child? You puttee back in garbage?"

I simmered her down, and told her that the girl-child would be taken to the nuns at their orphanage, and that she would be raised a "ploppa" lady. She left satisfied that I wasn't about to become a mother, but not with out eliciting my promise: "You keep word, you no never, no never, go catchee baby. Buddha take care of girl-child. You no go makee trouble with Buddha."

"Yes, Amah. Okay, I no never do." I had my fingers crossed behind my back.

☯   ☯   ☯

And then came April — unforgettable April, 1945. Max brought us the news that Iwo Jima was finally in the hands of the Americans. Both sides had incurred heavy losses. The invasion of Okinawa had begun. Rumors flew wildly about our District and that the invasion of the Japanese main land was being planned for the winter. Winter 1945. Another winter? — that seemed a long way off, and promised to be a bloody, bloody piece of war. Would it ever end? Would there always be wars? Would we ever learn?

Next, Max appeared, undone, with sorrow written all over his face. Unashamed, tears spilled down his cheeks as he reported the death of President Roosevelt. We were stunned. Shocked in disbelief. This man of power, who with his relentless drive to bring Hitler's Third Reich to its knees, was gone. Just like that. Gone! We sat in sober silence. Finally, Max spoke up, haltingly, as though trying out his words.

"Winston Churchill supposedly said 'there'll always be an England.' Well, I believe, there'll always be an America. The death of Roosevelt, sad and tragic as it is, particularly at this stage of the game, will not change America's policy, nor will it lessen America's war effort. It is just so sad that this man will not see the end, he will not see peace. I am sure it is a terrible blow to Americans, as it is to us, and the rest of the free world. But it is not going to change the course of events that are about to happen." Max sat down, the room fell silent again, each one of us wandering around in the maze of our thoughts.

I was at a loss about what to do with myself. I didn't want to sit around and mope and mourn. I didn't want to debate and discuss, and evaluate and predict, and assume and guess. I wanted to clear my head and free my soul. I wanted to walk, to run on a sunny beach. I wanted to breathe deeply of the clean, salty air and wash away the the stink of our ghetto.

I wanted to see the waves build into mountains of green glass, spend themselves on miles of white sand, retreat to again become part of the whole — and do it all over again … into eternity. I wanted that kind of assurance that there existed a plan, an orderliness of events, a reason and a purpose. I wanted to believe in a continuation of life as it changed form and substance. I wanted to believe that I was a part of it; I wanted to believe that I was not a mistake; I was not a joke. I needed that deep inner knowing that I, too, had purpose. I wanted to trust that knowing.

There was no beach, no ocean to experience. Worse than that, there was no quiet place, no place of solitude; no place to recharge, to refresh and reinvent one's self. It would have to be an "inside" job. Yuan Lin, all serene and wistful, diagnosed my internal upheavals as simply Weltschmerz and let it go at that.

That didn't help.

I was also looking for a special place to reflect on the passing of a great man, to connect with America in spirit, a place to honor America. I did the next best thing. I grabbed Eva and we walked around the corner to Tongshan Road to the big shop of Wong Fu, the "Sweet Man" who sold teeth-aching candied fruits, toasted nuts and sticky sweetmeats of unknown origin. An eight-foot long, metal Coca Cola sign, about four feet tall, all red, white and blue, stretched across a long counter facing the street. It may not have been the star spangled banner, but it was the closest thing to being American. We stopped at the Levysohns on the way and dragged two reluctant fellows along. Heinz and Wolf didn't think it was the best idea, but were good sports and joined us anyway.

The four of us lined up in front of the bold letters that spelled: "Drink Coca Cola," and flipped a sharp salute in unison, as I called visions of the American flag and FDR's face into my mind. I wonder what we looked like? No matter how ridiculous we may have appeared, our Chinese neighbors paid little attention to us and went about their way. They had long come to the conclusion that nakonings were strange, odd and according to their taste, smelled bad. We reached out to each other, held hands for a moment longer and turned to leave.

Just then two young Japanese soldiers in crumpled, ill-fitting uniforms walked by us. Suddenly they stopped, looked up, dropped to one knee, shouldered their rifles, aimed and blasted away at the late afternoon-blue of the sky. I looked up, and saw a formation of silvery flying fortresses, heading south, their noses in the air. I looked again at the two country bumpkins popping off their little rifles at a target they couldn't have reached with a cannon, and started to laugh and laugh. I couldn't turn off my hysterical outburst. Tears ran down my face, laughter roared out of me, letting go of all the bottled-up emotions I had kept hidden in secret places.

Unfortunately, the soldiers didn't care for my hilarity, straightened, up and with eyes blazing fury, shouted at me an endless stream of angry words. Even though I couldn't understand them, I realized I had insulted the Emperor, and pointed to my throat and to the sweets, making up an excuse in sign language, that my throat tickled from bits of sticky fruit. I was trying to make it clear that I was coughing in a funny way. Several kids had gathered about, and understood what was going on. They came to my rescue by laughing their little heads off. After all, the soldiers were their enemies as well. Nasty as the occupation forces could be, they were rarely mean to little people. Everyone was pointing at their throat giggling, until the soldiers gave in and marched off.

They had gone only a few steps, when one of them, with a brutal grin on his flat peasant face, turned back, stepped up to me, slid his rifle off his shoulders, grabbed it firmly with both hands and slammed the weapon's wooden stock down hard on my bare feet in their flimsy straw sandals. It all happened so fast, I didn't have time to get out of his way. The hard wood connected with my feet across the toes. A hot, searing, pain shot all the way through me, and forced a loud yell from my throat.

Not willing to give that bastard the satisfaction of having caused me great pain, I turned my back on him, and slowly putting one burning foot before the other, I walked down the crowded street. By the time I reached the corner, Wolf and Heinz had picked me up, and carrying me between them and returned to their house

I winced my way through Olga's gentle probing of my feet, which had turned an angry red. She came up with two elastic bandages and expertly wrapped both my feet tightly.

"This will help you walk. I don't think you have any broken bones. You would have yelled a lot louder by now. But," she added, shaking her head, "even if one of your toes were broken, there's not much one can do. You're young. You'll mend quickly. Just stay off your feet." She was most sympathetic, gave me hug and a cup of hot black tea — the cure-all.

Wolf, however, was really mad at me.

"You, of all people, you ought to know better," he scolded, "you don't joke around with these Japs. The soldiers are ignorant, cross and foul-tempered. They know the war has turned against them now and they hate us even more. And you're laughing at them. Laughing at their stupidity. You're lucky you haven't been hurt more." Concern and relief overshadowed his anger and showed up in his eyes.

He slipped my sandals back on my sore feet, and helped me up. Wincing with pain, I slowly hobbled home with Wolf on one side of me and Eva on the other. I wasn't looking forward to explaining my misfortune to my mother. I decided to tell her I tripped. I slipped. I skipped, I bumped — or something like that.

It took six days of complete rest, before I could begin to walk again — carefully. I kept wearing my coolie straw sandals and, as I told Eva in an attempt at humor, "I stayed secluded at my villa, and turned down an invitation to cruise the Aegean on Lady Astor's yacht." So much for that.

          ❧   ❧   ❧

May 10, 1945. The War Was Over. Hitler is dead. Goebbels is dead. Top Nazi officials arrested. And dead were the ones who perished at the hands of the Nazis. So many innocent ones … so many brave men dead. How could I rejoice in the death of one, mourn the death of others, and celebrate life at the same time? How could I do three opposites in one breath? And what had sanity got to do with anything?

On May 10, 1945, the President of the United States, Harry S. Truman accepted the surrender of Hitler's Germany, and with that the more than twelve years of unmeasurable terror had ended. Local newspapers reported the events in banner headlines, but we had gotten so used to Max Selig's daily updates and the ensuing lively debates and predictions, that we came to rely more on the accuracy of his news than that of the papers.

We celebrated, we rejoiced, we gave thanks, we cried and we prayed for the day Japan would follow in her Allies footsteps. Italy had fallen, Germany had surrendered. It was their turn. How much longer could we hold on?

It was a strange feeling, to come to a deeper understanding of the fact that there was an end to everything — good times and bad times alike. I was constantly wrestling with one big question or another. I had grown up with adults. I had lived in their world. Even though their physical world had changed drastically, they still owned what experiences had taught them. They owned their savvy, their knowledge and the wisdom of life's lessons. My childhood had ended abruptly. I skipped a whole set of classes, and graduated into adulthood — almost overnight. The few friends of my age had not fared differently. There were no carefree times, riding horseback with the wind on our faces, no picnics on grassy slopes, no moonlight swims, beach parties or movies, no holiday festivities, no dates, no dances, no whatever it was teens did, we didn't do it. We lived in one world only — the world of survival.

"When this is over. When you once again live in normal circumstances," Yuan Ling advised, his face bathed in serenity and kindness, "you will be able to recapture your childhood from within, and you will sweeten it with the wisdom of your years. We are everything we have ever been, only more so. We are own work."

Words. More words. They would have to do.

Chapter Thirteen

1945 Part Two
The Year of the Cock

The gruesome details that trickled in about Hitler's concentration camps were beyond comprehension, beyond the capacity of words to express, and our feelings went beyond mere mourning. Our senses raged against the crimes Hitler and his conscienceless underlings had committed against innocent people, and against God Himself. Death camps ... gas chambers ... firing squads ... torture ... starvation ... ovens ... the butchering of bodies ... babies ... the destruction of souls ... heinous crimes.

Man on the front porch of his cave.

"I'll never see my mother again ... my brother ... my family ... my friends. I just know they're gone." Mutti was inconsolable.

Vati's gaunt face looked even more haggard, if that was possible. "What about Helene, Toni and Ida, my brother Eugene? They already had helped their Jewish friends when we were still in Germany. Who knows? They may have been caught and," he paused for a moment, not able to say the words. When he continued, his eyes were dark with pain.

"I don't feel that they are alive. I feel a large hole inside of me." My father's laughter would not return for a long time.

"I'll never set foot into Germany again," I vowed.

We sat lost in our own thoughts, our own grief. Pictures of my beloved aunts, those tall, striking women in their stately homes, slender hands holding flowers, offering tiny cakes from old silver trays, pouring tea, sitting on satiny settees, smiling, ran through my mind. Huge Venetian mirrors reflecting the deep, rich colors in paintings by Dutch masters set in heavy golden frames, the sun creating brilliant sparkles on the massive chandeliers completed my dream scene for just a moment.

Then my mind played tricks on me, dropped a curtain over the lovely pictures and replaced them with crowds of nameless faces, distorted by silent terror, screaming ... screaming ... screaming. They were the same faces that tormented me during so many of my restless nights. I forced my eyes wide open. Perhaps I had the answer. They must be the faces, the thousands of nameless faces, that came to me in my dreams to tell me of the horror in their lives, the terror of the camps. the gas chambers. The ovens. Their lost children. Their broken lives. Death.

And here we were. We were alive. Why?

As though my mother read my mind, her voice broke the silence. "Only God knows why we have been spared. We will have to make our lives count; we have to live for those who died. We must remember them, always."

Tears and more tears. And after the tears came that all embracing, overwhelming and nourishing surge of power, that energy that made us move and laugh and love and cry — that life force that could not be denied. And life went on. It would be a life of purpose; a life of love.

❧   ❧   ❧

The humid summer heat ate away at our strength day and night, and left us listless and without energy. Wearily, we continued to battle mosquitoes, bedbugs and cockroaches. We sprinkled talcum powder on our sheets before going to sleep at night, if only to feel dry for a moment. We woke to linens that were wringing wet, and streaks of talcum dust decorated our moist bodies, and often — not unlike war paint — left spots and stripes on our faces as well. Even the refreshing effects of a cold-water rubdown didn't last but a few brief minutes. Soon perspiration beaded up on our skin again, and we experienced that never-feel-clean grubbiness for the rest of the day and into the night.

I didn't dare complain. All I had to do was look at the tired faces of my parents, and hear my father's unspoken advice: "Since we have nothing better, this has got to be the best." Not only that, but when I thought about what happened in Europe — how could I complain? I was ashamed. Compared to Hitler's death camps, his butchers, his ovens, his gas chambers — we had merely been inconvenienced! That was all.

Thank you God. No complaints.

But all wasn't over yet. Our lives were still in peril. Frightening gossip about the building of gas chambers by the Japanese occupation forces trickled like acid into conversations, eating away at us. Max clammed up and insisted it was simply scare politics and chaos propaganda. Hongkew had become a relentless rumor mill that churned out gossip around the clock.

"Separate the chaff from the grain," quoted Yuan Lin. "Do not give power to fear. Know that you have a sufficiency. Walk in the grandness of your nature." Oh, he was so full of it! The only thing that made it all real and believable, was the fact the he truly lived it. He walked his path clothed in serenity and goodness. He had quite a thing going with Buddha. It worked for him. I envied him a bit.

Rumors of an Allied invasion of Shanghai still hovered in the air like an angry swarm of bees. American bombing raids around Shanghai increased. Air raid sirens screamed their bone-rattling warning — but never on time. American planes could be heard long before the warning sounded. Sometimes those Yankee fly boys maneuvered their huge silver birds so low over Hongkew that one could see the teeth of the pilot, according to Kurt and Max. Our crazy friends would race to the roof of their house as soon as they heard the engines of approaching bombers, and scream and cheer and wave wildly at the planes. It was a miracle they were not hurt by flying shrapnel which the Japanese fired helter-skelter in all directions hoping to find a target. We were more worried about being hit by their fire than by the bombs. Surely, the Americans knew where we were.

The more hectic things got, the more conflicting the news, the more Max enjoyed it. Not a day went by, that he didn't pop in at the

Levysohns with the latest news — from world affairs to District gossip, to flaming rumors. Sometimes I wondered what he was going to do when all this was over. Perhaps he could become a reporter; he sure knew how to get the goods.

"It's no wonder the air raid sirens are always late," Max explained. "The Americans fly their planes low over the ocean to avoid radar detection, and voila! All of a sudden, there they are!"

Though still on his beggar's walk, Yuan Lin stayed close to us. Whether his travel was limited by the war, by the unrest and chaos in the interior, or if his presence in our lives had a deeper meaning, I wasn't certain. I hesitated asking him, he rarely spoke about himself. I had the feeling, however, that our European background satisfied the other half of his being, and gave him a sense of belonging. His choice of living the life of a Buddhist monk, his words of wisdom from his teachings could not quite obscure his English side, his years of living and studying abroad. There were times when he acted more like a British aristocrat in a monk's costume than a beggar. He would readily discuss and debate Nietzsche, Spinoza, Kant, Emerson, the Greeks, the condition of the Catholic Church, the Pope, as well as historical figures. What a brain! I just sat there and listened, maybe some of it would sink in and rub off on me.

From the Eastern side of Yuan Lin's thinking, there came the lesson that life was not about events, but about people. It revolved around understanding who we were what we "came" do to, and about becoming our "own work."

That was a mouthful to think about. At least it took my mind off the stinking heat, the washed-out-worn-out cotton blouse that stuck to my perspiring body, and the fact that my stomach growled and clamored for a real meal. I wanted to taste ice cream and fresh grapes again, crumbly, buttery cookies and whatever else my fancy dictated. Never mind! A cup of tea would have to fill the bill.

☯   ☯   ☯

The oppressive heat persisted, every motion was pure exhaustion; setting one foot in front of the other was a taxing effort. What was worse was that there was no place to go, nothing to do. Even though Wolf had some irritating intestinal problem, he went to work. So had Heinz and Paul. When I stopped in to see Olga at noon, she mentioned that she hoped the men would be back early; it was just too damn hot. She looked so very tired, that I felt even talking was too much of an effort for her and left.

"I'll be by early this evening," I said on my way out the door. "Maybe it will have cooled off, and we'll all feel better." Wishful thinking!

In spite of all my good intentions, my thoughts of gratitude, I was in a purple mood, as Olga called it, and was trying to shake off a combination of lassitude, boredom and resignation. The future was so far away, except for "tomorrow" of course, which no doubt would be more of the same. My misery looked for company, and I decided to go see Eva. Stripped down to her bra and panties, fanning herself with a ragged straw fan, she sat on a low stool, staring at the cement wall of her miniature courtyard. Her parents had gone out.

"I'm glad you came," she smiled wearily. "I hope you have a small glacier parked outside. I feel like a worn out, wet sponge with a high fever."

Lately she had been working for a refugee couple who made sauerkraut and kosher pickles, and I swore that her body exhaled vinegar and garlic, and her dark hair had turned to pickled cabbage. We both laughed about her latest choice of "perfume," and talked about what we were going to do when the endless war was over. We talked about what we were never, never going to do again — never going to wear, never going to eat, never again go hungry, never again feel like a piece of nothing, a piece of flotsam.

All of a sudden I sat up straight, Eva's eyes flew open, her fan dropped to the floor. There it was, that deep, distant hum of approaching aircraft. "They're at it again," Eva shouted, jumped up, reached for her short cotton shift, and swiftly pulled it over her skimpily attired body.

"What's the matter, Eva? Are you expecting company," I joked.

The words were hardly out of my mouth when that hum turned into a loud roar, and the patch of blue sky over the courtyard turned dark.

"They're right above us," I yelled. "I bet we're in for it." We heard a shrill whistling, whining sound ... silence ... then WHAMM!

The earth shook, the world exploded around us. Our better-late-than-never air raid sirens shrieked and howled. The twelve-foot cement walls, the tall wooden door of the courtyard took on lives of their own as they swayed and tilted and straightened again. Angry bursts of anti-aircraft guns acked-acked in shrill protest. I flew from my stool. The force of the explosion pushed me through the open door into the room with Eva at my side. We scrambled to our knees as more bombs exploded, and slid in unison under one of the beds. At least if the house came down, the mattresses, puny as they were, would catch the debris.

From under the bed next to me came Eva's bitter protest. "If this is what our friends do to us, what in the hell can we expect from our enemies?"

Another bomb exploded. the sirens were still wailing, the house was shaking, the noise was deafening. And then, as quickly as it had happened, the roar turned into a hum and then — silence.

"Don't get up yet. Stay were you are. They just might come back," Eva whispered hoarsely, as though imparting a great secret to me.

"The house is standing, we're in one piece," I observed. "I've got to see what's going on outside. I've got to see if my parents are all right, the Levysohns.... My God, our friends."

This had been not some little firework celebration. This had been a serious bombing raid. I slid out from under the bed, left Eva, and ran out the front door into the lane where people were lying face down in the filth and the dirt, turned a sharp left, and literally flew to my house. Still standing! Thank God. I pushed the door open, and there in the narrow strip of a hallway sat my parents on the floor, each clutching a big pillow. I didn't know who was more relieved at seeing each other. Mutti got her voice back, and explained that when they realized the planes were directly overhead, they each grabbed a pillow, the cardboard box with important papers, and headed for the stairs. Just then the first explosion picked them up; they tumbled down the stairs and they came to rest against the wall where I found them.

"I think it's over for today. If they intended to return, they would have been here by now," Vati suggested. I hoped he was right!

I helped Mutti up, Vati was already on his feet. No broken bones, no serious anything, just a bit shaken. They would probably discover a bruise here and there later on. Relieved, that they were all right and in good spirits, I walked upstairs. The glass roof over the bathroom had collapsed, and once again offered an unobstructed view of the facility. The Cohns were all right, the Lowenbergs were not at home. In our room a couple of pictures had fallen off the wall, the furniture had moved about a bit. But other than that, nothing was damaged.

Sure as rain, Amah came boiling in — hopping up and down like a magpie on fire, and yelling at the top of her voice. She shrieked a string of her favorite Chinese curses, her eyes flashing lightning. Mutti and I had long discovered that the more frightened and upset she was, the more this dear old heart worried about us, the more she yelled and screamed and threatened and thundered. That day was no different. She started right in.

"I tole you, Japanese no good. Plenny trouble. Why you no go Amelica before war come? Young Missy wantchee catch lich husband, no good here. Shanghai no good." On and on she went, not departing from her pattern of loving scolding. Finally Mutti handed her a cup of hot tea and settled her down. Amah knew exactly how silly she was, and grinned at me mischievously.

"So happy, my family good, no hurt. Amah feel good ... so happy."

"I'm going out. I have to see what's going on. I won't be far. I'm only going to the Levysohns."

I took off with Mutti's be-careful-watch-where-you're-going orders following me out the door. Not to be left out of it, Amah yelled another curse about "yellow apes, mother of turtles, foul wind from rear end, and something about men turning bluepants inside out," at my back.

Rubble greeted me everywhere, street vendors were scrambling around looking for their goods. Baskets, food, vegetables, fish, sweets, fried tofu cakes, peanuts, bits of paper, streaks of cooked rice, pieces of who-knows-what were strewn like confetti.

Scavengers already hustled for their share of ill-gotten gains, fighting off hordes of mangy dogs for scraps of food. In no time at all, there would not be a shred of anything edible or usable left lying in the street. That was one clean-up that needed no organizing, no direction or encouragement

Chinese, Japanese and refugees alike were running around in a fog — crying, shouting, confused. Dead bodies lay crumpled where they had fallen — most probably struck by flying shrapnel. Wounded men, women and children sat on the curbs, hovered on the stoops of store fronts, moaning in their blood-stained clothing — dazed, waiting for help.

I stopped at a heap of debris, when I thought I heard a human voice. I knelt down on the street. following the sound of the weak wailing, I started to remove rubble, pieces of cement and chunks of stucco with my bare hands from the spot. I dug deeper and there appeared a hand. I grabbed it, hoping to dislodge some debris and uncover a person. Gently, I pulled, The rubble gave and released a single bloody arm — no body attached to it. Just an arm. Horrified, I gasped, and flung it away from me as far as I could. Discarded, no longer of use, the arm came to rest on the silent figure of a dead Chinese woman.

Silence. The voice had stopped. Shocked, I slowly rose to my feet. No tears, just panic. I choked on my own breath. I shook my head in disbelief and did the next best thing. I ran on in the direction of the Levysohns. Here and there flames shot into the sky. Some of the flimsy houses had collapsed, others were on fire. Just before I turned in the Tongshan Road Lane, I saw several people on their knees, frantically digging and clawing at mounds of debris.

The outstretched arm of a refugee woman stopped me, tears streaked down her face as she begged for help. She had been walking down the busy street, when a bomb hit, and the explosion tore her baby from her arms. A wall had collapsed, and she believed her little girl was under the chunks of cement. Back I dropped on to the rubble, sharp rocks scraping my bare knees. I paid no attention to them.

Piece by piece, I removed sticks and stone, glass and pieces of metal, when I heard a human sound. Carefully, I continued digging where I thought someone might be buried alive — may be the child. Please God don't let it be another piece of a body.

Digging went slowly. My hands started to bleed, when all of a sudden, I felt something. Warm flesh. Little by little, I picked away at the rubble. Finally, I was looking into the face of a Chinese man. Gently, I brushed away the dust from his closed eyes and mouth. His eyes blinked open and he looked up at me. His voice rough and hoarse came from his dust-filled throat. In his language he asked, "How much to dig me out all the way?" He meant it. It was the way things were done. Buddah's way.

"Yuan Lin, today I don't like your Buddha!" I mumbled under my breath. Two young Chinese men appeared at my side, looked at the man's exposed face with great interest, and started to talk to him. I told them, he was all theirs.

Suddenly, a heart-wrenching wail tore itself from the young woman next to me. A man had found her child in the rubble just a few yards from where I had been digging. With sorrow etched on his face, helplessly, he handed the limp little body to the woman. With a sound something between a sob and moan, she grabbed the dusty bundle from the stranger, and cradled the dead little girl in her arms, rocking back and forth on her haunches, eyes vacant, murmuring words of love and promise. Suddenly an older woman, a friend perhaps, rushed to her side, squatted down next to her and wrapped her arms around the poor young mother and her dead child. The two huddled together cloaked in sorrow. I had to look away.

Who made the decisions of who was going to live and who was going to die? Who? Who was in charge? The God of the Jews? The God of the Christians? Buddha? Allah? Mohammed? Shiva? Who? I stopped the conversation with myself; this was not the time nor the place for playing questions and answers. People needed help, not puzzles.

I got to my feet and viewed the destruction around me. My knees were scratched and bleeding, my hands needed cleaning and bandaging. I couldn't dig with them any more. There was nothing I could do. I looked back once, and saw the gesturing going on between the two men and the talking face in the heap of debris. A big bargain for a life was in process. The would-be rescuers were working out a deal. That's China!

Tongshan Road was in shambles. A small bomb crater gaped in the middle of the street. Most of the open shops had been tossed by the explosions. Goods and the tools of the craftsmen's trade littered the sidewalks. My eyes fell on a low-rimmed wooden tub filled with peanut butter. Two small, naked children were sitting smack in the middle of the sticky sweetness. Their bodies were covered with peanut butter to which flocks of white cotton from the quilt maker's shop had adhered. Oblivious of the terror and tragedy around them, the little kids were happily licking away at their hands and arms in surprised delight, spitting out bits of cotton in between licks. Someone's misfortune was someone else's benefit. Karma!

I dashed into my friend's lane and except for trash littering the walks here and there, the houses were all standing. At the Levysohn's door, I was greeted by Wolf, who had just gotten home from the city, and who was on his way to my house. We assured each other of our families' safety, and stepped inside. Olga and Lee were standing by the window — minus a few panes — reassembling her makeshift kitchen. The first blast had tossed her pots and pans, utensils and dishes all over he place. Shards of glass littered the floor.

"Oh, Olga. Oh dear! Your pretty things...." I wailed.

"Never mind. Shards bring good luck," she announced cheerfully, as she scooped up pieces of broken glass. "Never cry over something that money can buy. Tears are for important things — for broken hearts" she philosophized. I just looked at her.

Paul and Heinz had arrived only minutes before the air raid, and were excitedly discussing the mysterious feeling that had prompted them to leave work and hurry home.

"All of a sudden I became restless, and I had butterflies in my stomach — not the good kind. More like a feeling of foreboding. All I knew, was that I had to get home." Paul was visibly shaken, but at the same time, relief flooded his voice.

Heinz said he had rarely ever seen him as disturbed. "He was driven," Heinz chuckled, as he picked up a picture off the floor, "just driven to get home. I'm glad he followed his urge."

"Always follow your inner nagging," Paul mused, "I fully believe that this voice is our divine guidance. I am not a religious man, as you know. But I am a Free Mason and I believe in the Architect of the Universe, and I consider this inner knowing the bond between myself and that ... that ... that architect."

His words touched something in me. A door opened a bit, allowing me a glimpse of something for which I had been looking. Maybe it was behind that door I would find the answers. So much to discover!

With everyone pitching in, it took no time to put the place back in order. Olga noticed my beat-up hands and scraped knees and her nurse's heart went to work at once. The iodine burnt like hell, but the vaseline soothed and the bandages felt great.

Wolf and I went back out on the street to see if the hot water man was still in business. Mr. Wu ching, dealer in boiling water, was open and operating. He pointed to some nasty blisters on his upper arms and bare torso where splashing boiling water had scalded him and left angry marks. He grinned and said, "Most lucky, no fire, but big wave hot water jump on me, burn velly bad. Next time, I tell Amelicans be mo' careful." He filled our four containers with boiling water, and to our great surprise, this thrifty merchant said, "Today Wu ching plenty lucky. Most happy Amelicans come, soon Japanese go. No charge fo' water."

Chien-Chien, Wu ching!

As it tuned out the Americans had been extremely careful in their bombing practices. Max, our Johnny-on-the-Spot reporter had the details about the air raid already — only three hours after the event. Olga was pouring the first round of tea, when Max and Kurt appeared on the scene. Satisfied that everyone was safe and unscathed, Max proceeded to tell us the latest news.

Some of the houses in his lane were still burning, several end-houses had simply collapsed from the air pressure of the explosions, burying their occupants in the rubble. Windows gaped empty-eyed, their glass panes shattered. Members of the Pao Chia were on the streets lending a helping hand keeping an eye out for looters. Volunteers pitched in at the hospital and hastily erected aid stations in tents, treating refugees and Chinese alike.

"Can you imagine," Max sounded exasperated, "when the fire engine arrived in our lane, the firemen wanted to get paid for putting out the fires. We managed to change their mind quickly."

"Well, that's nothing," I added, "I cleared a man's face from the debris, and he wanted to know how much I would charge to dig out the rest of him."

Max shrugged. "There are some things I'll never get used to. Ideologically, we're miles apart; and that isn't going to change."

He proceeded to tell us that Hongkew was a strategic target for the Americans.

"First of all, there are several buildings, as well as part of the jail that are used for ammunition storage. Somehow I don't believe they're gong to blow it all up. Loss of lives would be considerable, not to mention reducing our scanty homes and meager possession to zero. Our location is no secret to the Americans

"Next," he took a deep breath, "our underground people reported that there are several military installations cleverly hidden behind legitimate storefronts in our district. There are more than a handful of places that make parts for kamakazi planes and other weapons — all tucked out of sight. Today's bombing raid took out an important enemy radar school, I have been told."

He went on to say that we could expect more of the same.

"Be prepared to duck a lot," he joked feebly. "This is far from over, and we're smack in the middle of it. Lots of our people are homeless again. We don't have a count yet of how many dead. I know this, Chinese corpses are piling up on the streets at an alarming rate, and in this miserable heat, they're going to rot quickly."

More flies, more rats, more disease. The picture was grim.

The next day brought several waves of bombers, dropping their loads close to our District for nearly two hours. I was at home with my parents and our second-floor friends and as soon as we heard the hum of the engines, the agitated whine of the sirens, we dashed downstairs, and hovered in the narrow hallway, our bodies pressed together in the intense heat of the noon hour. With our nerve ends screaming, we held our breath when we heard the whine of an approaching bomb, bracing ourselves against the force of the anticipated explosion. Sometimes the "all-clear" sound came on the heels of the warning siren, and only added to the confusion of our chaotic lives.

The romance with moon-lit nights was over. The presence of a bright moon merely meant another run of bombers overhead. The whine of bombs looking for their target, followed by the roar of explosions was orchestrated by the sharp rattle of Japanese anti-aircraft guns. Again and again we expressed our mixed feelings about knowing how these raids would be a means to the end of war, but at the same we feared they also could bring an end to our lives. As scary as these air raids were, they meant that the Americans were on the move and the end of the war was in sight.

"We've made it this long," my optimistic father persisted in his rallies, "we're not going to die now. It's almost over," he promised. What a dear man, what a blooming optimist.

The following week, another big raid kept us jumpy, our frayed nerves barely holding us together. "Just think of what the poor people of London had to go through," Gerda said. "The Germans bombed them day and night for months."

"So they did, but at least the English had air raid shelters — underground cellars offered some protection. We have no place to go, except for hiding under the bed or sitting in an entrance way, all the while knowing it wouldn't do much for us in case the house collapsed," Helene said, her face a mask of fright. I didn't know what to say.

As Max had warned, it took forever to clean up the mess on the streets of Hongkew. The bodies of the air raid victims quickly decayed in the summer heat, and the rubble cooked in the sun as well. I heard the casualty count standing in line at the soup kitchen a few days later.

Forty refugees had been killed. The number of dead Chinese was estimated at more than four thousand. "There are probably a lot more dead Chinese," a lady offered in her soft Viennese dialect. "The way they live on top of each other, there's no way to get an accurate account. And," she added, her eyes sad, "they'll never dig up everybody from under those collapsed houses. The bones of those poor people will probably be part of the foundations for new buildings."

Karma!

Ever since the raid on July 17, the Levysohn men stayed home. Every day, Wolf, Heinz and I ventured to the hospital, or to an aid station and offered our help. I wasn't very good around sick and hurt people, so I took Rosa Goldberg's advise. Rosa had not relinquished her place in the open air in spite of the wildly flying shrapnel during the daytime air raids. The only concession she made to danger, was to move her stool against the wall next to the little box-like store. When I told her I was concerned about her safety, she just laughed.

"Now darlink, why would a piece of iron find me? I'm not that kind of a magnet. I only attract people. Nice people," she looked up at me with twinkling eyes. The serenity of a sleeping baby rested in her smile. She imparted another bit of wisdom to me, when I confessed my inability to work with bandages, blood and all the rest that went with nursing.

"So, don't play nurse, darlink. God made all kinds of people for all kinds of work. Be different. If God had made everybody a nurse, we'd have no builders, no farmers or butchers, no house-wives. Now, you go do what you do best."

I bent down and rested my cheek against hers for a second. She smelled of toasted apples and ginger. Her rough voice was warm, her sandpapery hand gave me that familiar pat on my backside, and her chuckle followed me for the rest of the day. She didn't have to make a miracle, she was one!

The next few days were a blur of worry, fear, heat, hunger and diarrhea. Or, as Yuan Lin so elegantly described the latter, "A deplorable display of a total lack of responsibility by the body's seating area." No matter the words, the condition was nasty, robbed us of strength, and made bags of bones out of us.

Chapter Fourteen

1945 Part Three
The Last Half of the Year of the Cock

"*B*etter an end with horror, than a horror without end," was Yuan Lin's sage comment to the heightened frequency of the bombing raids on Shanghai. More often than we liked, we heard the hum of the powerful engines of B-24s or B-29s, followed by the high-pitched wail of the sirens, trailed by the sound of bombs detonating in the distance, along with the peppering racket of the sharp ack-ack of Japanese anti aircraft guns.

The Lowenbergs were blessed with incredibly sound sleeping habits and managed to snooze through moonlit bombing raids, and the hacking of the accompanying gun fire. Our dear neighbors asked us not to wake them, after all, if it was their time, they joked, what better way to go than in their sleep. We weren't that ready to go, and made a mad, but quiet dash to the lower floor, hovered against the wall, waiting for the all-clear to sound. In spite of the heat, we slept in our clothes and even kept our shoes on, so we wouldn't have to waste a second getting ourselves downstairs during a night air raid.

By the end of July, cholera cases had popped up in the city. That's all we needed — one more deadly threat to our survival. Our resistance to sickness was low and we were vulnerable to the most puny bacillus. We paid even more attention to the presence of dirt and became relentless, neurotic cleaning machines.

Specific news about the war in the Pacific had dwindled. Even Max seemed unsure how to read the reports from both the local newspapers and the broadcasts from his friend's wireless set. One thing was certain, the war was being brought closer and closer to Japan's shores. Relentless bombing raids on Japan's major cities continued; most of Japan's navy had been sunk. Rumors of a string of top naval commanders committing harakiri made the rounds.

"Just where is the end?" Mutti questioned, her hands unoccupied with sewing. Trading alterations for food had stopped. There was little to trade anymore. People were running out of things to sell. Oh, but there were those who had "done well" during the war, collaborating with the enemy in some fashion.

"Well," Mutti declared, "we know who they are. They won't be going to America. Nobody is going to let them in," she added somewhat triumphantly.

"Don't fool yourself," Vati replied, a touch of sarcasm and resignation in his voice, "those ruthless, worthless pieces of dirt know their way around. They have no conscience. They play with opportunity, they gamble with the future, and they win. Just you wait," he almost snorted, "they're going to beat us to America. They're going to be the first to greet us when we finally get there."

"They may do all that, but I wouldn't want to live in their skin or walk in their shoes," Mutti concluded. " I still want to like myself when this is over."

There were those magic words again: when this is over." When?

But there was something else about to happen. One more adventure waited in the wings for us.

The Rescue

Mad! We were mad.We were crazy, out of our minds. What had possessed us to agree to Max' dangerous plan? What were we doing dressed as a couple of Chinese coolies, lying face-down on the bottom of a filthy djunk, that was probably as old as Noah's ark, and reeked of fish and rancid living? The murky waters of the river lapped softly against her ancient, wooden hull as she slowly inched her way across the Whangpoo, trying to avoid the criss-crossing beams of the searchlights from Japanese gunboats and river patrols. No doubt about it, we had lost our minds. It had all happened so quickly just a day ago.

Max had caught up with Wolf and me at Cafe Vienna, where over a cup of coffee he confessed that he had been involved with "a group of undergrounders" — made up of several refugees and a handful of Chinese. The group not only helped American and Englishmen escape from POW camps and the big Hongkew jail, but smuggled them out of Shanghai into Chungking. General Chenault operated his Flying Tigers out of this northern city which also served as headquarters for General Chiang Kai-Shek's shaky government.

Max went on to say that an American plane had been shot down across the river two nights ago. The pilot, co-pilot, navigator and bombardier had been rescued, and were hiding out in some herb merchant's godown until they could be brought across the Whangpoo. Fortunately, the four airmen had escaped serious injuries, and were only bruised and knocked about

"We haul them across river in a djunk that belongs to one of our guys, bring them to Hongkew and stash them for about twenty-four hours until our Chinese friends get back from up north. They'll turn right around and hustle the four Americans off to Chungking"

He paused for a moment, looking at us expectantly with big eyes.

"Well," he sighed. "There, the cat's out of the bag now."

"I had a suspicion all along that you were involved in that sort of thing," Wolf grinned. "You were always Johnny-on-the-spot with the kind of news that didn't make the papers until days later...." His voice hung in the air in a blend of admiration and exasperation. "What do you want us to do?"

"Here's how it works. And, don't worry, I've done it ten times now. This mission will be number eleven." He talked low, urgent and fast. "You come to my place and change into coolie clothes — make-up and everything. At dark, we leave the District at a safe spot not guarded by the Japs. The djunk is docked at one of the old shipyards a few blocks from here. We'll board her and cross the river." He paused and motioned for us to get our heads closer together. According to him, it was all so simple.

"I need two strong swimmers who speak Shanghai dialect. That's you," he looked at us trying to be order-of-the day matter-of-fact. He went on the explain that the djunk could only go so far in the shallows at the Nantao side of the river where the Americans were waiting to be picked up.

"You have about two hundred feet before you get to shore. Part of it you'll have to swim, the rest you can walk. But you have to keep low, out of the way of the searchlights. I hate to confess, but I cannot swim. Even with solid bottom under my feet, I'm petrified of that much water."

"Swim? Swim that filthy water? You're crazy! We could get typhoid, cholera, leprosy, the plague.God knows what," I hissed between clenched teeth, trying to keep my voice down.

"We'll wrap you from head to toe in ace bandages soaked in permanganate. And when we get back, you'll have a long hot bath at our place. You just have to remember to keep your head out of the water and your mouth closed. I know it's awful, but we've got to do it. Just this once," he pleaded.

"It's one more adventure to tell your kids," Max offered as consolation, and rolled his eyes to high heaven in an effort to make light of what lay ahead.

"Just one more futile episode in the vast epic of a futile war," Wolf commented with more than a touch of resignation in his voice as he lifted his tea cup in a mock toast.

The next thing we knew, we were two coolies on our way to Nantao.

                    ❧   ❧   ❧

The quiet Chinese woman whose big pole had guided the old djunk to our destination through the steamy summer-night darkness, had silently slipped the boat into a spot between two large sea-going vessels and braced her slender body against the pole to hold the djunk steady.

Max rummaged around in a small linen sack and finally handed Wolf and me each four tiny bits of natural sponge.

"Insert one piece gently into your ears and nostrils. The sponge will let you breathe, but it will keep insects and junk out of your ears and noses." Next, he offered us a jar of vaseline.

"Rub the vaseline thickly all over your faces and be especially generous around your eyes. It'll help. Your skin won't be able to absorb any water. It's the best we can do," he sighed apologetically.

"Lai-Lai! We're here," boat woman announced in a whisper.

Max gave us last minute instructions.

"Our friends are waiting for you. Do not under any circumstances speak English. They have been cautioned to keep their mouths shut. Your password is 'how win-chi' (good luck). It's easy to pronounce and easy to remember. Talk Chinese, make signs, whatever, just no talkee English! Savvy?" he warned.

"Good luck! Break a leg! Get going," he whispered hoarsely as he helped us over the side.

Slipping into the Whangpoo wasn't my idea of a refreshing dip. I shuddered at getting into the dirtiest river in the world. Hundreds of djunks carrying goods up and down river, and those headed for coastal travels sailed the Whangpoo daily, and docked at its shores at night. Their owners lived all of their lives on these djunks, bore their children, took care of their elders and dumped everything from chamber pots, to trash, to afterbirths, to unwanted pets and babies, overboard. The Whangpoo was a seething river of thick and dangerous refuse that no fresh spring could ever wash clean.

Slowly I lowered myself into the river behind Wolf who motioned me to follow him. Hidden by the thick cluster of djunks at anchor around us, we swam slowly toward the shore, Just as I was about to pass a large sea-going vessel on my left, when someone on board dumped a load of garbage over the side and barely missed me. I would probably encounter it on my way back.

Just then my hands touched a big, jelly-like hunk of unknown origin. I held my breath so I wouldn't scream, and with the last bit of courage, pushed the gooey lump out of my way. No sooner had I done that, when I felt something slithery and slimy wrap itself around my legs. I kicked furiously under the water, trying to dislodge what I was certain to be a horrible sea serpent. The thing slithered off my legs, regrouped and wrapped itself around my right leg — clear up to my crotch. Dear God, Buddha, Somebody, help! On final powerful kick and whatever it was wiggled off and was gone. I would thank my deities later.

Even though we were able to touch bottom after a few minutes, we kept swimming just to keep down, and finally crawled on shore. A few children were chasing each other in the moonless night, a couple of mongrels were snarling at us with false viciousness, when four figures loomed into sight, softly repeating, "how win-chi, how win-chi" like a holy mantra.

Wolf returned the greeting under his breath, put one finger over his lips, and motioned them to fall in behind us quickly, keeping down. We hoped they all could swim.

We ducked between the searchlights that criss-crossed over us like moonbeams gone wild. Seconds later, we were back in the slimy, warm river, soon to be swallowed up by the safe channel of passage between the two djunks. The whole rescue hadn't taken more than ten minutes, and we were back on board. Wei Fen, the women, released her hold on the pole, reversed her push and slowly began the trip back to the Shanghai side of the Whangpoo and the Hongkew dock.

Max handed us a couple of towels and a fresh set of coolie clothes, instructing us to strip and leave the wet ones behind. I disappeared into a dark corner, tore off my wet clothes and hastily unrolled the soaked bandages. The stink of the river water stayed in my nostrils, and I was glad for Max's advise not to eat before we left. Dressed in clean outfits, we joined the four "Joes" who lay face-down on the bottom of the djunk. Not a word had been exchanged between us. Conversation would have to wait.

A thump on the djunk's hull let us know that we had docked and were back in the District. Once again we followed Max through the maze of alleys, avoiding the checkpoints in the same manner as we had left. In less than an hour, two of the four grateful Joes were tucked away in Lee's spot under the stairs without waking Paul and Olga. Max took the other two to his place.

Americans! I was excited. Wolf and I squeezed into their tight quarters and in voices below a whisper, we found out that our guests were from New York, Kansas, Oklahoma and Idaho respectively. They talked about the hard-won American victories all through the China-Burma-India Theatre of War. They talked about the muck and the misery of fighting in the jungle that threatened to suck the very life out of the men. They wept about the buddies left behind. They spoke of their successful bombing raids over Japan, and assured us that the end of the war was in sight.

The boys thoughts turned to America and to their homes. They pulled out snapshots of their families and introduced us to sweetheart or wives, children, parents and grandparents, and thanked us endlessly for risking our skins to save theirs. Before we left them, they gave us their addresses and made us promise to get in touch with them when we got to the United States. Whenever!

Lee with his highly developed sense of secrecy and drama took care of the Americans during the next day, and when evening fell over Hongkew, three young Chinese men appeared and spirited our American Joes away. Max showed up for his routine visit to the Levysohns the next day, and acted as though we had not been together on a dangerous mission. Business as usual!

Well, it wasn't usual for me that night. I washed and scrubbed myself raw just to get the memory of the river water off my skin. I thought I'd never be clean again. In the darkness Mutti scolded me softly for coming home so late from our "theatre performance." She had made up my cot, and gratefully, I slipped between the clean sheets and closed my eyes. But I couldn't let go of the night. I played back the events of the evening on the screen behind my closed eyes, thanked God and Buddha for having kept us safe, and finally went to sleep.

It felt good. I had done something for the war — more than just praying for it to end. But end it did.

    ⦿   ⦿   ⦿

Surprise. Wonderful, gift-giving, life-giving surprise. "It" was going to be over — soon. On July 27, Max tore into the Levysohn's house, waving a piece of local newspaper like a flag.

"Here it is!" he shouted, "Read it and rejoice! America, England and China gave Hirohito an ultimatum to surrender, or be wiped off the face of the earth. Japan has run out of gas! It had to come. I bet you, we can count the days now." he wiped the heavy perspiration off his face, but couldn't remove the blissful grin on his features

And then it happened. On August the seventh several brief notices appeared in the Shanghai Times and the report was confirmed by our personal reporter, Max, that a powerful, new type of bomb had been dropped over Hiroshima, rumored to have devastated the city and killed and maimed thousands.

America's President Truman and England's Prime Minister Attlee later officially announced that an American aircraft, namely a B-29, had dropped an "atomic bomb" on Hiroshima. Within hours a frightening rumor burnt its way through our District.

Wolf came back from the soup kitchen reporting the latest Japanese threat. "If one more of these 'atomic bombs' are dropped over Japan, Jewish refugees will be rounded up and transported immediately to existing gas chambers," his face a shade paler than pale.

"If these bombs are as devastating as reported," Paul argued, "Hirohito will have to surrender, or see his country annihilated, laid to waste. He won't have any subjects left. A captain may go down with his ship, after all, he doesn't have any place else to go. But the Emperor of Japan has two choices. He can surrender and remain secluded behind the palace walls, an icon, a living symbol of past glory, or commit sibukku. I'm certain, he will surrender."

The guesswork was taken out of our hands. The next news flash was blinding, its consequences beyond comprehension: Nagasaki was the target of the second atomic bomb attack. Another Japanese city laid to ruins, thousands killed.

All I could of think of were words ... devastation ... destruction ... bombed ... destroyed ... burnt ... levelled ... dead ... wounded ... burnt.... What about all those innocent people who no more wanted a war with the world than we did? What about their shattered lives? They probably didn't even care who won, just so it was over. Hunger, disease, despair, sacrifices and heartbreaking losses are the dues of war. We'd paid our dues. Or had we? No one wins in war, my father said; no one.

It was in the middle of the night when the noise on the streets woke us, when neighbors pounded on doors shouting: "It's over! It's over! Japan has surrendered! The War Is Over!"

Vati and I piled out of our beds fully dressed, and roared into the street to make certain it was true. Crowds of shouting, laughing, hugging, dancing, bottle-swinging people milled about, not going anywhere — just celebrating. It was six long years that we had not known peace on our earth. Vati and I dashed over to our friends in Tongshan Road, where just a few days ago I had dug in the debris and rubble looking for a little girl. What a difference a day made!

The front door at the Levysohns stood wide open, lights were on, blackout-curtains had disappeared. The entry way was blocked by Kurt, Max, Eva and two total strangers singing God Bless America. Paul sat at the table pouring drinks from his bottle of "Victory Scotch." Wolf was wrapped in a sheet — he hadn't bothered to get dressed. From some secret hiding place, Heinz had retrieved a tiny American flag, which he was waving madly to the beat of the chorused tune in the hallway. Toasts and kisses and hugs and little victory jigs took on a theatrical air. We had practiced that moment so long in our minds that we actually were performing our dreams.

The mood had changed in a split second. Resignation turned into vibrancy, worries fled like scavengers at the sight of an eagle. Even the look of the Hongkew streets seemed to have improved. People were smiling, outgoing, jubilant. Chinese neighbors shook hands with nakonings and even went so far as to deliver friendly pats on the back of the foreign devils.

Subdued, Japanese soldiers remained quietly on the scene. We learned later that they awaited the arrival of American troops in order to formally surrender. The barricades were opened. We were free — in more ways than one. Our "King of the Jews," our camp commander, the Honorable Ghoya-san was beaten up by a bunch of young fellows, who didn't listen to his protest that he "just wanted to be friendly." His clothes in disarray, his face bruised, he stood at attention, one hand raised in a military salute, uttering a pitiful apology: "Sorry, sorry. So sorry!" I got my first look at fallen power, of having lost, of arrogance in the mud. Strangely enough, I felt sorry for him.

Finally, the first American army rescue mission arrived at Shanghai's airport and drove into Hongkew in a jeep, a vehicle we had not seen before. What a sight to watch the American flag being hoisted again. What a joy to cheer the bright colors of the British flag which once again whipped in the breeze over the Bund, along with the calling cards of the other Allied nations. Notably absent — Germany's cursed swastika and the stridently glaring red sun of the Japanese empire.

God Bless America, and Long Live the King!

The next several weeks played out just like the last part of a great drama with a happy ending and kept on playing. Airplanes brought in more American troops and equipment. American ships sailed into the harbor on the murky, yellow waters of the Whangpoo. Off the gangplanks swaggered America's navy — sailors dressed in impeccable white, bell-bottom trousers flapping at their ankles, round hats cocked smartly on well-trimmed heads, big grins on heir faces — ready for anything. And Shanghai was ready for them.

Combat rations and other food parcels made their way into our District, and we became re-acquainted with real food. Graham crackers, instant coffee, cheese spreads in tin cans, cocoa, chocolate bars, spam and even canned fruit. What luxuries! We could only nibble on these generous gifts; it would take some time for our bodies to accept rich foods again without getting sick.

Spirits were high as each day brought something else to celebrate. To my great surprise I felt a kind of depression take over, and I experienced a deep sense of let-down, a flatness to the moment, an inexplicable loss. I was disturbed and puzzled by these odd emotions and turned to Yuan Lin with my several variations on the theme of "Why?"

He was quiet for a moment, his startling turquoise eyes searched mine, exploring what lay behind. I was ready for my next lesson, which I knew was coming.

"Dear friend, an era has ended. All you've known since childhood was hate, fear, deprivation and war. That was the essence of your growing-up years. Now you must let go of them, and that leaves a void within. You must fill this void with the wholeness of life, with gratitude and love, with your dreams and your visions of the future.

"So many people are afraid to release the pain and suffering they have experienced; to let go of the past, because that is all they believe they have. They don't know with what to fill the hole that letting go leaves behind. I'm telling you different: Take the past and toss it! Toss it into the winds. Let the winds carry it away from you. You are ready to embrace the present and reach out to the future with joyful anticipation, with gratitude in your heart for all the gifts that await you.

"The past has given you strength and the future will give you wisdom. You see," he ended with one of his mysterious smiles hiding in the light of his eyes, "it's all the same, my dear friend, it's all the same. One day, you will know."

Again and again, I had to bow to Yuan Lin's truth, and accepted the unerring wisdom of his words. I didn't exactly let go of the past though, but at least I stored it for safekeeping far away at the very edge of my memory. One day I would come for it, take it out of storage, examine it, talk about it. And when I've done that, then I'll I toss it into the winds. The past made me what I am and what I would become.

"You are all you have lived," Yuan Lin lowered his dark head, and steepled hands at his forehead. "So, my dear friend, live well and wisely. Live peace. Live Love."

Chapter 15

1946
The year of the Dog

*T*he events of the last four months of the year 1945, the Year of the Cock, were exciting and were crowded with new patterns and images. The nightmares and the phantoms of terror who visited me nightly disappeared almost as swiftly as they had come. Our quiet moments were no longer interrupted by waves of fear in anticipation of impending disaster. We had time to reflect on our lives, gather ourselves, repair our bodies and, best of all, plan for the future. How reassuring, that after all, we did have a future waiting for us.

When the barricades to the Allied prisoner-of-war camps came down, and the gates opened, they revealed a beaten, starving, sick of body and spirit mass of people, many of whom had lost all pride and sense of being. I met up with the Langfords in a teary and heart-wrenching reunion. When I saw their emaciated bodies, got a good look at the conditions of the camp, when I heard their stories, I realized that the hardships of our years in Hongkew were nothing compared to what our friends had gone through. Three months later, the Langfords left for the United States. We would keep in touch, we promised. And, we did.

Millions of relief dollars, tons of food, medicine and equipment poured into Shanghai and trickled into the refugee community. We gratefully welcomed the gifts that eased living conditions, restored hope, mended bodies, and gave everyone a new lease on life. We remained in the Designated Area — no longer for some trumped-up reason of "military necessity," but simply for the fact that we had no money to move. But even living in Hongkew took on a different meaning. It was merely the waiting room for entry to America.

My parents had decided that not even a team of wild horses could drag them back to Germany. Official documentation had reached us via the Swiss Red Cross confirming the death of all my mother's family as well as the death of my fathers two sisters and his brother. My beloved Aunt Antonia and Uncle Erich were alive. They had fled on foot from the advancing Russian army, pulling a little wooden wagon with their few belongings behind them. Six weeks later, starving and exhausted, they arrived in a small town near the Rhein where they found shelter with old family friends.

No words could adequately describe the sorrow and the tears as we read and reread in disbelief the simple words written on a piece of impersonal paper telling us the approximate dates of our loved ones deaths and the names of the concentration camps were they lost their lives. No wonder my nights had been haunted with the silent cries from empty faces. They had come to tell me.

"There is nothing left for us in Germany. I could not live there anymore," Mutti mourned. "I would forever be suspicious of a people who 'didn't know what was going on.' People who conveniently looked the other way as their friends, their neighbors, were torn from their homes and disappeared. Would the man on the street, the butcher, the waiter, the policeman, the mailman, my neighbor, have worked in a concentration camp? I'd never stop to question. I won't be able to forget. I want no part of Germany." She did not have to convince my father.

For a while, the Levysohns had seriously considered emigrating to Australia, where old friends from Berlin had settled before the war and had described their life down under in glowing colors. But when Wolf and I announced that we wanted to be married the following year, (which came as no surprise to our families) and he insisted that our future lay in America, Paul and Olga quickly dropped the subject. The family would stay together, America it would be!

At first, my father was not that pleased with my choice of a husband, and a touch of the old aristocratic snobbery demanded a brief moment of attention. He suggested, sort of casually, sort of half-jokingly: "You're so young. Wouldn't you like to wait a bit longer? Perhaps meet a nice baron, a duke, a titled man ... an aristocrat? You know, they still make those...."

"To hell with settling for just a baron or a duke. I found a Prince! And, furthermore, you know it."

He never said another word. Not ever had I opposed my father openly, and when I looked at his face, I was relieved to see his eyes smile at me — a bit sadly perhaps, but just the same, he smiled.

My mother, however, couldn't help but have her say. "Martin, you know I'm not impressed by titles because they're man-made. I believe in only one kind of aristocracy — the aristocracy of the soul." Dear mutti, — she always had the last word.

A few weeks later, a letter addressed to my mother reached us through the continued efforts of the Swiss Red Cross. As Mutti started to read, she caught her breath, her eyes flew over the flimsy paper, her hands shook and when she finished, the pages fluttered silently to the floor.

"It's from Hedwig," she managed to say. "Someone wrote the letter for her. She lost both hands and part of her arms in an air raid. She almost died. She wants to be forgiven for having stolen the jewelry from us,"

Dead silence. The three of us just looked at each other. Finally, my father, his voice rough and raw, began to speak haltingly, shaking his head from side to side.

"Never wish anyone evil. Never seek revenge. Leave it to the Almighty, He does such a thorough job. Hedwig stole bracelets and rings. Isn't it ironic, that she has no hands and arms now to wear them?"

Not another word was spoken. But in spite of it all, my heart hurt for Hedwig — the real Hedwig, the kind and loving one who lived behind the shadow of the dark one. The silence in our little room was oppressive and I took off for the Levysohns. I had lot of questions. I wondered if Yuan Lin had some answers.

❧   ❧   ❧

All of a sudden the hordes of short, stocky soldiers in their crumpled dun-colored garb and the flag with the blood-red sun on white canvas were gone, wiped off the scenery in the passing of a night. The flow of American khaki sprinkled with sparkling white navy uniforms filled the streets of Shanghai. American troops poured in from the China-Burma-India Theatre of War. Tall and lanky, fueled by the euphoria of victory, filled with visions of going home, these combat-seasoned Yankees simply boiled over with life. Night and day, the city sizzled as it played host to a new brand of customers who came from Nebraska, Ohio, North Dakota, Texas, Mississippi, you name it. All the boys were after was fun, and Shanghai obliged them.

The men were billeted in hotels and buildings formerly inhabited by Japanese occupation forces. A former factory-warehouse in Hongkew, served as a processing center where GIs and officers, according to the army's "point system," were assigned to their next post, or scheduled to be sent home and discharged.

Since all army installations, billets as well as the distribution center of UNRA goods, were being administered by the American government, all kinds of jobs became available. Offices needed secretarial and clerical help, there were maintenance jobs to be had, the PXs were hiring sales and stock clerks and the airfield needed drivers and mechanics. Hundreds of refugees, including most of our friends and myself, were earning money again.

As soon as the American Consulate re-opened its doors, the line of Europeans waiting to register for entry into the United States snaked clear around the block week after week. Our families stood in line for several days, until we made it through the front door of the consulate. Grinning from ear to ear, wrapped in gratitude with eyes misty, we received our quota number that would eventually open the doors to our new home — to our future life. Once our new affidavits arrived from America, we would be duly processed, and given that coveted American visa It would take some time; perhaps a year, perhaps more. But we'd get there!

In the meantime, I practiced living in America, by being around Americans all day long. I worked in the China Theatre Replacement Service, CTRS for short, as a record clerk in the dispensary. I added years to my age in order to get the job of handling the venereal disease records of the men being processed for reassignment. What a howl that was. I had to ask Olga to explain these diseases to me. I had not heard of them. Neither Amah nor my friends from the House of Flowers had ever talked about that subject. Fortunately, I was quick to learn.

Aside from all the awkward and often humorous situations that came with this odd and crazy job of mine, my greatest thrill was in living in an American outpost as I called it. It was a preview of life in America for me. Like a sponge, I soaked up traditions and customs, American music, comic strips and national holidays. I tasted food and drink; I incorporated expressions into my English vocabulary. I counted American coins in nickels, dimes and two bits. I was touched by the openness, friendliness and the casual camaraderie of these young men. I loved their carefree ways, their jokes and their generosity — the way they talked. Not a day went by that someone didn't leave a candy bar, a bottle of vitamins, a tube of toothpaste, or an American magazine on my desk. I never knew whom to thank. But I knew one thing with absolute certainty: The day I would put my my foot down on American soil, I would be coming home in every sense of the word.

Max, Kurt and Eva all had jobs with the army. Wolf landed a position with Special Services and Heinz worked at the airfield. We got together often in the evenings to talk about our day, our bosses, expounded on the wonder of the United States and all the new things that we discovered at every turn. The longer we were around Americans, the more impatient we became to get to America. We had lost so much time and we were anxious to make life happen.

"Patience. Patience. Patience," Yuan Lin coached. "Only in patience lies the key to fulfillment. Never hurry the seasons." I looked at him and made a face; he had to laugh at himself.

"No, no!" he protested, "don't blame Buddha for these words. I made them up," he confessed. "But, all joking aside," he continued, "I'm going to miss you all terribly. I might have to continue my walk in America."

I didn't put it past him. Yuan Lin was in a class all by himself.

Wolf and I were married in a simple Chinese civil ceremony and celebrated the event at the Levysohns with cups of American coffee and generous servings of Cafe Vienna's famous nut torte. We toasted to good luck and good life with the help of two bottles of Scotch "confiscated" by Wolf's boss from the Officers Club. The note that accompanied the gift read: "Another Service of Special Services. Drink up — Le chaim! Best Wishes, Colonel James Chasser."

The second-floor room at the Levysohn's had become available and the landlord was glad to rent it at a reasonable price. Things had changed. Key money left with the arrival of the first American jeep. Hongkew landlords no longer could charge premium prices for their rental properties. Soon, the refugee population would be gone all together.

We celebrated Christmas and New Year's Eve with our regular crowd, plus several American soldiers with whom we worked. Most of the men had not seen home for four years, and being around a family, any kind of family, eased their loneliness a bit. They talked about their wives and children, about their sweethearts and best girls. They talked about their parents, the farm, their grandfather's hardware store, their fathers' insurance business, the farm, college, Sunday morning church, their plans, their dreams. They gave us their addresses, and made us promise to "be sure to visit when you get to America." I couldn't wait!

Chapter 16

1947
The Year of New Beginnings

*A*ll of a sudden the year was 1947, the month was July — almost two years after the end of the war. Wolf and I were the first in our family to receive our visas to America. What a day to celebrate. What a time it had been.

Max and Kurt, Eva and her family and several other friends had already left for the United States. Some people went to New Zealand, Australia and Palestine, a few even returned to Austria and Germany — to reclaim their properties.

"If and when we get anything back," Vati announced, "they can send it to us in America. I don't trust myself to even visit." There was a threat in his voice and his eyes were wide open and angry.

"Don't get him started," Mutti interrupted, "he said it all a hundred times already."

Finally the day arrived when Wolf and I boarded the American troop transport, the SS Gordon. On August the eighth, in the midst of a Tiger Heat, I stood on deck of this big ship, and looked at the Shanghai Bund for the last time. The years fell away and I saw myself — I saw that young girl and her parents walk off the *Gneisenau*'s gangplank eight years and three months before.

The scene hadn't changed at all. Coolies in sweat-stained rags were hauling loads suspended from bamboo poles, children shrieked and chased each other on the docks; heavy traffic, bicycles, rickshaws and throngs of pedestrians clogged the streets. It hadn't changed.

Only I had changed. I had grown up. And as I looked at the city that had sheltered us from the horrors of Hitler's war against the Jews and against the world, a huge wave of gratitude engulfed me. Tears washed my eyes and cleared my vision.

All I saw in front of me was a fine city bathed in sunlight under a China-blue sky, with handsome buildings lining the broad street on the waterfront. In the sun-dappled shade of blossoming trees, I saw dainty Chinese ladies in long silk gowns, their shiny black hair piled on top of their heads secured with pieces of ivory and jade, carrying colorful umbrellas. They walked in fragrant gardens and stopped on graceful bridges that arched over sparkling ponds to catch their reflection in the water. All the ugliness fell away; only a deep gratitude remained.

The ship's whistle let out a long hooooot, the large troop carrier slowly moved away from the dock, all chains undone, all ties gone. Free and unhindered, she headed for the open sea.

Wolf put his arm around me, and in silence, with my eyes still glued to the land I was leaving, I made a vow:

"I shall never hate anybody ever! Not a group, not an individual."

I had witnessed what hate had done to the whole world. And I knew what hate had wrought not just in this century, but in all the centuries before.

I didn't hate the Germans. I didn't hate the Japanese. I didn't like what had been done to us. I didn't like that we had been judged, classified and stamped sub-humans, that we had been robbed of our identity, of living a life of purpose — of following our star.

Yuan Lin had taught me to be grateful for everything I experienced, because: "I am everything I've ever been. I am everything I have lived. I am my own work."

I didn't hate anyone.

Finally, I was free to follow my star.

Epilogue

*W*hen San Francisco opened its Golden Gate to the several thousand Shanghai Jews who arrived on crowded World War II troop carriers, hospitality, friendship and compassion greeted the weary masses. These refugees had traveled over their elbow to get to their knee and finally set foot onto the land they had dreamt about for so long.

Speaking for myself—well, I truly had come home. The moment I touched American soil my heart was at peace and I knew that the future was mine to live. Marienhall became a fond and treasured memory, but no longer was it the destination of my dreams. I lived happily in a little white cottage with the proverbial picket fence hugged by rambling red roses, a real bathroom and Gold Bond Stamps.

Our two families settled in Denver, Colorado where both my parents and the Levysohns (who changed their name to Lansing according to Paul's wishes) led a life of deep content and boundless gratitude for many, many years. Each day, we counted our blessings, viewed with awe the magnificent snow-covered Rocky Mountains, and felt a great deal more like delayed pilgrims than displaced persons.

Our children, Ron and Marly, were born in the mile-high city and made our happiness complete. The kids were American citizens before we were. Our families attended citizenship classes, and in May of 1953, the Lansings (Levysohns) and the Blombergs were the largest family ever to be sworn in as American citizens in Denver. What a day that was.

My father just grinned and grinned. He never stopped. "Aren't we so glad we didn't give in?" was all he said with tears glistening in his hazel eyes. He, too had come home. Vati found employment with a printer, where he put to use his typesetting skills from the past. Later on, he took a job with the *Denver Post* and worked there until he retired at the age of 75. He didn't even give in to aging. Although he added a great number of words to his vocabulary the sing-song rhythm of his Pidgin English never left him. And that was all right. If anything it made him more appealing.

Heinz eventually married a young refugee girl from Frankfurt, raised two wonderful children and remained close to the family. The pictures that accompany this story were the results of his relentless pursuit to document the Shanghai years. He, too, left his gifts behind. I treasure the gifts.

We stayed in touch with Max Selig.who made his home in San Francisco while his room mate, Kurt Vogel, joined his relatives in Boston. Max remained a bachelor, but Kurt married a young widow with two small boys, and like a fairy tale — they lived happily ever after. Both our friends enjoyed successful business careers.

Eva and her parents settled in Chicago where she married a young attorney, raised a daughter, and became an interior designer. We corresponded faithfully through the years, talked on the telephone and whenever possible, we visited with each other. As with the rest of our little group — and just like the memories of the seasons — an uncharted rhythm brought us together with astonishing regularity.

After nine long years, the Schillers, who decided to make New York City their home, were finally reunited with their daughters. The two girls had grown into lovely teenagers with clipped British accents, and a strong desire to make up for the lost years. Joseph worked as an accountant for a large corporation, and every once in a while he and Lucy came to Colorado to ski. We cherished their visits.

My mother's family, the Schafers eventually made their home in San Francisco. The two sister kept up a brisk corresponence and saw each other at least every other year. Wild horses couldn't keep the Cohns away from my parents, and when they arrived in America in early 1948, our faithful friends made a beeline for Denver. The Shanghai bonds ran deep and strong.

It was always a special day when a letter from Yuan Lin arrived. I couldn't wait to open the envelope, because the moment I lifted the flap, his gentle presence flowed into the room. The memories of his startling turquoise eyes lit up my heart and his warm voice brought his gifts of love and wisdom. He reported on his travels, on settling down in Taiwan and becoming a teacher. Before I tucked his letter in a special place in my desk, I'd swear I saw him steeple his hands, touch his forehead, and say: "Peace, dear friend. Remember, it's all the same."

Distance could not diminish the power of his persona. I missed him terribly.

I called on all the wisdom and faith Yuan Lin had taught me to hold me up, when Wolf left us suddenly in 1970. The past surfaced and I could hear my teacher's soft voice saying, "Dear friend, always remember, we don't come here to stay. We come here to go."

Life in all its goodness and splendor unfolded once again when I met and later married my husband, Thorn, who with his big heart and gentle hand opened new and different doors for me. And I grew some more.

All in all, I have been one lucky girl-child.